WICCA AND THE
CHRISTIAN HERITAGE

What is Wicca? Is it witchcraft or Paganism? Occultism or esotericism? Are Wiccans witches?

Since it was first publicised in 1954 by Gerald Gardner, Wicca has been associated with magic, spirituality, mysticism, nature religions, secrecy, gnosis, the exotic and the Other. Over the past thirty years, anthropologists, sociologists and historians have defined and explored Wicca within all these contexts, but there has been a tendency to sublimate and negate the role of Christianity in Wicca's historical and contemporary incarnations.

Joanne Pearson 'prowls the borderlands of Christianity' to uncover the untold history of Wicca. She argues that Christian traditions are inherent in the development of contemporary Wicca, and makes a groundbreaking analysis of Wicca's relationship with Christianity. Focusing on the accusations which have been levelled against Catholicism, heterodoxy and witchcraft throughout history, Pearson explores the importance of ritual, deviant sexuality and magic in Christian and Wiccan contexts, and addresses the problematic nature of the Wiccan claim of marginality.

Joanne Pearson, a scholar of contemporary Wicca and its history, is author of *A Popular Dictionary of Paganism* (Routledge, 2002) and editor of *Nature Religion Today: Paganism in the Modern World* (1998) and *Belief Beyond Boundaries: Wicca, Celtic Spirituality and the New Age* (2002).

WICCA AND THE CHRISTIAN HERITAGE

Ritual, sex and magic

Joanne Pearson

Routledge
Taylor & Francis Group

LONDON AND NEW YORK

First published 2007
by Routledge
2 Park Square, Milton Park, Abingdon, Oxon OX14 4RN

Simultaneously published in the USA and Canada
by Routledge
270 Madison Ave, New York, NY 10016

Routledge is an imprint of the Taylor & Francis Group, an informa business

© 2007 Joanne Pearson

Typeset in Sabon by
HWA Text and Data Management, Tunbridge Wells
Printed and bound in Great Britain by
Antony Rowe Ltd, Chippenham, Wiltshire

British Library Cataloguing in Publication Data
A catalogue record for this book is available from the British Library

Library of Congress Cataloging-in-Publication Data
Pearson, Joanne.
Wicca and the Christian heritage : ritual, sex, and magic /
Joanne Pearson.
p.   cm.
Includes bibliographical references (p.   ) and index.
1. Witchcraft–History. 2. Neopaganism–Relations–Christianity.
3. Christianity and other religions–Neopaganism. I. Title.
BF1566.P43 2007
299´.94–dc22   2006034909

ISBN10: 0–415–25413–2 (hbk)
ISBN10: 0–415–25414–0 (pbk)
ISBN10: 0–203–96198–6 (ebk)

ISBN13: 978–0–415–25413–7 (hbk)
ISBN13: 978–0–415–25414–4 (pbk)
ISBN13: 978–0–203–96198–8 (ebk)

Shall I give up the friend I have valued and tried,
If he kneel not before the same altar with me?
From the heretic girl of my soul should I fly,
To seek somewhere else a more orthodox kiss?
No! perish the hearts, and the laws that try
Truth, valour, or love, by a standard like this!

Come, Send Round the Wine
Thomas Moore (1779–1852)

CONTENTS

Preface   ix

Introduction   1

1 England's 'old religions'   11

2 *Episcopi vagantes* and heterodox Christianity   27

3 Churches gnostic and agnostic   43

4 Rediscovering ritual   59

5 Sex and the sacred   77

6 The magic of the margins   94

Afterword: the Christian heritage?   112
Notes   114
Bibliography   151
Index   169

PREFACE

Over the past thirty years Wicca has been explored by scholars in a variety of fields. Anthropologists have found within it fertile ground for a new investigation of magic, a subject which has appeared in anthropological literature since its beginnings as a discipline,[1] and Wicca has appeared in the ethnographies of Paganism which have emerged in the last decade.[2] Historians have regarded it as an 'undiscovered country', a religion or spirituality with little knowledge of its own origins and thus ripe for investigation.[3] Sociologists have categorised it in terms of earlier studies of occult deviance,[4] or have regarded it as a signifier of closure in the late/high modernism-postmodernism debate.[5] The present book is primarily a work of cultural and religious history. This is partly as a result of assessing the literature on Wicca produced over the past twelve years, and partly as a consequence of looking back at my own contribution to that literature. In the former, I detected a distinct tendency to sublimate or otherwise negate the role of Christianity in the historical and contemporary contexts of Wicca.[6] In the latter, I recognised traces of an interest in the various contributions to Wicca that might be accredited to Christianity. The present study thus had a long gestation period, which with hindsight I am now able to recognise.

My first academic conference was also one that I organised – Nature Religion Today, hosted by Lancaster University at their Ambleside centre in April 1996. Here, the Christian theologian Linda Woodhead presented a paper in which she outlined an argument suggesting that Wicca was not a new religion, but a new reformation. Also present was the Wiccan priestess and scholar Vivianne Crowley, who delivered a paper on Wicca as Nature Religion. In this paper, she discussed the attraction of Wicca, speculating 'that Wicca's emphasis on the feminine in the form of the Goddess and its use of ritual might be more novel and therefore attractive features to those of a Protestant background' (Crowley, 1998: 171). In the process of editing the book that emerged from the conference, I was reminded of this again and became increasingly convinced that there might be something in it. Possibly this was because my own religious upbringing had been within a Methodist church which seemed to me to be devoid of any ritual. At the same time, however, I was receiving responses to a questionnaire I had circulated in 1995 and 1996, which seemed to suggest that it was not just my own personal feelings and that there could be some truth in Crowley's assertion. Aside from the early modern association of witches with a conspiracy against Christendom, and the identification of 'Pagan' as non- or anti-Christian, I was also becoming aware of the prevalence of esoteric and heterodox Christianity among key figures in the occult world of late-Victorian England and fin de siècle France.[7] In this world, only Aleister Crowley and Helena Blavatsky seemed virulently anti-Christian, and even in these cases fault was laid at the door of the Church rather than at the foot of the cross.

In a paper delivered at the Sociology of Religion conference held at Exeter University in April 2000, I therefore raised questions concerning the relationship between Wicca and Christianity. I had noted the very small number of respondents of Catholic background to my questionnaire, together with the fact that responses from Europe outside Britain arrived from Wiccans in Scandinavia, Germany and the Netherlands rather than Spain, Portugal and Italy,[8] and this suggested that Vivianne Crowley's speculation might be correct. I sought to explore the relationship between Wicca and Christianity in two ways. The first was to outline the location of Wicca in the religious milieu of the late twentieth century, noting the spectrum of Wiccan responses to Christianity, from outright rejection to involvement in interfaith forums. The second was to provide a few examples of the ways in which Christianity and occultism were either combined or considered compatible by members of those magical orders which were influential in the development of Wicca. Since it formed only a small part of a much broader paper – later published as a chapter in an edited volume from the conference proceedings in 2003 (Pearson, 2003a) – this exploration was limited to a section of just over a thousand words. It seemed to me, even at the time, to warrant deeper investigation.

Processes of de-Christianisation in post-Revolutionary France and Victorian Britain have been well documented in scholarly and other literature.[9] Likewise, the place of esoteric Christianity in the occult subculture of Britain and France from the late nineteenth to the mid-twentieth centuries has been included in studies of occultism, witchcraft and Wicca.[10] What is left unnoted, however, is the prevalence of practising and lapsed Roman Catholics within this occult subculture, and the latter's overlap with Anglo-Catholicism and heterodox forms of Christianity. The first omission may well be in keeping with the general tendency in British scholarship to dismiss Roman Catholicism as irrelevant and to ignore its influence on the development of modern society. As David Blackbourn has pointed out, the Roman Catholic Church has been consigned to an historiographical ghetto for the past two centuries:

> [h]istorians in the mainstream have commonly considered Catholicism, if they considered it at all, as a hopelessly obscurantist force at odds with the more serious isms that have shaped the modern age.[11]
>
> (Blackbourn, 1991: 779)

This situation, as he notes, is now changing, with studies being produced which do concern themselves with the interaction between church, culture and society in the years after the French Revolution, and it is of course an essential component of the study of sixteenth-century Europe. However, it is as a result of the ascendancy of Protestantism in England during that century that the impact of Roman Catholicism has tended to be marginalised or ignored. It is perhaps unsurprising, then, that Roman Catholics and the Anglo-Catholic wing of the Church of England, equally as important elements in the Christian subculture of Victorian England as Christian esotericism, remain largely unconsidered in historical studies of Wicca's antecedents. Even less noticed are the heterodox variants of Christianity that also formed part of both the Christian and occult subcultures.

The present work thus seeks to explore a part of Wiccan history that has only recently come to light. The involvement of Gerald Gardner in traditions of Christian heterodoxy has been noted only to be dismissed. However, with the work of Jone Salomonsen (2002) revealing the dual religious identities of Jewish and Catholic witches, and Kathryn Rountree's recent study of witches and pagans operating within the mainstream Roman Catholic culture of Malta (2006), it seems to me to be time to explore the Christian inheritance of Wicca in greater detail. At the same time, expressions of marginality by Anglican priests perhaps indicate that the borderlands traditionally associated with the 'other' have shifted, and that it is time to explore these marginal regions.

I should like to thank the Arts and Humanities Research Council (AHRC) for providing me with a grant under their Research Leave Scheme that finally gave me the time to complete this work, and my former colleagues at Liverpool Hope University who enabled me to take this leave despite having been there for a very short time. Jennifer Monds and Helen Tandy at Sarum College Library have been immensely helpful, as have staff at Cardiff University Library in facilitating access to early books in the Salisbury Collection. I should like to thank the Dean and Chapter of Salisbury Cathedral for granting access to the Cathedral library, and Suzanne Edward for being so accommodating. At Routledge, my thanks to all who have contributed to the book's production, especially Lesley Riddle, Senior Editor for Religious Studies and Theology, and Gemma Dunn, Editorial Assistant; both have been immensely supportive and encouraging.

Ronald Hutton has supported and encouraged my career since postgraduate days. My thanks to him for sharing ideas, for his willingness to offer comments and feedback on drafts, and for opening up the field of Wiccan history to an extent that I had not imagined possible back in 1995. Although far removed from the thesis submitted for my PhD at the end of 1999, my supervisor Richard H. Roberts will no doubt understand how much he not only helped me through that process but also enabled the present work to be conceived. Geoffrey Samuel and Santi Rozario have been great friends and inspiring academic companions now for over a decade, and I thank them for many conversations, and for Geoffrey's willingness to respond to emails simply entitled 'Help!'. Kathryn Rountree shared with me some of her thoughts on witches and pagans in Malta at the tail-end of the process of writing this book, which provided me with an invigorating boost. I very much look forward to the publication of the book based on her fieldwork.

My thanks for the encouragement of the Church of England clergy who took part in my workshop on 'Pagans and Christians in the Twenty-First Century' at the Diocese of Salisbury Conference in Derbyshire in July 2006, as this book was drawing to a close, and to all at Salisbury Cathedral from whom I have learned so much. Long live bonfires at dawn! Thanks to Dave, Allan and John who shared memories of earlier forums that enabled Wiccans and Christians to talk together, and to Steve, Fred, and Fiona for useful comments along the way, and particularly to Philip Heselton, who provided me with valuable information as well as copies of Gerald Gardner's ordination certificate. Indeed, to those who trained me and to all the Wiccans whom I have met and worked with over the past twelve years, my heartfelt thanks.

I acknowledge here a great debt to my parents. I have only recently come to appreciate what a gift it is to have been given time and space to read, think and study, which they always ensured I had. Without their encouragement and belief in me I would not be where I am today. To my beloved husband, Paul, I owe a huge debt of gratitude. It was he who first showed me that ritual does indeed exist within Christianity, and without the constant ability to ransack his brain as well as his library, this book simply couldn't have been written. This book is dedicated to him.

Pages 2–6 of the Introduction to this book contain a proportion of material previously included in a chapter entitled 'The History and Development of Wicca and Paganism' in Joanne Pearson (ed.) (2002b) *Belief Beyond Boundaries: Wicca, Celtic Spirituality and the New Age*. It is reprinted here by permission of Ashgate Publishing Ltd. A small amount of the material in Chapter 4 was originally part of a conference paper for 'William James and The Varieties of Religious Experience: Centenary Conference in Celebration of the 1901–1902 Gifford Lectures', held at Old College, University of Edinburgh in July 2002. It was later published in *CrossCurrents*, Fall, 2003, 53(3): 413–23. Part of Chapter 5 began life as a paper delivered at the conference 'Dangerous Sex: Contesting the Spaces of Theology and Sexuality', held at the University of Glasgow in April 2002. I should like to thank Alison Jasper and Heather Walton for providing me with the opportunity to air my thoughts in such an encouraging environment. The paper was published in an article entitled 'Inappropriate Sexuality? Sex Magic, S/M, and Wicca (or "Whipping Harry Potter's Arse!")', in *Theology & Sexuality*, 11(2): 31–42. Material drawn from it is reprinted here by permission of SAGE Publications Ltd (SAGE Publications, 2005). A portion of Chapter 6 was delivered as 'Magic, Witchcraft and Occultism in Contemporary Paganism', a keynote lecture for the Dutch Association for the Study of

Religion Annual Conference, in Utrecht, in May 2003. It was subsequently published in the association's newsletter, Nederlands Genootschap voor Godsdienstwetenschap, Nieuwsbrief 2004/2, pp. 3–16. I am deeply grateful to Wouter Hanegraaff for inviting me to this stimulating conference.

INTRODUCTION

Witchcraft 'prowls the borderlands of Christianity', to borrow a phrase from Michel Foucault (1987: 16). To the Protestant reformers, it followed in the wake of heresy as surely as night follows dusk. Regarding the magic of witchcraft as different to that of Catholic priest-craft only in intent, the rituals of witchcraft were perceived as inversions of the latter's quasi-magical liturgy. Familiarity, it is said, breeds contempt, and the witchcraft of the contemporary Western world has sought to distance itself from the Christian traditions of the reformations, both Protestant and Catholic, deemed responsible for the persecution of those accused of witchcraft. Yet within these Christian traditions are contained not only many themes drawn upon in modern witchcraft, but also an inheritance that is both personal – in the sense that varieties of Christianity remain the religion in which the majority of witches were raised – and influential in the development of contemporary Wicca. Drawing on evidence that has only recently come to light, and which heretofore has received only cursory attention, this book seeks to explore the borderlands between Wicca and the marginal forms of Christianity in England and France, both heterodox and Catholic. The book thus uncovers a part of Wiccan history that has either been unknown or studiously ignored, a history found in the borderland, marginal region where Christianity and Wicca meet.

The use of the labels 'witchcraft', 'witches' and 'Wicca' above may be confusing, referring as they do to those 'witches' accused of practising 'witchcraft' in the early modern period, to modern Western people who call themselves witches practising various forms of witchcraft, and to the contemporary initiatory religion called Wicca, whose initiates identify as both witches and Wiccans, as well as priestesses and priests. The focus of this book is a religion that is approximately sixty years old. It is 'the only religion which England has ever given the world' (Hutton, 1999: vii). This religion, known as Wicca, was formulated by Gerald Gardner (1884–1964), among others,[1] in England in the 1940s, slowly becoming more widespread and public after the repeal of the Witchcraft Act in 1951. Gardner was born in 1884, in Crosby, Liverpool. After spending most of his life working in the colonies of Sri Lanka and the Far East, he returned to England in 1936

1

and retired to the New Forest with his wife, Dorothea – usually known as Donna – daughter of an Anglican clergyman. Here, he claimed to have been initiated into an hereditary witchcraft coven in 1939. However, although Gardner was certainly interested in witchcraft at this time, there is no solid evidence of the existence of any pagan witch covens prior to 1948, by which time Gardner's basic framework for a religion he called 'Wica'[2] was in place and Gardner was leading a coven in Hertfordshire with his close friend Dafo. More recently, Chas Clifton (2004: 269) has proposed '[p]ostponing the accepted creation date of Wicca to about 1951' in order to better explain the differences between the fictional witchcraft of Gardner's novel, *High Magic's Aid* (1949), and his later portrayal of witchcraft as a surviving ancient religion, a portrayal gleaned from the work of Egyptologist and fellow folklorist, Margaret Murray.[3]

The later portrayals to which Clifton refers were contained in two volumes, *Witchcraft Today* (1954), and *The Meaning of Witchcraft* (1959). The first of these brought Gardner to the attention of the media, and whilst this may have been unexpected, Gerald apparently revelled in the publicity. Doreen Valiente, Gardner's high priestess and collaborator in the early 1950s, reports that Gerald,

> started posing before the cameras of the press and preening himself on his great discovery of the survival of witchcraft. ... [His] motives were, I believe, basically good. He was desperately anxious that the Old Religion should not die ... [but] he had a considerable love of the limelight and of being the centre of attention.
>
> (Valiente, 1989: 65–6)

Believing witchcraft to be a dying religion, then, Gardner propelled it into the public domain, initiated many new witches, and encouraged the establishment of covens, operating according to the outlines provided in his books.

In the 1960s, Alex Sanders (1926–88) established a slightly different version of Wicca, which became known as Alexandrian Wicca. Like Gardner, Sanders hailed from the Liverpool region, born in Birkenhead then growing up in Manchester. Also like Gardner, Sanders was a prolific initiator, and took the religion formed in England into Europe: many covens in Germany and Scandinavia sprang from his visits to the continent. Sanders was by all accounts as much a publicity seeker as Gardner had been, though many Gardnerian witches reacted against him in the 1960s and 1970s.[4] Despite sensationalist media coverage and a decidedly salacious 1969 film *Legend of the Witches: Their Secrets Revealed ...*,[5] Sanders' moves to make Wicca more accessible now tend to be appreciated rather than berated. Gardnerian and Alexandrian Wicca were combined in the 1980s by Vivianne Crowley, an initiate of both forms. The Gardnerian, Alexandrian and combined traditions of Wicca are those that are discussed in this book. However, Wicca is by no means the only type of witchcraft. A variety of forms derived from it have emerged since the late 1970s.

From Britain, Wicca spread to North America and Europe; from America, various derivations spread back across northern Europe, Canada, Australia, New Zealand, and South Africa.[6] In the process, Wicca has evolved and, at times, mutated quite dramatically into completely different forms. Influences have come and gone, having a distinct impact in some countries and leaving little recognisable mark in others. In some areas, debates have raged as Wicca has acclimatised: in the southern hemisphere, for example, discussions continue as to how the seasonal rituals of the Wheel of the Year should be celebrated, given that Midwinter/Yule in the northern hemisphere is Midsummer in the southern.[7] In the USA and Canada, practices borrowed from First Nations peoples have been adopted by Wiccans which mean little to some Europeans, who may instead opt for Celtic, Saxon or Germanic inspiration, making a syncretic identification with what are regarded as the indigenous traditions of northern European ancestry. At the same time, these latter form an important part of the identity of some North Americans of European descent, with alleged Celtic pagan concepts proving particularly popular. Likewise, feminist witchcraft, which emerged from the feminist consciousness movement in the USA, has had a profound impact on Wicca in that country and on practices in, for example, New Zealand.[8] Whilst feminism has certainly influenced English Wicca, feminist witchcraft itself is far less pronounced.[9]

British Gardnerian Wicca was exported to the United States by an initiate of Gardner, Raymond Buckland, in 1967. Once there, according to Orion (1995: 143), it was transformed into a 'very different kind of religion'.[10] In particular, Wicca was adapted by the women's spirituality movement, resulting in the development of Pagan Goddess spirituality and feminist witchcraft traditions such as Dianic and Reclaiming witchcraft. This feminist witchcraft developed largely out of the feminist consciousness raising movement combined with Wicca, and is quite distinct from British Alexandrian and Gardnerian Wicca. Feminist witchcraft, for example, explicitly emphasises the Goddess as representative of divinity, attempts to maintain an explicitly non-hierarchical organisation inherited from the feminist consciousness movement (in which women rotate leadership and make collective decisions), and engages in political activism after the feminist rubric 'the personal is political is spiritual' (Culpepper, 1978: 222). Alexandrian and Gardnerian Wicca, however, emphasise both Gods and Goddesses as representative of divinity, allow a 'hierarchy of experience' (implicit in their organisation in covens led by a High Priestess and/or High Priest and the structure of three degrees of initiation), and tend to maintain a distance between spirituality and politics.

In *Wicca and the Christian Heritage*, 'Wicca' refers to Alexandrian and Gardnerian Wicca. When feminist witchcraft is referred to, it is as 'witchcraft' rather than 'Wicca'. This distinction in part reflects the terminology used by practitioners.[11] On the one hand, Wiccans use the term 'Wicca' to denote a mystery religion involving a process of initiation and rigorous training within a cosmos polarised between male and female forces, all of which is an inheritance from the magical secret societies from which Wicca is descended. The term is also used in order to differentiate between the anthropological study of primitive, tribal witchcraft and the Wiccan religion of Western, literate, post-industrial society (re)invented by Gerald Gardner and developed since that time into its contemporary forms. On the other hand, feminist witches prefer the term 'witchcraft', using it to describe a religious practice based upon the human (female) witch becoming empowered through interaction with the Goddess as divine counterpart of the witch, an empowerment which is sought in order to provide personal liberation for the individual woman and thus sustain women in their struggle against patriarchy. Feminist witchcraft is thus located within the wider feminist spirituality and Goddess movements, making use of a constructed image based on a feminist reading of the witchcraft persecutions of the sixteenth and seventeenth centuries and a myth of matriarchy, both of which are preferred alternatives to a legacy from secret societies, which are regarded as a predominantly male preserve, and having Gerald Gardner as founding father.

Wicca has also been instrumental in the subsequent development of a variety of forms of Paganism. Indeed, Hutton goes so far as to claim that Wicca is the classical form from which all other contemporary Pagan groups evolved.[12] Thus, whilst contemporary Wicca may have *originated* in mid-

of a 'relatively self-contained, England-
f, 1998: 85), an increasing variety of
as now become established. From this
er Pagan traditions and other varieties
isingly syncretistic and nondogmatic
hip between Wicca and Paganism has
leed, the notion of Wicca as a form of
l.

ented by a myriad of self-consciously
ie contemporary world. These include
spirituality, shamanism, Heathenism
hip, non-aligned Paganism, feminist
of witchcraft, all of which heavily
5, of the estimated 110,000–120,000
nitiated Wiccans.[13] Initiatory Wicca in
growth of Paganism, and this is partly
subverts the non-hierarchical, anti-

elitist attitudes held by the majority of Pagan groups. Wicca's presentation of itself as the esoteric centre of which Paganism constitutes an exoteric manifestation[14] has at times exacerbated the tensions implied by what are perceived to be elitist distinctions made by Wiccans.[15] However, such self-identification as members of an esoteric, initiatory religion also reflects the roots of Wicca in occult societies.

In his formulation of Wicca, Gardner drew on traditions of high ritual magic derived from those practised in occult societies since the last decade of the nineteenth century, and particularly from the published work of Aleister Crowley. Despite Gardner's claims to the contrary it is clear that a proportion of Crowley's work did indeed enter Wicca,[16] and the high ritual magic practised within the secret, magical societies of the British occult revival at the turn of the twentieth century was highly influential. That the teachings and practices drawn together under the auspices of the Hermetic Order of the Golden Dawn and developed by Crowley were of particular importance is indicated by Gardner's library. Twelve of Crowley's works are listed among the library's contents, along with Mather's translation of the Key of Solomon (1888), Ellic Howe's *The Magicians of the Golden Dawn* (1922), Israel Regardie's publications of Golden Dawn rituals (in three volumes, 1937–9), and the more practical of Dion Fortune's books – *Sane Occultism* (1938) and *The Mystical Qabalah* (1935). The stories of these individuals and the organisations which they founded or to which they belonged are well documented,[17] and their influence on Gardner and Wicca is generally accepted by practitioners of Wicca in Britain whilst, as noted above, still being rejected by many feminist witches in the United States. Partly as a result of their influence, Hanegraaff has argued that Wicca is not specifically Pagan, being rather,

> a neo-pagan development of traditional occultist ritual magic, but ... the latter movement is not itself pagan. In other words ... [Wicca] gradually and almost imperceptibly shades into a non-pagan domain.
>
> (Hanegraaff, 1998: 86)

Such a claim is supported by the fact that there are a significant number of Wiccans who do not consider themselves to be 'Pagan' at all. The old aphorism once popular in Wiccan circles – 'All Wiccans are Pagans, but not all Pagans are Wiccans' – can no longer be considered to be a general reflection of Wiccan identity. Gardner's attraction to the secret societies and ritual magic of his era, and the initiatory mystery religions of the classical ancient world, overlaid Wicca with certain characteristics as it emerged in the 1950s. Not least of these is that initiation, secrecy and intimate community maintain strong boundaries that firmly demarcate who is an 'insider' and who is an 'outsider', an important means of maintaining Wicca's distinctiveness.[18] In this, Wicca differs from other forms of witchcraft and Paganism in which 'inside' and 'outside' status is not such an issue.[19] That Wicca is most often classed as 'Pagan' by both practitioners and scholars may not, therefore, be particularly accurate, for identification as Pagan has never been a requirement for Wiccan initiation. Thus, although making up 10 per cent of the British Pagan population in 1999,[20] in many ways initiatory Wicca can be regarded as existing on the margins of Paganism, as well as on the margins of the occult.

In other contexts, however, Wicca has become increasingly less marginal. At the level at which Wicca interacts with popular culture, there appears to be a certain amount of 'trendiness' attached to identifying oneself as Wiccan or as a witch. Throughout the 1990s the 'teen witch' image was increasing in popularity, with Silver Ravenwolf's book *Teen Witch: Wicca For A New Generation* (1998) proving to be a bestseller in the United States, whilst the film *The Craft* (1996) was especially influential with teenagers. Teenage girls, in particular, wrote to the Pagan Federation for advice about joining a coven after watching the film. The all-pervasive publishing machine ensured that the steady stream of publications on Wicca and witchcraft became a flood that smothered everything and threw up all kinds of debris in its wake: book store shelves were inundated with volumes on kitchen witches, bedroom witches, teenage witches, satanic witches, and the seemingly ubiquitous velvet-covered tomes by 'Titania'.[21] No longer were there Gardnerian witches, Alexandrian witches, solitaries (hedge witches) and hereditaries. They had been joined by

> white witches, grey witches, black witches, green witches, teen witches, feminist witches, media witches, hedge witches, kitchen witches, New Age witches, and even weekend witches.
>
> (*The Cauldron*, February 1999, 91: 30)[22]

This list reflects a growing awareness that 'witchcraft' and 'Wicca' can be used as labels for very different groups and individuals. On the one hand, 'Wicca' is used to refer to 'covens' of friends who have no initiation or training but gather together to celebrate the seasons or full moons, a practice that could perhaps be labelled more accurately as 'non-aligned Paganism'. On the other hand, 'Wicca' is styled as an esoteric religion and mystery tradition operating in small, closed groups to which entry is solely by initiation ceremonies which include oaths of secrecy and which are designed to trigger personal transformation and the experience of transmutation. The appropriation of 'Wicca' by uninitiated people has proved irritating to Wiccan initiates,

serious religion which demands
)n. The proliferation of 'how-to'
 age or level of experience, with
 a move from the margins to the
 ;sful marketing of what some see
 for consumption by all.[23] Whilst
)le who seek out initiatory Wicca
 ; facilitated by this dissemination
 that the trivialising DIY versions
 me adepts without the difficult
 ; that Wicca is being diluted and

trivialised through the commodification of witchcraft, there is a sense in which the growing popularity of witchcraft is perceived to be 'eroding the previously closely guarded secrecy of Wicca' (Harrington, 2000: 7). As a consequence, many Wiccans feel that the identity of Wicca as an initiatory religion needs to be re-established and protected.

The diversification of Paganism, variants of witchcraft and Wicca, and the position of British Wicca on the margins of both these expressions of spirituality and of occult magic make it necessary to spell out the type of Wicca with which this book is concerned. It also makes increasingly necessary those studies of specific communities that Jone Salomonsen pointed to in her work on the Reclaiming witches of San Francisco. As she observes,

> lack of differentiation between feminist and nonfeminist versions of Witchcraft, between Californian, East Coast and British customs, or between visionary texts and social practices, is like quoting from Luther when describing the Catholics.
>
> (Salomonsen, 2002: 10)

Such conflation is concomitant with early studies of newly emergent religious groupings, and reflects the thematic studies covering a range of Pagan groups, synthesised and generalised, rather than in-depth studies. More comprehensive, in-depth studies have begun to emerge, led, as were the earlier, thematic studies, largely by North American scholars studying North American groups.[24] To some extent, this has resulted in the characteristics of North American Wicca and feminist witchcraft being perceived as in some way normative, or as a template which can be imposed on, or which has superseded British Wicca. Such a presentation of Wicca often stems from scholars who have not worked with British Wiccans. In this book, the opposite is true. Although I have had conversations with North American Wiccans both in person and via forums such as the Nature Religions Scholars List, I have not had the opportunity to work with them. This lack of involvement with variants of Wicca or witchcraft in the US, coupled with the fact that I am British, with a background predominantly in English history, leads naturally to a focus on Britain. More importantly, the Wiccans among whom I have worked have all been British and European, and those who formed the Wicca which they practise – Gerald Gardner, Doreen Valiente, Alex and Maxine Sanders, Janet and Stewart Farrar, Vivianne and Chris Crowley – are all British. My concern in this book is therefore with British Wiccans initiated into one of the three streams outlined above: Gardnerian, Alexandrian, or a combination of the two. In this, I rely partly on fieldwork conducted for my PhD in the period 1995–2000, and partly on ongoing interaction with the community. Such ongoing involvement has included observation of practitioner understanding of Wiccan history.[25]

Stories of witchcraft as the original, pre-Christian, indigenous religion of Western Europe, of the 'burning times', of the Golden Age of Matriarchy, as well as histories situating Wicca's roots in Freemasonry and magical secret societies, reflect to a large extent the development of Wicca. The story of the survival of a pre-Christian religion persecuted during the witch hunts of early modern Europe began to give way under the onslaught of historical study in Britain in the 1970s.[26] However, at the same time it was receiving renewed impetus in the USA through the development of feminist witchcraft, emerging from the feminist consciousness movement and Gardnerian Wicca, even if the latter was/is unacknowledged.[27] Its development as a mainstay of feminist witches' identity was combined with a myth of matriarchy, and both remain extremely powerful. One should be wary of generalisation, however. Not all practitioners of feminist witchcraft are resident in the US, and not all of them continue to believe in Murray's (and Gardner's) theory or in the myth of matriarchy. Likewise, many Wiccans in Britain still believe they are connected to an age-old fertility religion of which those persecuted in the witch hunts were also representatives. They are often unaware of the latest research on witchcraft, and they have not all been delighted by the research which they have been keen to access, like that of Hutton. The 'genuine scholarly rigour' and willingness of Wiccans to re-evaluate their history, to which Hutton referred in the introduction to the 1993 edition of *Pagan Religions* (p. xiii), is by no means universally valued and has been challenged by his later work.[28]

This is demonstrated in two rival reviews published in the Beltane (May) 2000 issue of *Pagan Dawn*, in which Tony Geraghty (2000: 37) describes Hutton as 'the gentle iconoclast ... [who has] banished our illusions'. After this book, he claims,

> the Craft will never be quite the same again. ... That we can believe in the Craft in future without Gardner's bluff or Murray's blindfold is no bad thing. For that, we should thank Hutton, while rubbing some soothing oil ... onto the affected parts of our collective ego.
>
> (Geraghty, 2000: 38)

'Gardner's bluff' and 'Murray's blindfold' are, however, precisely those parts of the myth which Hutton (2003b: 265) claims had been debunked in Wiccan circles well before the publication of his book, and indeed, this point is picked up by the second reviewer, John Macintyre, who criticises Geraghty's 'apparent belief that the historical claims advanced by Gardner are not only still generally accepted amongst Wiccans but that they constitute a cornerstone of the Craft' (Macintyre, 2000: 39). *The Triumph of the Moon* has not, argues Macintyre, 'burst upon us like a bolt from the blue, to shatter the tower of our "cherished concepts" into ruin' (ibid.). He asserts that early historical claims have been disintegrating for the past twenty years, as indeed they had in academic circles. Many Wiccans were in the process of, or had already, abandoned their myths of origin, as Macintyre argued. Those who still adhered to the idea of Wicca as the ancient religion of the British Isles simply ignored Hutton's research.[29] I have no doubt that the new historical material contained in the present work will elicit the same spectrum of responses.

In the course of his investigations into the history of Pagan witchcraft, Hutton came to the conclusion that Wicca represented,

> not a marginal, isolated, and thoroughly eccentric creed, arguably produced by one rather odd ex-colonial, but an extreme distillation and combination of important cultural currents within mainstream British society which had developed or been imported during the previous two hundred years.[30]
>
> (Hutton, 2003b: 268)

That he did not cover all such currents to his satisfaction, and that further research remained to be conducted is borne out by his comment, '... my own suspicion is that the greatest invisible player in the story [of the emergence of Wicca] is spiritualism' (Hutton, 1999: xi). But whilst spiritualism may not have received the same attention as other influential currents upon Wicca, it has hardly remained invisible.[31] Not least, spiritualism was certainly instrumental in bringing about the repeal of the 1736 Witchcraft Act and its replacement with the Fraudulent Mediums Act of 1951,[32] which signalled to Gardner that the time was now ripe for publicising witchcraft. Indeed, Gardner ([1959] 2004: 195) opined that, '[t]he Spiritualists hailed it as their charter of freedom', and he saw in spiritualism vestiges of witchcraft.[33] However, a further current, and one that has not been subjected to any extensive exploration, is to be found in developments within European Christianity, particularly in England and France. My own contention is that the real 'invisible player' is heterodox Christianity, particularly as it developed out of the Catholic revival of the nineteenth century. Although representing only a small ingredient in the 'cauldron of inspiration' on which Gardner drew, the heterodox variants of Christianity have been influential on what might be considered more substantial – and certainly well-documented – elements of Wicca's history such as Freemasonry, spiritualism, Druidry, and occult/secret societies.[34] Its place in the story of Wicca, therefore, now needs to be examined.

The present work therefore seeks to uncover this other untold history of Wicca. It begins with the English reformations of the sixteenth century for, as Nigel Yates has argued (2000: 10), the Catholic revival in England was not without precedent and thus, '[t]he teachings of the Tractarians and the innovations of the early ritualists cannot ... be understood without a better appreciation of the nature of Anglicanism in the three centuries between the Reformation and the Oxford Movement'. Chapter 1 thus considers the emergence of the Church of England and its associated myths of the ancient British church, concerns with issues of validity and authenticity, and the use of the terms 'old religion' and 'new religion'. This opening chapter sets out the background to themes drawn on later in the book. Importantly, it includes the characterisation of the Church of England as reformed Catholic rather than wholly Protestant, thus undermining to some extent Crowley's claims for the attraction of Wicca to those of Protestant backgrounds, at least as far as English Wiccans are concerned. The desire to find validity for orders and the radical attempt to revitalise an ancient British Christianity were shared by other .Christians, both Catholic and heterodox, including Anglo-Catholics and the churches of the *episcopi vagantes*, and this forms the main body of Chapter 2. Gerald Gardner, Ross Nichols and other figures important to the development of Wicca were not merely members of, but were ordained as deacons, priests, and even bishops and archbishops of heterodox Christian churches in England and France, and this is explored in Chapter 3. Chapters 2 and 3 also refute the claim made by Davis and Heselton that Ward and Gardner were part of the Old Catholic Church. The remaining chapters are concerned with three accusations that have been levelled against Catholicism, heterodoxy and witchcraft – ritual, (deviant) sexuality, and magic.

This recovery of the untold story of Gardner's interests in heterodox Christianity might prove to be an issue of controversy for some Christians, not to mention some Wiccans. Uncovering a Christian heritage may be uncomfortable to those who – in spite of Hutton's work – have not yet 'proved capable of re-evaluating' Wicca in light of his findings. It may also irritate feminist witches who may find here another suggestion of patriarchal origins in Christian heterodoxy, as well as those who have considered Wicca to be somehow opposed to ideas of Christianity, yet here find its origins indebted to some of the historical contingencies in Christianity. Time will tell whether the writing of the story of Christian influences on Wicca can be accommodated by Wiccans themselves, whether this history will be incorporated into Wiccans' celebrated version of their past.

1

ENGLAND'S 'OLD RELIGIONS'

Wicca is commonly called the 'old religion' by its practitioners, a designation that is intended to claim historical ancestry to validate some of its practices. However, this chapter argues that this term does more than retrace or reread a past (*religare*) and claim to maintain rituals of an ancient Wiccan ancestry (its *traditio*). 'Old' and 'new' religion are value-laden terms that have links with a political history dating from the time of the Tudor reformations in England, for the term had earlier served both the Church of England and the Catholic traditions of Christianity in the period between the reformations and the nineteenth century. In continental Europe, the various forms of Protestantism that arose in the course of the sixteenth century were seen to offer new experiences of Christianity. Characterised as throwing off the shackles of popery, magic, superstition and monasticism, the reformed Protestant traditions relegated the tropes of Roman Catholicism to the 'dark ages' of Christianity and looked to the future. However, a deep concern of the new Church of England was to demonstrate that English Christianity was not dependent on the Catholic Mission of Augustine of Canterbury (597 CE) for its claims to be apostolic, and it therefore sought to retrace older apostolic origins and 'Celtic' influences.[1]

There are, then, at least three 'old religions' to which England has laid claim. Two of these are constructs of the Christian church formulated during the period of the reformations, both Protestant and Catholic. During and after the establishment of the Protestant 'new religion', Roman Catholicism was referred to as the 'old religion', both affectionately by lay people who sought comfort from what they knew, and disparagingly by the reformers. Of course, Roman Catholicism cannot be regarded as one of *England's* 'old religions', but with the revival of English Catholicism in the nineteenth-century Oxford Movement and the development of Anglo-Catholicism, there emerged a more positive reclaiming of the 'old religion', with a concomitant critique of Protestantism as the 'new religion'.[2] However, this 'new religion' in the form of the Church of England sought to provide itself with a line of continuity stretching back to the apostolic era in order to substantiate its claim to be an 'old religion'. The third version of an 'old religion', constructed partly in response to institutionalised Christianity in the twentieth century, was of course Wicca. In order to explore the political valorising of 'old' and 'new' it is necessary to demonstrate the uses of these terms in the struggles over authenticity in Anglicanism, before returning to their uses in the development of Wicca.

The 'new religion' of 'Protestant' Christianity in England emerged and developed during the reigns of Henry VIII (1509–47), Edward VI (1547–53) and Elizabeth I (1558–1603), rather than springing fully-formed as a result of Henry's 'divorce question' in 1530. It developed over a period of some seventy years, five of which saw a reversion to the Roman Catholic Church and Papal authority under Mary Tudor (1553–8). Indeed, the new Church of England was never fully Protestant. Henry had wanted a break with Roman authority, not with Catholic traditions of piety and ritual, to the despair of his more Protestant-minded reforming ministers, Thomas Cranmer[3] (1489–1556) Archbishop of Canterbury (1532) and Thomas Cromwell[4] (c.1485–1540). Later, Elizabeth continually sought to occupy a middle ground between the Protestant Puritans on the one side, and Roman Catholicism on the other. Only during the short reign of Edward were the Protestant reformers able to follow their own agenda, an agenda that was overthrown during the reign of Mary. By the seventeenth century, then, the Church of England had become 'a fusion of Catholic and Protestant positions in which most Christians, apart from extreme Calvinists and Catholics, could find a home' (Waite, 2003: 77). As will be seen later in this chapter and in Chapter 4, it was the inclusivity of this 'broad church' that allowed for the revival of Catholicism in an English form in the Oxford Movement of the 1830s, and its later Anglo-Catholic and Ritualist developments. The complexity of the religio-political manoeuverings under the Tudor monarchs is not, however, the subject of extensive discussion here; suffice it to say that the general population would not necessarily have been aware of each and every shift or the intricacies of debates and intrigues.[5] However, some awareness of the Protestant colouring of Edward and Elizabeth, and the Catholicism of Mary, would have been enough to engender anxieties and expectations as each reign drew to a close, and events such as the 1536 Pilgrimage of Grace and the dissolution of the local monastery would not have gone unnoticed. Indeed, the latter would have been as likely to be celebrated as mourned, given the often harsh treatment of local populations by their monastic landlords.[6]

If Protestantism emerged as the new people's religion, full of hope for the future, it did so partly by casting Catholicism as the old-fashioned religion, full of superstition and administered by a priesthood that not only performed sacramental magic, but also practised angelic or demonic magic (Waite, 2003: 229). Indeed, to one anonymous reformer writing in 1556,

> the sorcerers who conjure demons are more holy than you who are the whorish Church ... you command Christ to enter into a piece of bread and believe that you could have him as often as you say the words, 'this is my body'.
>
> (cited in Waite, 2003: 102)

12

Anticipating theories of religion and magic that were formulated in the nineteenth century, magic was not simply un-Christian but a survival from the backward, primitive culture associated in the minds of the reformers with the Middle Ages. That there was a general tendency to refer to Roman Catholicism as 'the old religion' need not refer, then, to a nostalgic remembering of a recent past, nor can it necessarily be read as a yearning for an authentic Christianity, particularly in the 1530s and 1540s when the break with Rome was not strictly a break with Catholicism. A certain amount of time had to pass before it was possible for people to look back to 'the good old days', and certainly there is evidence of this after the passing of centuries. In *Witchcraft, Magic and Culture, 1736–1951*, Owen Davies cites the example of a Yorkshire Anglican priest in 1825 who was asked to 'lay' a spirit which was troubling an old woman (i.e. she thought she was possessed). He said he couldn't 'lay spirits' to which she responded: 'if I had sent for a priest o' t' au'd church, he wad a dean it' (1999: 23). Davies asserts that there was a popular memory of spirit-laying powers of the Catholic clergy by the eighteenth century in England, though 'Catholic worshippers and priests were rather thin on the ground' (ibid.). Closer to the period in question, in 1593 Thomas Bell could remark on 'the sad fact that the "common people for the greater part", insist on calling Protestantism "the new religion"'.[7] No study of instances of Catholicism being referred to as the 'old religion' and Protestantism as the 'new religion' has yet been conducted, and such an investigation would be out of place here. That there were instances of such labelling is, however, beyond doubt as shown by the examples given above.

Picking up on the anxiety that seems to have attended the labelling of Protestantism as the 'new religion', the emerging Church of England responded with a particular ambition for antiquity, an anxiety for ancestors. This takes us to the second of our examples, the Church of England's desire to promote itself as an authentic expression of the earliest formulations of the Christian religion. As indicated above, the Reformation in England was not accomplished primarily via Henry VIII's marital problems.[8] Rather, it emerged and developed[9] with many twists and turns throughout the Tudor period and on into that of the Stuart monarchs. A continual theme, however, was the search for, and invention of a tradition of English Protestantism. With the 'old religion' continuing to assert itself through papal interference at one extreme and popular appeal at the other,[10] the leaders of the 'new religion' found it necessary to remake a history for the English church that would legitimate the break with Rome and validate their own orders. In order to subvert the attempts of Catholic propagandists to undermine Protestantism by contrasting the antiquity of Roman Catholicism with Protestantism's novelty, they needed to find a precedent: an older 'old religion'.[11]

Cromwell, as Henry VIII's Lord Chancellor, began this process in his preambles to the Act in Restraint of Appeals (1533) and the Act of Supremacy (1534).[12] In the Act in Restraint of Appeals, England is declared 'an empire' according to 'divers sundry old authentic histories and chronicles', and the English Church 'hath been always thought, and is also at this hour, sufficient and meet of itself without the intermeddling of any exterior person or persons'.[13] The Act was to conserve the imperial prerogatives of the imperial crown, both temporal and spiritual, 'to keep it from the annoyance ... of the see of Rome'.[14] The purpose of these Reformation statutes was 'to separate the English from Western Christendom and provide them with a new identity, derived from a new view of their past' (Jones, 2003: 18). A new, official version of English history was constructed to meet the needs of the new church, the church which had delivered the English from the 'slavery' of papal authority asserted during the Middle Ages, restoring the nation 'to its original imperial state in which the English king had reigned supreme over all aspects of national life' (ibid.: 22). The underlying concept was that England was independent and had therefore developed an indigenous English culture, religion and institutions, untainted by outside influence, power and authority.

The characterisation of England as an imperial realm rests on the legend of the unhistorical King Lucius, portrayed as an English equivalent of Constantine. Cromwell made use of the claim that Christianity was brought to England by Joseph of Arimathea and disciples of St Philip. After the crucifixion, Joseph of Arimathea had supposedly become a missionary, working with the apostle Philip in France before being made leader of a mission to Britain. Arriving in Glastonbury, he was alleged to have built the first English Church, the *vetusta ecclesia*,[15] *c.*64 CE, from wattle and daub.[16] Once he and his companions had died, the church was unused until 166 CE when King Lucius wrote to Pope Eleutherius (174–189 CE) of his own volition, asking him to send Christian missionaries to convert him and all his people.[17] These missionaries, St Phagan and St Deruvian, refounded a small community at the church and built a second of stone, which became a monastery under St Patrick who arrived from Ireland in the fifth century. English Christianity, it was claimed, thus came straight from the early apostles, straight from Jerusalem, not via Rome.

The story reflects the struggles of the monks of Glastonbury during the high Middle Ages.[18] The association with the apostles had first appeared in William of Malmesbury's *De Antiquitate Glastoniensis Ecclesiae*, *c.*1130, but although the passage on Joseph of Arimathea is an interpolation dating from at least a century later,[19] the legend seems to have emerged from an already traditional belief in the apostolic conversion of Britain.[20] Such works as Malmesbury's *De Antiquitate* and John of Glastonbury's *Cronica sive Antiquitates Glastoniensis Ecclesie* (*c.*1400) were often commissioned for the purposes of increasing the prestige of monastic houses by demonstrating their claims to ancient historical foundation. But they also had another purpose, a political one. The date of a country's conversion to Christianity determined its precedence in the general councils of Europe, apostolic conversion being the most prestigious. Thus, the legend of St Joseph at Glastonbury enabled

14

claims to be made for the apostolic conversion of England, and it was 'cited by the English party to back its claim to precedence at a series of general councils – at Pisa (1409), Constance (1417), Siena (1424) and Basle (1434)' (Gransden, 1980: 362).

However, the impact of the Glastonbury legends continued to be felt well into Cromwell's lifetime.[21] In 1520, a life of Joseph of Arimathea in verse had been printed to reinforce his connection with Glastonbury,[22] which the reigning abbot, Richard de Bere (1494–1525), wanted to promote.[23] The need to increase revenue from pilgrims in the fourteenth century,[24] and rivalries over claims to antiquity and precedence within the church in the fifteenth, had meant that the 'status of Joseph at Glastonbury rose accordingly, and reached its apogee in the early sixteenth century' (Hutton, 2003a: 69), just in time for Cromwell to make full use of it for the establishment of the new Anglican Church which was to see the dissolution of Glastonbury Abbey, along with all the other monastic establishments. Thus, though the abbey would be dissolved six years after the 1533 Act,[25] the story was both readily available and had a proven track record of success in promoting not just an independent English national church, but one which had successfully claimed precedence in the conciliar movement of fifteenth century Europe.[26] That Joseph of Arimathea did not enter the *Roman Martyrology* until 1545 would simply have given further credence to the idea that English Christianity existed, and always had existed, independently from Rome.

From Cromwell's time onwards, according to Jones (2003: 60), 'the history of England was the story of the heroic struggle of its native kings and people, valiantly defending *true Christianity* against alien invaders who in various guises represented the forces of "Anti-Christ"' (emphasis added). These invaders included not just the heathen Saxons from Germany, but also St Augustine of Canterbury – portrayed as a corrupting agent from Rome – and the arrival of monks and friars following the Norman Conquest. But this was nothing new. As mentioned above, the importance of the idea of an independent English national church, free from Rome, was already traditional before the twelfth century. What *was* new was that there now existed the institution of such a church, national and erastian in character, broken away from Rome, and backed by the power of the state propaganda machine: the *Ecclesia Anglicana* was no longer the Catholic Church *in England*, but the Church *of England*. The legend was reworked to give England a destiny: to defend the national church which 'had been retained in spite of interference from abroad by the Papacy during the medieval period' (ibid.: 77) – a period which was now to be ignored and dismissed as backward and decadent – and restored to its native state by the Henrician reformation. To aid this effort, those condemned as heretics by the old religion were transformed into native guardians of the true faith – figures such as John Wycliffe (*c.*1330–84) and the Lollards were now portrayed as suffering persecution in order to preserve the pure and untainted 'English' Christianity. Thus was born the idea of the proto-Protestant martyr.

Marian exiles such as John Bale (1495–1563) portrayed old heretics and heretical sects as new Protestant, or proto-Protestant, martyrs and heroes in an attempt to provide a continuous lineage leading up to the reformers of the sixteenth century. Bale's vision of England's history was one of a golden age of purity characterised by the acceptance of Christianity from a pure source, during Joseph of Arimathea's visit to Britain in 63 CE. Coming from Jerusalem rather than Rome, 'The Brytains toke the christen faithe at ye very spring or fyrst going forth of the Gospel, whan the church was moste perfit, and had moste strengthe of the holy ghost'.[27] This purity lasted until the division of Britain into dioceses under Diocletian (regarded as the first sign of institutional rigidity), at which point the second stage of decay and degeneration set in, particularly after the mission of St Augustine. This 'minion of Antichrist' introduced 'candelstyckes, vestymentes, surplices, alter clothes, synyng bookes, rellyckes'.[28] Even worse, Augustine and, after him, Theodore of Tarsus, supported the Saxon invaders against the native Britons. The final signs of decay were Dunstan's enforcement of clerical celibacy *c.*1000, and the Danish invasions, the latter supposedly aided by treasonous monks. England was now completely overrun by papal corruption, which was to last until the 'morning star' of Protestant theology, John Wycliffe, began the third stage of English history by throwing off the yoke of Romish doctrine, followed by the ending of slavery to Rome under Henry VIII. It was claimed, then, that for almost five hundred years the ancient British church had been subverted by the power of Rome; but in the whole of Europe, 'England had withstood subversion the longest, and thrown it off the soonest' (Fairfield, 1976: 106). In purifying the Catholic cult of saints and adapting it for Protestant use, Bale attempted to re-establish continuity with a past golden age of the pre-Augustinian ancient British church and provided the goal of its revival under the sixteenth century reformers. His vision was taken up by another Marian exile, John Foxe (1517–87) in a far more famous work, *The Actes and Monuments of these latter and perilous days,*[29] published in England in 1563 and more popularly known as Foxe's *Book of Martyrs.*

During the six years of Edward VI's reign (1547–53), Foxe began writing *The Actes and Monuments* as an historical justification of the Reformation. Like Bale's 1545 work *The Image of Both Churches*, Foxe depicted this history as one of conflict between the forces of good and evil, or Christ and Antichrist, England and Rome. When Elizabeth I came to the throne in 1558, Foxe reworked his book as a propaganda weapon of over 1,800 folio pages for her 'Protestant' establishment. New editions appeared in 1570, 1576 and 1583, and by the time of his death in 1587, 'his book was a national institution … it became a foundation stone of English Protestant nationalism',[30] and fuelled hostility towards Catholics and Catholicism for generations.[31] An abridged version was issued in 1589, and new full editions in 1596 and 1610. The 1570 edition contained some 500 pages reconstructing English history to suit the reformation under Elizabeth, and the Privy Council ordered it to be set up alongside the English Bible in cathedrals. It was seen as vital that Protestant historiography provide a tradition for the reformers, that 'they might be regarded as continuators of those who through a long persecuted past had been defending the cause of the true primitive church in England' (Aston, 1964: 150; cited in Jones, 2003: 63). *The Book of Martyrs* occupied Foxe for the last thirty years of his life and, as noted, continued to be influential well into the nineteenth century. At the same time, however, Elizabeth's Archbishop of Canterbury, Matthew Parker (1504–75; consecrated Archbishop 1559), was attempting a similar project, 'revealing' the alleged ancient apostolic roots of the English Church via antiquarian research, rather than through a spiritual ancestry based on martyrology.[32]

Parker 'interested himself, particularly, in "the Ancient British Church" in which he found an independence from Rome that justified his lonely position in Catholic Christendom' (Whitebrook, 1945: 45). Unlike Foxe and the Puritans influenced by his work, however, Parker realised the problem in pronouncing as proto-Protestant those medieval sects that were strictly anti-episcopal. Instead, during the 1560s and 1570s, Parker employed historians and textual scholars whose remit was to demonstrate the roots of Anglican practices in the ancient precedent of an English church of antiquity, via what Robinson has called, '... a fantasy narrative of Englishness that could discover itself in Saxons and Britons' (Robinson, 1998: 1079). Under his direction, they

> set out to reform the English past by reforming its texts, purging them of the 'corruptions' of Catholic writers, readers, and scholars ... [and demonstrate] the proximity of 'our ordinances and rites' to those of the first English Christians.
>
> (Robinson, 1998: 1061, 1080)

Through focusing on the national character of the Church, the episcopal nature of Anglicanism was neatly side-stepped – it was not, after all, simply the validity of Anglican orders that was at issue.[33] By the time of Parker's death in 1575, his scholars had transformed England's past and,

> whatever the instincts and nostalgia of their seniors, a generation was growing up which had known nothing else, which believed the Pope to be Anti-Christ, the Mass a mummery, which did not look back to the Catholic past as their own, but another country, another world.
>
> (Duffy, 1992: 593)

The longevity of Elizabeth's reign was to do the rest.

The idea of a Saxon golden age continued to be mined by Anglican churchmen desperate to avoid 'negotiating the dangerous straits of anti-episcopal views' (Barnett, 1999: 30) held by the Waldenses and other medieval sects cast as proto-Protestant. Whilst Puritans vilified the history of the church as 'pagano-papism'[34] and condemned its descent into 'priestcraft', Anglicans such as Richard Field[35] (1561–1616) portrayed Wycliffe and Huss, for example, as champions of independent national churches rather than as critics of Rome's unchristian episcopal hierarchy. A century later, in 1708, Jeremy Collier (1650–1726), in *An Ecclesiastical History of Great Britain, Chiefly of England*, was still using the idea of an independent Saxon church to claim a spiritually legitimate lineage for the Anglican episcopate. Yet even among Anglicans, Protestant identity was still defined in anti-Catholic, anti-popery terms via 'the vilification of Catholic Church history and the assertion of a definably Protestant spiritual route through the labyrinth of medieval priestcraft' (Barnett, 1999: 35). As the Church of England became more secure and established, it was the promotion of this idea of a Protestant spiritual route which grew in importance as Anglicanism asserted its identity: anti-Catholicism as 'Englishness' continued to have a very public existence whilst the idea of the ancient British church receded into an important, but no longer dominant, bass note.

A legalistic form of anti-Catholicism had emerged with the recusancy laws of the late sixteenth century,[36] the product of legitimate fears brought about as a consequence of the excommunication of Elizabeth I by Pope Pius V, which justified plots against her. It centred on an emerging national identity and personal fears stemming from the queen's childhood during the reigns of her three predecessors, Henry VIII, Edward VI, and Mary, and the constant threats to her throne particularly during the first thirty years of her reign. It was to be another 200 years before Catholics were permitted to own land on taking an oath that did not include denial of Roman Catholicism, priests were no longer subject to persecution, and the punishment of life imprisonment for keeping a Catholic school was abolished.[37] The 1778 Catholic Emancipation Act provoked the Gordon Riots against 'popery' in 1780, in which anti-Catholics led by Lord George Gordon[38] took control of the streets of London for a week, damaging the property of Catholics and their known sympathisers. It took 10,000 soldiers and 285 deaths to suppress the riots. In 1791, Catholics willing to take the prescribed oath were freed from the recusancy statutes and the Oath of Supremacy, certain legal and military posts were opened up, and Catholic worship and schools tolerated. Two years later in 1793, Catholics in Ireland were granted the right to vote, and admitted to universities and the professions. It was not until 1829, however, that the Roman Catholic Relief Act removed the disabling laws against Roman Catholics in Britain, and only as recently as 1926 were the remaining disabilities revoked.[39] The period from the English Reformation to the inter-war years was therefore a time of crisis for Roman Catholics living in Britain as well as for British Roman Catholics who had felt compelled to live outside the realm. Religious dissent was still equated with treason, providing a hothouse for political subversion and social disorder, and Catholicism was equated with a descent into chaos.

Catholicism had also been equated with witchcraft in the minds of Protestants since the period of the Reformation,[40] and they continued to be linked in the (anti-Catholic) public mind of the late nineteenth and early twentieth centuries.[41] For Catholics who remained in England, secrecy was a necessity and essential for priests such as Richard Challoner (1691–1781) who ministered to the scattered flock.[42] Challoner set out to ensure the survival of the old religion, constructing an identity for British recusants by 'stressing their continuity with the primitive Church and, in particular, the unbroken continuity of that primitive Church with the British and Irish churches of the Middle Ages, the Reformation era, and his own day' (Hyland, 2006: 2). In tracts such as *The Touchstone of the New Religion* (1734) and *A Roman Catholick's Reasons why he cannot conform to the Protestant Religion* (1747), he argued that Protestantism was a new religion which, having broken with the primitive Church, left Catholicism as the only Church which retained the continuity so important to Protestants. In seeking to defend the antiquity of the Catholic Church and its traditions against Protestant charges of novelty, in works such as *The Grounds of the Old Religion* (1742), Challoner was also providing Catholics with an historical consciousness, just as the Tudor propaganda machine had sought to do for Protestants. Indeed, in 1741 he supplied Catholics with two volumes of their own martyrology to rival that of Foxe – *Memoirs of Missionary Priests and other Catholicks of both Sexes who suffered Death or Imprisonment in England on account of their Religion, from the year 1577 till the end of the reign of Charles II*. His work prepared the way for the revival of Catholicism in England in the nineteenth century.

This revival continued the emphasis on Catholicism as 'the old religion',[43] leading to sustained competition with the established national church in its claims to continuity with antiquity. Thus, William Lockhart (1820–92), one of the first of the Tractarians[44] to convert to Roman Catholicism (in 1845), wrote *The Old Religion; or, How shall we find Primitive Christianity. A journey from New York to Old Rome* (London: Burns and Oates, 1870), whilst the Anglican Thomas Lathbury (1798–1865) authored *Protestantism the old religion, Popery the new* in 1838. Challoner's *The Grounds of the Old Religion* had been reissued in 1820, and Hall's (1574–1656) treatise on the differences between 'the reformed and Roman Church', *The Old Religion*, was republished in 1837. In 1912 the English Benedictine monk and historian, and member of the Pontifical Commission to study the validity of Anglican orders (1896), Cardinal Francis Aidan Gasquet (1846–1929), published *England under the Old Religion, and other essays*. All of these publications indicate a positive identification with antiquity and a valorising of 'the old'.

Although the influx of Irish immigrants to Britain in the nineteenth century was responsible for much of the growth of Roman Catholicism, it was largely the growth of Catholic doctrines and practices within the State church that concerned Protestant statesmen. Beginning with the Oxford Movement (1833–45)[45] of John Keble (1792–1866), Edward Pusey

(1800–82), John Henry (Cardinal) Newman (1801–90) and Henry Edward (Cardinal) Manning (1808–92), the Catholic revival fostered both conversion to the Roman Church[46] and the development of Anglo-Catholicism[47] within the Church of England. Beginning with Keble's Assize Sermon on 'National Apostasy' of 14 July 1833, in which he attacked the government's proposal to reduce the number of Irish bishoprics by ten following the 1832 Reform Act, the Oxford Movement of the Tractarians fought against the attempted reform of the Church by the state in the 1820s and 1830s,[48] and against theological liberalism. They also drew on the interest in elements of primitive and medieval Christianity of the Romantic Movement, and revived the earlier concern of the Church of England to demonstrate direct descent from the apostles. This interest in the origins of the English church led to a reconsideration of the relationship between the Church of England and the Roman Catholic Church – in the final, ninetieth *Tract*, Newman had argued that the Thirty Nine Articles of the Church of England, defined in the sixteenth century, were clearly compatible with Roman Catholic doctrine as defined by the Council of Trent. Having come to this conclusion, and having had his work condemned by many bishops, Newman retired to his community at Littlemore in 1842. When William George Ward's *The Ideal of a Christian Church* (1844) was censured by the Convocation of Oxford on 13 February 1845 – 777 votes to 386 – Ward, Frederick William Faber and others associated with the Movement were received into the Church of Rome. Newman followed in the Autumn of 1845. After the Gorham Case of 1850,[49] other Tractarians converted to Roman Catholicism, including Manning in 1851. As a consequence, the Oxford Movement was attacked for its Romanising tendencies, including the establishment of Anglican religious orders, first for women and later for men, its emphasis on ceremonial, and its introduction of the research and insights of the Liturgical Movement into the liturgy of the Church of England: the Eucharist became more central to worship, vestments were re-introduced, and Catholic practices became more common in worship.[50]

None of this was particularly new – there had always been Anglicans who identified closely with Roman Catholic thought and practice, and who emphasised continuity with Catholic tradition. As noted above, during the various Tudor reformations the fortunes of those retaining aspects of Catholicism waxed and waned. Under the Stuarts, however, the Catholic faction of the Church of England flourished, particularly under Charles I[51] (1625–49), during the Interregnum (1649–60), and in the reign of Charles II (1660–85), 'a Golden Age for Catholic Anglican doctrinal writing, liturgy and spirituality', according to the Society of King Charles the Martyr.[52] The Anglican theologians living during this period, known as the Caroline Divines, defended the continuity of the Church of England with the pre-Reformation *Ecclesia Anglicana*, as well as upholding the doctrine of the Real Presence, and the importance of auricular confession and religious observance at fasts and festivals. Among them was Lancelot Andrewes (1555–1626), Bishop of

Winchester, an opponent of Puritan rigidity with an aversion to Calvinism who urged ceremonial worship for the Church of England and used the mixed chalice, incense and altar lights in his own chapel. The Non-Juror[53] Bishop of Bath and Wells, Thomas Ken (1637–1711), one-time chaplain to Charles II, provides a clear expression of the typical position held by the Caroline Divines in his will. He wrote:

> I die in the Holy Catholic and Apostolic Faith, professed by the whole Church, before the disunion of East and West: more particularly, I die in the communion of the Church of England, as it stands distinguished from all Papal and Puritan innovations.
>
> (cited in Cross and Livingstone, 1983: 776)

This reversion to the authority of the ecumenical councils prior to the schism between East and West, as well as the rejection of the claims of Rome and refusal to adopt Continental, specifically Calvinist reforms were predominant themes in the formulation of Anglicanism under the Caroline Divines, continuing and developing the doctrinal system that had emerged during the reign of Elizabeth I. The most famous of the Divines was, of course, William Laud (1573–1645), Charles I's Archbishop of Canterbury from 1633. Laud affirmed the apostolic succession, thereby winning the enmity of the strong Calvinist faction that had emerged in the reign of James I and VI (1603–25). As usual, the expression of Catholic tendencies led to accusations of popery even though Laud was a loyal Anglican Englishman, and his intolerance of the Presbyterians in Scotland gave impetus to the Covenanter movement[54] and led to the Bishops' Wars of 1639 and 1640.[55] He was subsequently accused of treason by the Long Parliament of 1640 and imprisoned in the Tower of London before being executed under a bill of attainder on 10 January 1645.

The work of Archbishop Laud and other Caroline Divines was an important legacy for Anglo-Catholics, and their writings were collected by members of the Oxford Movement for the Library of Anglo-Catholic Theology.[56] The Tractarians continued to argue that, since the Church of England had preserved the apostolic succession of priests and bishops and thus the Catholic sacraments, it was not a Protestant denomination but a branch of the church catholic, along with the Roman Catholic Church and the Eastern Orthodox Church. Such claims are, of course, contested. On the one hand, neither the Roman Catholic nor the Eastern Orthodox churches accept the branch theory of the 'church catholic', and the Anglican claim to valid apostolic succession and sacraments is rejected by the Roman Catholic Church.[57] On the other, the evangelical wing of the Church of England fought against Catholic doctrines and practices within Anglicanism, stressing the essentially Protestant nature of the church. Catholic beliefs and practices thus remained a matter of private opinion rather than official doctrine, leading to the high profile conversions to Rome of Newman and

Manning. Most Anglo-Catholics remained within the Church of England, however, but the development – or reclamation – of an English Catholicism was regarded as 'unEnglish' for much the same reasons as Catholics had been treated as such since the English church was reformed: they encouraged papal interference. This was felt particularly in the years following Pius IX's *Rescript* of 1850 which created (or 'restored', according to Catholics) a Catholic hierarchy in England. *The Times*[58] reported the appointment of the Archbishop of Westminster as 'a clumsy joke, one of the grossest acts of folly and impertinence which the court at Rome had ventured to commit since the Crown and people of England had thrown off its yoke', and Lord John Russell provides a good example of an English Protestant response to the *Rescript*. He wrote:

> [t]here is an assumption of power in all the documents which have come from Rome; a pretension of supremacy over the realm of England, and a claim to sole and undivided sway, which is inconsistent with the Queen's supremacy, with the rights of our bishops and clergy, and with the spiritual independence of the nation.[59]
>
> (*English Historical Documents*, vol. XII (I), p. 368, quoted in Norman, 1968: 57)

The Reformation Journal, in the preface to its first volume, went further still, depicting nothing less than a papal conspiracy to reconquer Britain: '[i]t is now beyond all question that the entire power and policy of Rome is being directed against Britain, with a view to its being subjected again to the degrading slavery of the Vatican'.[60]

The 'enormities of the Pope' were linked with the 'excesses of the "Puseyites" in the State Church' (Norman, 1968: 57), which rather than being 'the bulwark of Protestantism, turns out to be a huge manufactory of a national or home-made Popery',[61] and there were suspicions that the 'Puseyites' and Irish Catholics were linked in a Roman conspiracy. In 1868, Benjamin Disraeli asserted to the House of Commons that 'High Church Ritualists[62] and the Irish followers of the Pope have long been in secret combination and are now in open confederacy'.[63] To Catholic converts such as the leader of the Gothic revival movement in architecture, Augustus Welby Northmore Pugin (1812–52), 'the calumnies, the denunciations against the old religion [had become] more rabid than ever'.[64] To Pugin, Catholicism was truly the 'old religion', which would 'never remain satisfied with the mere shadow of antiquity' as found in Protestantism.[65]

It is hardly surprising then, that after his conversion to Roman Catholicism in 1922, G. K. Chesterton (1874–1936) felt it necessary to write on the question of Catholicism as a new or old religion in the 'Introductory: A New Religion' of his 1926 work *The Catholic Church and Conversion*. Chesterton begins with the observation that '[t]he Catholic faith used to be called the Old Religion; but at the present moment it has a recognized place among the

New Religions' (1926: 1). It has, he argues, become a novelty, 'an innovation and not merely a survival', with no claim to antiquity or tradition. It is a fad, like Socialism, Spiritualism, or Christian Science – it is 'one of the wild passions of youth', an 'indecent indulgence', in which monastic meditations or ascetic manuals are treated as if they were 'bad books' of pornographic content by which an undergraduate might '[wallow] in the sensual pleasure of Nones or [inflame] his lusts by contemplating an incorrect number of candles'. Any religion recognised as 'old' is acceptable, he claims; but new religions are annoying, even frightening, and

> [a]mong these annoying new religions, one is rather an old religion; but it is the only old religion that is so new. … It is coming in again as something fresh and disturbing … the religion that is two thousand years old now appearing as a rival of the new religions.
>
> (Chesterton, 1926: 2)

Of course, Chesterton was not to know that a 'fresh and disturbing' 'new religion' was waiting in the wings to appear as a rival of the old religions. It was to emerge within the next thirty years, claiming to be far older than the mere 2,000 years of Catholic history, and to be not just *an* 'old religion', but *the* 'old religion'. As stated in the Introduction, it was formulated by a retired civil servant called Gerald Gardner, among others, and emerged as a religious entity called Wicca sometime around 1951. This newly-emergent tradition was to draw on the value-laden term 'old religion' in ways that can now be explored in light of the term's previous usage.

The use of the term 'old religion' in Wicca is usually regarded as deriving from American folklorist Charles Godfrey Leland's use of it in *Aradia, or the Gospel of the Witches*, published by the Folklore Society in England in 1899. In it, Leland produced an account of the beliefs and rituals of the 'old religion' of witchcraft in Tuscany – *la vecchia religione* – that he claimed had been reported to him by a witch named Maddelena.[66] The religion was purported to be centred on the goddess Aradia, sent down to earth by her mother Diana to teach witchcraft to peasants in order that they might fight their oppressors – feudal landlords and the Roman Catholic Church. According to Leland, in 1890s Tuscany, 'the witches even yet form a fragmentary secret society or sect, … they call it that of the Old Religion, and … there are in the Romagna entire villages in which the people are completely heathen' (Leland, 1990: 116). Whether Leland's claims to have uncovered an old surviving witchcraft religion were true or not is beyond the concerns of this chapter. Suffice it to say that his use of the term 'old religion' is as likely to have been borrowed from Roman Catholicism as it is to have derived from the stories of Maddelena.

Whatever the provenance of Wicca as 'the old religion', the story of a surviving pre-Christian religion called 'Wicca' or witchcraft has exerted a huge influence on the development of Wicca. The idea of witchcraft as a surviving old religion was first presented by two Catholics, Karl Ernst Jarcke in 1828 and Franz Josef Mone in 1839, both of whom were antagonistic to the witch cult they purported to describe. Attempting to make the witch hunt seem perfectly justifiable, they suggested that those persecuted as witches in the early modern period were indeed practitioners of a surviving pagan religion.[67] This link with the past was used in the opposite way in 1862 by the radical French historian Jules Michelet, who portrayed the 'surviving witch cult' as a priestess-led, feminist, peaceful and nature loving movement, 'the repository of liberty all through the tyranny and obscurantism of the Middle Ages' (Hutton, 1996: 11). His book, *La Sorcière*, was commercially successful (as he had intended), and was published in English in 1904 as *Satanism and Witchcraft*, five years after Leland's Michelet-inspired account appeared.

The story of a surviving pre-Christian pagan witch cult was made most famous, however, by the Egyptologist Margaret Alice Murray in her 1921 publication *The Witch Cult in Western Europe: A Study in Anthropology*. In this, and her later book *The God of the Witches* (1933), Murray wove together ideas of rural fertility religion popularised by Frazer, the witch cult as described by Michelet and Leland, and folk customs, as well as asserting her belief that a female goddess was the original deity of the witches, the veneration of the horned god dating from the later, decadent era in which the cult was recorded. Her theory was that the witch cult contained the vestigial remnants of a pre-Christian European fertility religion, which Murray thought had perhaps first developed in Egypt and which she called 'Dianic'.[68] It became, in Britain, the more popular and influential version of a story that was by 1921 already almost 100 years old. As Caroline Oates and Juliette Wood have argued, it is easy to see why her version became popular:

> Where Mone, Jarcke, Michelet and Leland had all written about secret societies of witches in Germany, France and Italy, Murray made the cult British and, following Pearson,[69] extended its secret history much further back in time. Here was an image of ancient British culture just begging to be revived.
>
> (Oates and Wood, 1998: 25)

Gardner could not resist the opportunity to initiate such a revival. The Folklore Society's stress on lore as living and dynamic, rather than a dead thing of the past, in the period immediately before and during his membership of the society, would certainly have encouraged him to take Murray's ancient but dead religion and make it live again in the traditions, customs and beliefs of modern people.[70] Gardner therefore had no hesitation in perpetuating the inaccurate thesis which Murray had made so popular in Britain in his own books *Witchcraft Today* (1954) and *The Meaning of Witchcraft* (1959). *Witchcraft Today* contained an introduction by Murray and closely followed her theory, with chapters claiming that 'There have been Witches in all Ages', and an outline of Gardner's belief that witchcraft 'was directly descended from the Northern European culture of the Stone Age', uninfluenced by anything except 'the Greek and Roman mysteries which originally may have come from Egypt' (Gardner, 1954: 54). *The Meaning of Witchcraft* begins with an outline of three schools of thought on the origins of witchcraft. Two are summarily dismissed – Gardner ([1959] 2004: 1) does not believe that witchcraft was either 'a kind of mass hysteria' or 'the worship and service of Satan'. Instead, he praises Murray's presentation of witchcraft as 'simply the remains of the old pagan religion of Western Europe, dating back to the Stone Age' and persecuted by the Church as 'a dangerous rival' (ibid.). He continues:

> I personally belong to this third school, because its findings accord with *my own experience*, and because it is the only theory which seems to me to make sense when viewed in the light *of the facts of history*.
> (Gardner, [1959] 2004: 1, emphasis added)

Gardner seems to have felt that he had found academic authority that supported and validated his experiential 'knowing' with historical facts. Like Cromwell and Parker, Gardner had sought 'a return to the origin; a leap beyond history, [which] simultaneously requires that this leap be made through history, [and] be mediated by an immense historical and textual labor' (Robinson, 1998: 1083). He seems to have been convinced that this labour that enabled the leap through history had been provided by Murray. Always aware of his own lack of formal education and qualifications, it may well have been important for Gardner to feel that Wicca had an academically credible historical context. He was probably unaware that Murray's theory was heavily criticised from the time of its publication,[71] though he may have known of later critiques by R. H. Robbins (1959: 116–17) and E. E. Rose (1962), both of which are listed among the contents of Gardner's library.[72] Of course, their publication came too late for their criticisms to be included in any of Gardner's books, even had he wanted to make reference to them.

In claiming an unbroken witchcraft tradition reaching back into antiquity, a cult which had survived from pre-Christian times, Gardner not only reflected, but extended, the claims of both Catholicism and the Church of England to be manifestations of the 'old religion'. He had provided Wicca with a powerfully romanticised fiction that made it attractive to newcomers and ensured its survival, in just the same way as had the emerging Anglican Church of the sixteenth century and the Catholic minority in England. Of course, recourse to a secretly preserved past is typical of new forms of religion, and of esoteric societies. However, through this consideration of the politicisation of the value-laden terms 'old religion' and 'new religion', the development of Wiccan myths of origin can be seen to be predicated on a Catholic view that 'old' is good, in reaction to a Protestant view that 'old' is outdated, that the 'new' has superseded the magical, mystical life. Not only that, but claims of ancient origin carried with them associated claims of precedence; in claiming to pre-date English Christianity as the indigenous religion of Britain, Murray and Gardner can also be seen to be claiming precedence in the spiritual life of the nation. In the Anglican struggle for authenticity and in the Catholic response to that struggle, 'old' and 'new' had become categories of political expediency. The Anglican compromise, the *via media* between the opposing factions of (old) Catholic Rome and (new) Protestant Geneva, had led the Church of England to claim its own ancient origins and apostolic succession. But claims to ancient origins and the consequent assurance of valid apostolic succession were the concern of another group of religious organisations with which Gardner was involved. The same concern with ancient, indigenous religions emerging and operating independently of the Church of Rome characterises the heterodox Christian churches of the *episcopi vagantes* in England, Wales and France. Under the auspices of two of these 'wandering bishops', the literary fantasm of the Ancient British Church, so useful to Cromwell, Bale and Parker, was to see two further revivals, in the nineteenth century under Rev. Richard Williams Morgan, and in the twentieth under Frederic 'Dorian' Herbert. It was a theme that was to influence the development of Druidry and Wicca, in both of which Gardner was involved.

2

EPISCOPI VAGANTES AND HETERODOX CHRISTIANITY

In his 2003 publication *Gerald Gardner and the Cauldron of Inspiration*, Philip Heselton briefly mentions Gardner's links and involvement with a body called the Ancient British Church,[1] admitting that it has yet to be studied in depth.[2] The short-lived Ancient British Church to which Heselton refers is in fact the second of that name to be revived but, as is clear from the previous chapter, the ideas that underlie it constituted part of both the myth of the Church of England and that of the nation. The earlier revival of the Ancient British Church is addressed later in this chapter. First, its intriguing connections to the backwaters of the mid-nineteenth to mid-twentieth century ecclesiastical underworld of England, Wales and France need elucidating. This was an underworld populated by, and in part constructed by, the 'wandering bishops', or *episcopi vagantes*, and the various heterodox churches they sought to establish attracted such key figures in the history of modern Paganism and magic as Ross Nichols, Gerald Gardner, W. B. Crow and Theodor Reuss.

The search for evidence about both the churches and some of their bishops has, however, been limited by a dearth of available sources. This chapter is therefore based largely on two volumes of material. The first is a study produced by Fr Henry R. T. Brandreth, a Priest of the Oratory of the Good Shepherd, for the Lambeth Conference of 1948.[3] It was published by SPCK in 1947 as *Episcopi Vagantes and the Anglican Church*. Brandreth's book seems to have been written on the premise that irregular episcopacy was a problem with which the Church of England should be concerned. As such, one might expect his work to be particularly unfavourable to the wandering bishops. However, Brandreth had many friends among the *episcopi vagantes* and rather commendably refused to be drawn into the kind of character assassination that might be expected from such a report. The second source is a more substantial account of the activities and lineages of the *episcopi vagantes* by Peter Anson, a noted investigator of the ecclesiastical underworld of the Church of England who also made studies of Anglo-Catholic religious communities in *The Call of the Cloister* (1955), and in particular of the monks of Caldey Island and their founder in *The Benedictines of Caldey* (1940) and *Abbot Extraordinary* (1958).[4] Entitled *Bishops at Large* and originally published in 1964, Anson's study of the wandering bishops has been difficult to obtain. However, in February 2006 it was reprinted by Apocryphile Press of Berkeley, California as part of The Independent Catholic Heritage Series. The Press proclaims the volume to be 'the classic history of the various successions claimed by most independent jurisdictions ... the most sought-after book in the movement's history' (back cover). Anson's work is partly based on documents made available to him by Brandreth in Paris, the pioneer in this area of study, and the book is dedicated to him. Other sources include both the writings of some of the bishops, none of which I have been able to locate, and sources written in French, a language which I unfortunately do not read even had I been able to obtain them.[5] Nevertheless, the works produced by Anson and Brandreth have provided sufficient material for the purpose of this and the following chapter.

Episcopi vagantes have existed in church history since the fourth century, occasionally with doubtful orders but more commonly lacking diocesan jurisdiction, i.e. they were not confined to reside in a particular cathedral city. Later, during the crusading era, exiled bishops sought refuge in various European towns where, acting as *episcopus in partibus*, 'they often lived under the expectation of being appointed to a vacant titular see' (Macdonald, 1945: 21) on the death of the incumbent,[6] thus encouraging such wandering. The situation relating to bishops was not effectively regularised until 1882, when a decree of Propaganda was issued replacing *episcopus in partibus* with *episcopus titularis*. The bishops of the past two centuries considered in this chapter, however, are defined by either their irregular orders or their irregular exercise of them. According to *The Oxford Dictionary of the Christian Church*, the *episcopi vagantes* are men

> who have been consecrated bishop in an irregular or clandestine manner or who, having been regularly consecrated, have been excommunicated by the Church that consecrated them and are in communion with no recognized see. A man[7] is also included in this group when the number in communion with him is so small that his sect appears to exist solely for his own sake.
>
> (Cross and Livingstone, 1983: 465)

According to Brandreth (1947: 1), their 'episcopal status is doubtful, and ... even if his orders be valid, the exercise of them is not legitimate'.

The bishops, and the autocephalous churches they founded, mushroomed from the 1860s, in England partly as a by-product of the Anglo-Catholic revival which spawned a desire for the validation of Anglican orders,[8] and partly, like Anglo-Catholicism itself, as a legacy of the Non-Jurors of the seventeenth and eighteenth centuries. The Non-Jurors were so called because, in the period after the Protestant-named 'Glorious Revolution' of 1688, they refused to take the oath of allegiance to William III and Mary II, having already given the same oath to the deposed Roman Catholic monarch

James II and his successors.[9] They numbered nine bishops,[10] including the then Archbishop of Canterbury William Sancroft, and some 400 priests along with their flocks. Deprived of their benefices, the Non-Jurors held secret services of their own whenever possible, and held to the belief that it was incumbent upon them to preserve the true Anglican succession, for, following the Caroline divines, the Non-Jurors emphasised the continuity of the English Church with the Catholic and Apostolic Church, signified by the apostolic succession of bishops. To ensure the Non-Juring succession, Sancroft delegated his archepiscopal authority to William Lloyd, Bishop of Norwich in February 1692 and, upon receipt of the *congé d'élire*[11] from the exiled James II, on 24 February 1694 George Hickes and John Wagstaffe were secretly consecrated. On 29 May 1713, Hickes consecrated three more Non-Jurors, Jeremy Collier, Samuel Hawes and Nathaniel Spinkes, and the regular line continued until the death of Robert Gordon in 1779. Through an irregular line, however, the line continued until Charles Booth's death in 1805, though by this time the Non-Jurors had largely been absorbed back into the established church.

After the deaths of the original Non-Juring bishops, including Thomas Ken, Bishop of Bath and Wells, who had opposed the consecration of further Non-Juring bishops, the newly consecrated bishops 'did not even pretend to be the legitimate successors of the deprived bishops in their several sees, for they never assumed territorial titles' (Langford, 2001).[12] Nevertheless, titles were in fact being assumed in a manner which would later become commonplace among the *episcopi vagantes*: Jeremy Collier, for example, styled himself 'Primus Anglo-Britanniae Episcopus'. Unaware of the doubtful legitimacy of the later Non-Jurors and the schismatic nature of their existence,[13] the Orthodox Church, from 1716 to 1725, entered into correspondence with the Non-Jurors, correspondence which the latter had initiated with a view to reunion, though the Orthodox Church clearly only ever wanted complete submission to the patriarch.[14] In this correspondence, the Non-Jurors referred to themselves as '[t]he "Catholic remnant of the British Churches" [which] claims descent from Jerusalem prior to the mission from Rome' (Langford, 2001).[15] In this can be seen an appeal to the Glastonbury legend, and the beginnings of overtures by schismatic groups led by irregular bishops seeking validation of their orders from the Orthodox Church, both of which continued throughout the nineteenth and twentieth centuries and remain evident today. The Glastonbury legend has been touched upon in the previous chapter. As this chapter makes clear, to the wandering bishops the importance attached to the validation of orders by various branches of the Orthodox Church, as a recourse to old, even original Christianity, is enormous. As such, it continues the emphasis on pre-schismatic unified Christianity as represented in the first four ecumenical councils[16] identified by Elizabethan and Caroline Divines such as Richard Hooker and Lancelot Andrewes, Tractarians, and Anglo-Catholics, discussed in the previous chapter.

The Non-Jurors had, of course, seceded from the Church of England,[17] itself considered a schismatic body by Rome. Likewise, a variety of Catholic and reformed Catholic churches have, at various times, separated themselves from communion with Rome whilst maintaining apostolic succession and adhering to basic Catholic doctrines, such as the seven sacraments. The Church of Utrecht, for example, with three bishops, separated from Rome in 1724, leading to the formation of the Old Catholic Churches. 'Old Catholics' became, in the eighteenth and nineteenth centuries, increasingly agitated by attempts to secure the centralised authority of the Church in Rome. They fought against such positions as Ultramontanism,[18] and rejected the 'new' Roman Catholic doctrines such as the bodily assumption of Mary (1850) and the Immaculate Conception (1854). However, it was as a reaction to the declaration of Papal Infallibility by Pope Pius IX (1792–1878) at the First Vatican Council (1869–70) that a large number of such groups separated from Rome, and it is at this point that an Old Catholic Movement formed. The Movement turned to the Jansenist Church of Holland[19] in order to maintain apostolic succession for the consecration of its bishops, and was formalised in the 1899 Declaration of Utrecht.

Division was sought not from Catholicism in general, but from Rome, and the two became increasingly distinct in the eyes of the Old Catholics, just as they were in the minds of many Anglo-Catholics. In Germany, Austria, and Switzerland, parish communities refused to accept the new decrees and joined together in common councils to reaffirm their faith in the Scriptures and what they saw as the 'authentic' Catholic Tradition of the church which, to them, Rome no longer represented. In response, Rome attempted to force Old Catholics into submission, cutting off priests from their pensions unless they subscribed to Papal Infallibility. The Old Catholics continued in their refusal to submit, and found in the Catholic Church of Holland the legitimate apostolic succession which would allow bishops of the Old Catholic Churches[20] to be consecrated, thus preserving Catholicism without recourse to Rome. In Austria, Germany, Switzerland, Czechoslovakia, Italy, Switzerland, France, Yugoslavia and Poland the movement grew and took root, with bishops being consecrated, for the most part, in Utrecht. It later spread to the United States, and for a very short time had a somewhat problematic existence in Britain. It was never a large movement in Britain; those who desired a Catholic liturgy without the dogma and authority of Rome were already provided for, and thus there was little need for another form of British 'Old Catholicism' once Anglo-Catholicism had established itself within the Church of England.[21]

On 28 April 1908, Dr Arnold Harris Mathew, son of an Anglican father and a Catholic mother, was consecrated at the Cathedral Church of Saint Gertrude, Utrecht, by Archbishop Gul assisted by the Old Catholic bishops of Haarlem (J. J. van Thiel), Deventer (N. B. P. Spit) and Germany (J. Demmel). Three years later, in 1911, he was elected Archbishop and Metropolitan of Great Britain. Originally destined for Anglican orders, he had instead trained as a Roman Catholic priest, received his ordination in 1878, and after some years left the Catholic Church and married. He then acted as an Anglican curate at Holy Trinity Church, Sloane, until forced to retire into lay life by the immoral behaviour of his incumbent, Rev. Robert Eyton. It was not until 1907 that he approached the Archbishop of Canterbury, Dr Randall Davidson, proposing – unsuccessfully – that he take on some ministerial function in the Church of England.

At the end of that year he was approached by one Richard O'Halloran, an ex-Catholic priest, who claimed that 250 priests and congregations required an Old Catholic bishop, and had elected him to that office. After negotiations with Utrecht, of which Mathew kept Archbishop Davidson informed, he was duly consecrated as described above. On his immediate return to England, Mathew discovered that O'Halloran's information was false and in fact only a handful of Old Catholics required his ministrations. He informed Utrecht of the correct state of affairs, and asked to retire, but this was refused and he was exonerated from all blame. He thus remained in full communion with Utrecht, assisting at the consecrations of other bishops and attending the Old Catholic Congress at Vienna in 1909, where he came across differences between the Old Catholics of Germany and Switzerland and the Church in the Netherlands.[22] As a result, by December 1910 Mathew had declared his 'autonomy and independence'.[23] He established ecumenical relations between the English Old Catholics and the Patriarchal See of Antioch through his Eminence the Most Reverend Archbishop Gearrasimos Messara of Beruit, Syria, who on 5 August 1911, received the Old Catholics under Bishop Mathew into union and full communion with the Orthodox Patriarch of Antioch.

It was not until ten years later, in 1920, that the Old Catholic bishops, assembled at Utrecht, stated that his consecration was null and void, by virtue of the fact that it was obtained surreptitiously through false information – the responsibility for which had previously rested on O'Halloran. In his Foreword to Brandreth's *Episcopi Vagantes*, Rev. Canon J. A. Douglas[24] relates Archbishop Kennick[25] of Utrecht's description of Mathew. Kennick claimed that,

> Mathew simply hypnotised the Dutch Old Catholic hierarchy into believing that the Church of England was actually in the process of breaking up, and that the great majority of Anglo-Catholics would be eager to unite under his leadership, and with them a large secession of English Roman Catholics. All that they were waiting for was his own consecration to be their bishop.
>
> (Brandreth, 1947: xvi)

The reality, as Douglas notes, was very different: 'his English adherents never numbered more than a few hundred, and the English Old Catholic Church, of which he proclaimed himself the founder, never assumed reality' (ibid.: xvi).

The Lambeth Conference of the same year (1920) examined the case of Mathew and expressed doubts as to the validity of the orders stemming from him, noting that

> [e]ven the perfectly orthodox, respectable and self-contained Rite presided over by Mgr. Bernard M. Williams, Bishop Mathew's successor, is not in communion with any historic See, and is, in fact, repudiated by the Western Patriarchate of which it claims to be a part.
>
> (Brandreth, 1947: 4)

Within a year of his break from Utrecht, Mathew had consecrated five bishops, without a See or flock between them. Two of them had been excommunicated by the Church of Rome in February 1911, owing to irregularities, and appear to have undergone the rite of consecration simply in order to regain their position and continue their struggle with Rome. Bernard Mary Williams, mentioned above, was consecrated, with right of succession,[26] in April 1916. Some eighteen months earlier, on 28 October 1914, Mathew consecrated Frederick Samuel Willoughby, an ex-Anglican priest who had been forced to resign when charged with sexual misconduct but who had presented himself as persecuted by his bishop. Of this, Mathew seems to have been unaware but once the truth came out about Willoughby he expelled him, before the latter had a chance to perform any consecrations. However, once outside Mathew's Old Catholic Church, within a year Willoughby consecrated Bernard Edward Rupert Gauntlett and Robert King on 26 September 1915 and, on 13 February 1916, James Ingall Wedgwood (1883–1950). It is through the disreputable Willoughby that the most widespread of the Mathew lines of succession was established.[27] It was (and still is) known as the Liberal Catholic Church. Loosely connected with the Theosophical Society, it is characterised by a combination of Roman Catholic ceremonial and occultism.

According to Peter Anson, by 1915 the majority of Mathew's clergy had become members of the Theosophical Society and the Order of the Star in the East, and were shocked when, in a Pastoral Letter dated 6 August that year, Mathew ordered them to resign from these organisations, something which no Anglican bishop had required of his clergy.[28] Within five weeks of this letter, they had broken with Archbishop Mathew, and elected two of their number to the episcopate. These were Gauntlett, Secretary of the Theosophical Society Order of Healers, and King, a consulting psychic and astrologer. Both had been ordained by Mathew prior to their consecration by Willoughby. The effective leader of the schism, however, was Bishop James Ingall Wedgwood, who initiated reforms which led to the establishment of the Liberal Catholic Church, becoming its founder and first presiding bishop.

Wedgwood was an Anglo-Catholic who at one time had decided to train for ordination in the Church of England. After hearing a lecture by Annie Besant in York, however, he joined the Theosophical Society and left his church. He went on to become General Secretary of the Society in England and Wales (1911–13), before taking up the office of Grand Secretary of the British Jurisdiction of the Co-Masonic Order.[29] It was at this point, in 1913, that he communicated with Mathew and was ordained by him as a priest of the Old Catholic Church on 22 July the same year, a year before Willoughby's consecration. It was the latter, however, who raised Wedgwood to the episcopate in 1916, and thus Wedgwood's consecration was not that of the Old Catholic Church. Wedgwood travelled extensively between England, India, Australia, New Zealand and the USA. It was during a visit to Australia in 1915 that he met Charles Webster Leadbeater (1854–1934) and initiated him into Freemasonry. Like Wedgwood, Leadbeater had been attracted to Holy Orders, but unlike the former he had completed his training and had been ordained an Anglican priest by the Bishop of Winchester, Dr Harold Browne, in 1879. In 1883, whilst serving his curacy at Bramshott, Hampshire, he met Madame Blavatsky and, like Wedgwood, left the Church of England and became a Theosophist.

Apart from an interim period when he was suspended due to sexual impropriety with young boys,[30] Leadbeater spent the rest of his life working for the Theosophical Society. In 1913, he moved to Australia, where he received his consecration as a Bishop of the Liberal Catholic Church from Wedgwood on 22 July 1916. Together Wedgwood and Leadbeater set out to revise the liturgy of the Church, using Mathew's 1909 publication of *The Old Catholic Missal and Ritual* but eliminating references to fear of God, everlasting damnation, the insistence on sinfulness and appeals for mercy. Instead, they stressed the idea of co-operation with God. It was completed and published on 21 June 1918. Later that year, at a synod held in London on 6 September, the church was officially renamed 'Liberal Catholic'.

Leadbeater remained a leading figure in the Theosophical Society, working alongside Annie Besant, and was the 'discoverer' of the World Teacher, Jiddu Krishnamurti, in a village near the Society's headquarters in Ayodhya. The Church was to be used as 'one of the vehicles for [the World Teacher's] force, and a channel for the preparation of His Coming'.[31] Leadbeater was also a 33° Co-Mason, and became the second presiding bishop of the Liberal Catholic Church, after Wedgwood. According to Jocelyn Godwin (1994: 368), '[a]t heart, he was a magician, and the Mass was his preferred rite of ceremonial magic'. The Liberal Catholic Church, like the Theosophical Society, is still in existence today and is one of the most successful of the churches founded by an irregular bishop, both in terms of numbers of adherents, geographical spread, and longevity. Given its links with Theosophy[32] and Co-Masonry, its stress on ritual and gender equality,[33] and its lack of doctrinal dogmatism and authority, this is perhaps not surprising. In fact, apart from its liberal theology and promotion of women's ordination, the LCC contained many similarities to Anglo-Catholicism, one branch of which continues to fight against the legitimacy of women priests.[34] In terms of liturgical practice, Wedgwood and Leadbeater stressed that the LCC was neither Roman Catholic nor Protestant, but Catholic, and it aimed at 'combining the traditional sacramental form of Catholic worship – with its ritual, its deep mysticism, and its abiding witness – to the reality of sacramental grace' (Anson, 1964: 352). As Godwin (1994: 368) remarks, the LCC 'preserved all the glory of Catholic ritual for those whose tastes ran in that direction, minus the discomforts of papal authority and dogma'. Of course, it also avoided the discomforts of Church of England authority and dogma.

The legacy of the Theosophical Society for twentieth century occultism and Wicca has been well documented. It was not, however, from this scion of the Mathew succession, via the Liberal Catholic Church, that Gardner and his friends and associates received their ordinations and consecrations. According to Brandreth (1947: 2), in 1947 there were 120 *episcopi vagantes*, and over thirty of them were resident in Great Britain. Quite how many there were in the 1930s I have been unable to ascertain, but there are two other lines of succession which are of importance to the present study – the first from Jules Ferrette (d. 1903),[35] and the second from Joseph René Vilatte (1854–1929). Each shall be taken in turn.

Jules Ferrette entered the novitiate of the Friars Preachers at Flavigny in 1851, and was professed the following year. He was ordained deacon on 7 April 1855, and raised to the priesthood the same year, on 2 June, in the Lateran Basilica, Rome. Within a year, he apostatised – on 17 June 1856 he wrote to Père Jandel, Vicar General of the Dominican Order, that he no longer believed in Catholicism and did not regard himself as a member of the Order. A few days later, he left bound for India, but actually went to Damascus where he appears to have worked with the Irish Presbyterian Mission. In 1865, he published a liturgy in Arabic, and became friendly with a bishop of the Syrian Jacobite[36] Church, Mar Bedros, Bishop of Emesa (Homs).[37] The following year he arrived in England, claiming to have been consecrated as 'Mar Julius, Bishop of Iona' by Mar Bedros.[38] No proof of his consecration has ever emerged, the only evidence being a printed document which he claimed was a translation of his certificate of consecration, dated 22 June 1866 (Old Style). In September 1866 he published *The Eastern Liturgy adapted for Use in the West*, and declared himself ready 'to give Holy Orders to pious and learned men, who, being duly elected, will declare themselves willing to conform to this Liturgy'.[39] With little response even among the advanced Anglo-Catholics with whom he consorted,[40] and having been charged as an imposter, Ferrette disappeared for some years before emerging to consecrate a successor in 1874, after which he left England for the United States. He died in Switzerland, shortly after publishing *Les Rites Essentiels du Christianisme* in 1903.[41]

Richard Williams Morgan (1815–89), Ferrette's alleged successor, was born in Bala, North Wales, and 'seems to have inherited Welsh nationalism, Jacobitism,[42] and Nonjuring interests from his ancestors on both sides' (Anson, 1964: 43).[43] In 1841 and 1842 he was ordained deacon and priest respectively by the Bishop of St Davids, Dr Connop Thirlwall, after which he served in parishes in Wales and became increasingly nationalistic.[44] He was described in the *Church Times* as 'a genius and eccentric ... obsessed with the vision of a British Church which should restore the doctrine and discipline of the days before St. Augustine'.[45] This 'obsession' was shared by Morgan's cousin, John Williams ab Ithel, who had written extensively on the idea of the Ancient British Church. Anson (1964: 43), however, claims that Morgan was 'a tireless but uncritical research worker, ready to believe anything that took his fancy and indifferent to the lack of documentary evidence'. Evidence of this is clear in his publications. In *The British Kymry, or Britons of Cambria: Outlines of their history and institutions from the earliest to the present times* (re-issued in 1857), he talks of 'Christo-Druidic Bards', and the merging of Druidism into Christianity and claims Caerleon as one of the three ancient Arch-Druidic seats of Britain. Much of this material was drawn from the writings of Edward Williams (1747–1822), better known by his bardic name of Iolo Morganwg, and such claims were widespread among nineteenth-century Welsh Anglican clergy. In an echo of the 'official version' of history promulgated in the Tudor reformations, Morgan appealed to British institutions in distinction to those of continental Europe, claiming that,

[t]he Roman Catholic Church has no pretensions to being the primitive or apostolic church of Britain. It came in so late as a century and a half after the Saxon, and four centuries after the national establishment of the native British church.

(Morgan, 1857 'Introduction')[47]

In 1860 he published *St. Paul in Britain, or The Origin of British as Opposed to Papal Christianity*, a book that was reprinted nine times between 1861 and 1984 partly due to its adoption by the British Israelite Society.[47] In the Preface, Morgan sounded the now familiar refrain: 'The leading principles of her laws and liberties are of pure indigenous growth; and her evangelical faith was received by her directly from Jerusalem and the East, from the lips of the first disciples themselves of Christ' (1861: v–vi). The claims are repeated in his Conclusion, with Joseph of Arimathea, Simon Zelotes, and Saint Paul named as the planters of British Christianity. Clearly, his version echoes that of earlier ages, but Morgan's lifetime saw both the heyday and the demise of the story in Wales. In the year of his birth, 1815, Thomas Burgess, Bishop of St David's, published *Tracts on the Origin and Independence of the Ancient British Church*, which argued for St Paul's conversion of Britain. Just prior to Morgan's death, the Vicar of Bangor, John Pryce, won the competition for the best essay submitted to the National Eisteddfod of 1876 on the subject of the Ancient British Church, in which he refuted all the legends concerning the introduction of Christianity to Britain.[48]

After 1858, Morgan found himself serving in parishes in England and it was whilst undertaking occasional duties in Oxfordshire that Mar Julius

(Ferrette) is supposed to have conditionally baptised, confirmed, ordained and consecrated him as the first Patriarch of a restored Ancient British Church, with the title of Mar Pelagius I, Hierarch of Caerleon-on-Usk. According to the unsupported claims of Mar Georgius (Hugh George de Willmott Newman), in *The Man From Antioch* (1958), Morgan and Ferrette had been in contact for some time, discussing the restoration of the pre-Augustinian tradition in Britain as part of a world-wide Orthodox Movement which would eventually lead to the reunion of Christendom.[49] Thus began the second attempt to establish a church the purpose of which was the revival of the mythical ancient British Christianity. It contained all the same ingredients – apostolic foundation via Joseph of Arimathea, roots in Jerusalem rather than Rome, independence and indigenous institutions – but this time it was explicitly Welsh.[50] As Thomann (2001: 1, 15) notes, '[w]ith the advent of Jules Ferrete ... Morgan's dreams and desire of restoring the ancient British church began (or rather seemed) to materialize', though the Ancient British Church itself 'always remained rather shadowy, rather an idea than a community'. Morgan is, however, alleged to have consecrated a successor – Charles Isaac Stevens – in 1879, who in turn is supposed to have consecrated Leon Chechemain, a former Catholic Armenian *vartapet*,[51] and so, with or without a community, the idea, no matter how 'shadowy', was to survive.

For the purposes of this study, few important consecrations took place in the Ferrette line of succession until the 1920s when Herbert James Monzani Heard, an ex-Anglican deacon, decided to relinquish his orders in a post-reformation church in favour of priesthood in an Ancient British Church supposedly older than any Christian church apart from Antioch and Jerusalem. He was consecrated 'Archbishop of Selsey' on 4 June 1922, and set out to try to revive the remnant of the Britonnic Church of Mar Pelagius (Morgan); apparently, he was 'so kind-hearted that he was always ready to impart either the Syrian-Antiochene or the Free Protestant Episcopal succession to almost anybody who asked for one or the other of them' (Anson, 1964: 235). In 1938, he re-consecrated Mar Frederic (Harrington) of the Vilatte succession, founder of the Orthodox-Keltic Church of the British Commonwealth of Nations, in an effort to unite the lines of succession. Later, Heard consecrated the biology lecturer, Theosophist and priest of the Liberal Catholic Church (ordained 1935) William Bernard Crow (13 June 1943).[52]

Crow also knew Harrington who, as Primate of the Orthodox-Keltic Church, had granted a charter to the Order of the Holy Wisdom, founded by Crow in 1939. The Order taught that the teachings and symbols of the older non-Christian religions 'found their perfect fulfilment and consummation in the Person of Jesus Christ and in His Church' (Anson, 1964: 236). In a leaflet issued by Crow in October 1943, the Order is described as follows:

> The Order is not a Church, but an organisation within the Universal
> Church, which seeks to reproduce, as fully as possible within its own
> sphere, for the benefit of its members and humanity in general, the deep

spiritual experience enshrined in ritual and symbols. ... It endeavours
to teach the doctrines and practices of the Ancient Wisdom Religion ...
[and] utilizes the knowledge passed on in the great streams of sacred
tradition, not excluding those of the Far East, the Brahminic-Yogic, the
Ancient Egyptian, Zoroastrian-Magian, Kabbalistic, Gnostic-Masonic,
Gothic-Rosicrucian, Druidic-Bacchic, Chaldean, Buddhist-Lamaistic,
and Islamic-Sufic.

(cited in Anson, 1964: 237)

Crow stressed that his Order had no connection with any other Masonic
or Rosicrucian body, though it is clearly styled on such, with degrees of
initiation and Crow titling himself 'Grand Master'. Within a year of his
consecration, Crow was corresponding with Aleister Crowley, sending
the latter some of his pamphlets.[53] It is not known whether Crow became
involved in Crowley's Thelema, the Ordo Templi Orientis (OTO), or the
Ecclesiae Gnosticae Catholicae associated with the latter, though it may well
be true that Crowley thought him a useful aid in promoting all three.[54] What
is certain is that, in a letter dated 30 May 1947, Crowley suggested that
Crow send his followers to Gerald Gardner for initiation into the OTO, and
that 'Gardner realised that he already knew [Crow] through his friendship
with J. S. M. Ward'.[55] Mar Frederic (Harrington) had consecrated Ward
(1935) and Frederic 'Dorian' Herbert (1937), of whom more later, but
died before he could raise Crow to the episcopate. Heard stepped in and
consecrated Crow as Mar Bernard, Bishop of Santa Sophia, in the latter's
private oratory.

Crow in turn consecrated Hugh George de Willmott Newman, on 10 April
1944, as 'Mar Georgius, Archbishop and Metropolitan of Glastonbury and
Catholicos of the West'.[56] It is he who constructed, or at least wrote down,
the pseudo-history of the Ferrette line. De Willmott Newman and Heard,
for the most part, were the main consecrators of others, including Colin
Mackenzie on 6 June 1946 (de Willmott Newman consecrated), the member
of Ward's Abbey of Christ the King who it is claimed re-ordained Gardner in
1949 during a visit to Cyprus.[57] De Willmott Newman had previously been
ordained a priest in the Mathew succession, and was the main driving force
behind the union between various lines of succession, largely via mutual re-
consecrations, originally started by Harrington.

On 17 October 1943, prelates of the Ancient British Church, the British
Orthodox Catholic Church, the Apostolic Episcopal Church, the Old
Catholic Orthodox Church, the Order of the Holy Wisdom, and the Order of
Antioch met together as 'the Council of London', in response to resolutions
passed by the Lambeth Conference of 1920[58] and to a repudiation issued
by the Syrian Church on 10 December 1938 (perhaps as a consequence of
Harrington's re-consecration into the Ferrette line). The Syrian Patriarchate
of Antioch and All the East had issued a notice against schismatic bodies
who 'make public statements claiming without truth to derive their origin

and apostolic succession from some ancient Apostolic Church of the East, the attractive rites and ceremonies of which they adopt and with which they claim to have a relationship'. Harrington and 'all the sects claiming succession through Vilatte' are specifically named as examples of 'schismatic bodies which have come into existence after direct expulsion from official Christian communities and have devised for themselves a common creed and system of jurisdiction of their own invention'. The notice ends by

> deny[ing] any and every relation whatsoever with these schismatic bodies and repudiate[s] them and their claims absolutely … forbids any and every relationship and, above all, intercommunion with all and any of these schismatic sects and warns the public that their statements and pretensions as above are altogether without truth.[59]

The 'Council of London', in return, disclaimed any connection with the Syrian patriarchate, no longer recognised the patriarch as holding office, declared themselves 'The Ancient Orthodox Catholic Church', and elected Crow to the now vacant (as they saw it) patriarchal see with the glorious title of 'His Holiness Mohoran Mar Basilius Abdullah III, Sovereign Prince Patriarch of the God-protected city of Antioch, and of all the Domain of the Apostolic Throne, both in the East and in the West' (Anson, 1964: 241). In addition, they protested against resolutions 27 and 28 of the 1920 Lambeth Conference[60] as an attack on their orders and a hindrance to the reunion of Christendom. A few months later, on 23 March 1944, the Ancient British Church and the British Orthodox Catholic Church united with the Old Catholic Orthodox Church,[61] derived from the Mathew succession via Willoughby, and together became the Western Orthodox Catholic Church. Constituted as the Catholicate of the West under Patriarch Basilius Abdullah III (Crow), it claimed to be a fully autonomous and autocephalous Orthodox Church with territorial jurisdiction in Britain and Western Europe.

It should come as no surprise to find that, like the Church of England, none of the Eastern Churches recognised the Western Orthodox Catholic Church or its jurisdiction, and nor did the Old Catholic Council of Utrecht. Rather, it belongs to a tradition – which itself did not emerge until the 1960s – that the apostate French Dominican Julius Ferrette was consecrated Bishop of Iona by Mar Bedros, Bishop of Emesa (Homs), and appointed his Legate in Europe for the purpose of establishing an autocephalous British Patriarchate. As Anson argues, the Council of London and its resolutions

> are of the stuff that dreams are reminiscent of … none of the prelates who took part in its brief session could claim jurisdiction over more than perhaps a dozen followers, and some of the Churches had only a paper existence. They did, on the other hand, take themselves quite seriously.
>
> (Anson, 1964: 243)

A similar story can be told with regard to the twenty or so churches claiming succession from the Jacobite Patriarchate of Antioch, via the Independent Catholic Church of Goa and Ceylon by way of Joseph René Vilatte (Mar Timotheos).

Vilatte was a Parisian émigré to the USA, who appears to have changed his religious affiliation at the drop of a hat. After training for the Roman Catholic priesthood, he left but returned four times to the Church, became a Methodist twice, a Presbyterian twice, and was for a time a Congregationalist minister. In 1885 he sought to become a priest of the Protestant Episcopal Church under Dr Hobart Brown, Anglican Bishop of Fond du Lac. Brown sent him to work among the Belgian Old Catholics in Wisconsin, for which purpose he was ordained deacon and priest on 6 and 7 June 1885 by the Old Catholic Bishop Herzog in Berne, Switzerland, although his oaths of obedience were made to Brown. After Brown's death in 1888, however, Vilatte sought to be consecrated bishop in the Old Catholic Church. This ambition was thwarted by Grafton, Brown's successor, who also refused to consecrate Vilatte as 'Bishop-Abbot' of the American Old Catholics. Seeking alternative avenues, Vilatte approached the Russian Archbishop Vladimir and then the Roman Catholic Bishop of Milwaukee, both of whom refused him. After repudiating the jurisdiction of Grafton, he was degraded from the priesthood and excommunicated by the Protestant Episcopal Church on 21 March 1892.

By this time, Vilatte was styling himself '*Supérior, de l'Eglise vieille-catholique d'Amerique*', and claimed to have been elected to the Old Catholic episcopate, a claim which is almost certainly false.[62] Learning of a Fr Antonio Francisco-Xavier Alvares, Archbishop of the Independent Catholic Church of Ceylon, Vilatte set out for Ceylon in July 1891. Alvares, a Brahmin Goan priest, had been elected by the 'Patronado Association'[63] as first bishop of a schismatic church in 1888. He was duly consecrated by Mar Ignatius Peter III, Jacobite Patriarch of Antioch, the same man who, as Bishop of Emesa (Homs), had earlier consecrated Ferrette as Bishop of Iona (1866). Alvares thereafter styled himself Mar Julius I, Metropolitan of the Independent Catholic Church of Ceylon, Goa and India. After a wait of almost a year, whilst Mar Julius consulted with Mar Ignatius Peter III, Vilatte was finally consecrated in Colombo by Mar Julius, assisted by Mar Paul Athanasius, Bishop of Kottayam, and Mar George Gregorius, Bishop of Niranam, on 29 May 1892. Vilatte took the title Mar Timotheos, Archbishop of the Old Catholic Church of America, conferred by a certificate of consecration dated 5 June 1892 with which he claimed to have been presented. As with Ferrette, no such certificate has ever been produced.

Vilatte then went on to consecrate others, ignoring the Canon Laws of the Syrian Church which do not allow the consecration of a bishop by one bishop acting alone. He continued to perform such consecrations even after his excommunication by the Patriarch of Antioch. Needless to say, all orders conferred by Vilatte are not recognised as valid and, being excommunicate, are not accepted into communion with the Syrian Church. In addition, in 1892 the General Convention of the Protestant Episcopal Church resolved that it would not recognise that any episcopal character was conferred on Vilatte, and sent a statement of the facts as they knew them to the Archbishop of Utrecht, the Old Catholics of Germany and Switzerland, and to the Metropolitans and Primates of the Anglican Communion. Not to be stopped, Vilatte travelled to England and Wales in 1898, and ordained the Anglo-Catholic deacon Fr Ignatius of Llanthony (Rev. Joseph Leycester Lyne, 1837–1908)[64] to the priesthood, after which he went on to Milan to start an 'Italian National Episcopal Church', for which purposes he consecrated Don Miraglia Gulotti as 'Bishop of Piacenza'. During this time, his application to return to Rome was *sub judice*; not surprisingly, the judgement of the Holy See was to place both Vilatte and Gulotti under major excommunication by decree dated 13 June 1900.

Over the next few years, he carried on travelling and consecrating, truly a 'wandering bishop', and 1906 found him back in his native France, attracted by the chance of establishing a national Gallican Church. Here, he took advantage of the anti-clerical legislation of Waldeck-Rousseau and Combes, by which the state could take control of church property and pass it on to welfare and charitable institutions. Vilatte managed to get hold of the old Barnabite church in Paris and reopen it for Old Catholic services. In 1907, he ordained as priest the magician Louis-Marie-François Giraud, who was associated with the Universal Gnostic Church.[65] However, Vilatte's national church failed to overcome Catholic opposition, and having been excommunicated by the Archbishop of Paris, refused ordination by the Romanian Orthodox Church, and denounced as a pseudo-American bishop, he left France and returned once more to America.

Here, he consecrated F. E. J. Lloyd in 1915, with whom he incorporated his movement as The American Catholic Church under the laws of the State of Illinois, with Vilatte as Archbishop. In 1920, he retired, leaving Lloyd as Archbishop, and returned to France and to the Holy See, with which he was reconciled in 1925. For the remaining four years of his life, he lived near Versailles at the Abbey of Pont Colbert. He died of heart failure on 8 July 1929, and was buried without episcopal vestments and with a requiem mass celebrated as for a layman. Described early in his career as a character of 'piety, sobriety, purity, intelligence and prudence' by Bishop Brown in 1885, he was latterly known as an ecclesiastical adventurer and 'an opportunist psychopath'.[66] He was most certainly a very active, widely-travelled *episcopus vagans*, and two widespread lines of succession stem from him, in the American Catholic Church and the African Orthodox Church. Neither of these churches is particularly relevant to this study, however. Rather, it is the two lines that entered England, and churches derived from Vilatte in France that are of far greater importance. They are therefore considered at length in the next chapter.

In general terms, the heterodox churches and their bishops emphasise claims to apostolicity, orthodoxy, and catholicity, this latter being either simply without, or explicitly against, the Papacy and Rome. Thus far, they echo the concerns of the Tudor reformers, Caroline Divines, and Anglo-Catholics discussed in Chapter 1. Many of the *episcopi vagantes* also shared with Cromwell and Parker a desire to locate their version of Christianity in the purity of an untainted past, as the earliest form of Christianity after Jerusalem and Antioch, and stemming directly from these ancient seats rather than arriving via papal missionaries from Rome. Often, a similar nationalist flavour as that of the English reformations is to be found, though this tends to be more localised, without the power of the state behind it. Thus, Mar Georgius (de Willmott Newman) titles himself Patriarch of Glastonbury and Catholicos of the West, and Harrington styles himself Primate of the Orthodox-Keltic Church. Mar Pelagius (Morgan) is an extreme example, combining a fervent Welsh nationalism with the most extreme myths of the foundations of Anglicanism, and beyond: the Druids were the forerunners of Christianity, the Trojans discovered Britain, the British are descended from one of the ten tribes of Israel, St Paul, as well as Joseph of Arimathea, had been to Britain etc. etc. Whatever else had happened, to the Welsh Protestant clergy of the nineteenth century, the Reformation had swept away the corruptions of Rome, and to Morgan this enabled the Welsh Church to return to its state of primitive purity in the shape of the Ancient British Church.

Unlike the separation from Rome of the English reformations, however, the *episcopi vagantes* were almost obsessed with the idea of the restoration of Christian unity. In this, they mirrored the preoccupations of the Non-Jurors and the various incarnations of the Order of Corporate Reunion. The means by which they sought to bring about this unity was not through long negotiations and debate, but by the widespread, often indiscriminate propagation of what they considered to be episcopal and priestly orders. These are, however, 'divorced from almost every consideration but a mechanical conception of validity',[67] i.e. they are not connected to any form of ministry, and often the churches to which their titles related existed only on paper, sometimes only in the imagination of the bishop. Where churches and pro-Cathedrals did exist, they were often rooms in private houses, with some exceptions.[68] The titles themselves – both of the prelates and the churches – are unbelievably extravagant, mixing aristocratic and ecclesiastical pretensions which far exceed a simple 'my lord Bishop': Prince-Patriarch, Mar, Catholicos, Metropolitan, Primate, Hierarch, even Pontifex.

To these were often added doctorates and other degrees from their own 'universities' – Crow's Doctor of Divinity was from the International Orthodox Catholic University, of which Patriarch Heard was Chancellor. The latter was also Chancellor of the Université Philotechnique Internationale on Bond Street. Also in existence were the University of St John and the Western Orthodox University, which had replaced the University of Sulgrave,

Northamptonshire. Both were under the jurisdiction of the Catholicos of the West, Mar Georgius (de Willmott Newman). Doctorates of Divinity were sold for £15 15s; Master of Arts degrees were £10 10s. De Willmott Newman himself claimed the following degrees: MA, DCL and PhD (Apostolic Academy of St Peter at Antioch); DD (International Orthodox University); LLD (Université Philotechnique Internationale); and DLitt (The Keltic University).[69] Needless to say, none of these foundations obtained recognition as degree-giving universities in Britain, nor did they apply for financial aid from the University Grants Committee. Neither were they concerned with offering any pre-ordination training – priestly and episcopal orders were, by and large, given on a whim, the latter to men who, having found fault with the bodies to which they belonged, saw no option but to set up a rival church. Far from promoting Christian unity, this often involved mutual excommunications and frequent changes of church names; thus the world of the wandering bishops represents a mass of confused and complex relations not seen even in the period of the reformations.

It was, of course, the schism from Rome particularly during the Elizabethan reformation[70] that brought into question the validity of Anglican orders, though it was not until Leo XIII's *Apostolicae Curae* of 1896 that a declaration concerning their invalidity was finally made. After this, those within the Church of England, as well as those outside, who wanted unquestionably valid orders had to go elsewhere – either to Rome, with all the inherent problems of foreign power, or to the Eastern churches which seemed to facilitate a combination of apostolicity alongside autocephalous status. The Anglican position as regards the *episcopi vagantes* and their churches is thus somewhat ironic. After all, they had rejected the Roman concept of apostolic succession of the historic episcopate at the Reformation,[71] and their own claims to it are invalid in the eyes of Rome. Sympathetic to their own schism (with Rome), they discredit any schism from their own ranks. This notwithstanding, the problem was not simply a question of validity, but of the irregular exercise of these orders, for the churches were largely made up of bishops and priests, with little or no laity to whom to minister. In addition, the churches of the *episcopi vagantes* were often ahead of their time, in allowing for the ordination of women, for example. Perhaps more importantly, they were linked with occultism, the magical fringes of Freemasonry, and a variety of neo-gnostic traditions. This was especially true of the French heterodox churches and the third revival of the Ancient British (now labelled Agnostic) Church, which are the subject of the next chapter.

3

CHURCHES GNOSTIC
AND AGNOSTIC

In the century prior to Mar Timotheos' (Vilatte's) sojourns in his native country, many attempts had been made to provide a substitute for the orthodox Catholicism that had been suppressed and marginalised in the aftermath of the French Revolution. A year after the violent anti-clericalism of 1789, which led to the deaths of 2–3,000 clergy[1] and the exile of over 30,000 more, a Constitutional Church had been established by the National Assembly. The tithe was abolished, and church property nationalised and sold off. Those clergy who filled the vacuum were willing to adhere to and maintain the Civil Constitution, the exile leaving the way clear for the consecration of new bishops in the Constitutional Church who were supportive of, and supported by, the government. Under an agreement between Napoleon and Rome in 1801, twelve Constitutional bishops were allowed to submit to Pope Pius VII and retain their sees, but many priests and laity remained loyal to the bishops in exile who refused to return to their dioceses. These French Catholics formed the *Petite Église*. With the restoration of the Bourbon monarchy after the downfall of Napoleon in 1815, most of the exiled bishops were reconciled with Rome, but the *Petite Église* continued even after its last priest died in 1847. Vilatte's parents were members of this Church, and it is still extant today.[2]

By the nineteenth century, the Church's hold on everyday life had been severely weakened and, '[e]mancipated from formal religious observance, new believers sought new systems to replace the old, adopted the language of the old to present the new' (Weber, 1988: 402). An extensive underground of secret organisations flourished in the ensuing religious anarchy, to such an extent that the nineteenth century could be characterised as

> rife with superstition, with occult cults, with counter religions. All had existed before 1789; now the difficulties of orthodox religion gave them a chance to flourish – no longer underground, but visibly, at all levels of society.
>
> (Weber, 1988: 415)

Often combining heterodox Christianity, occultism, Freemasonry and spiritualism, these cults and counter religions existed alongside the short-lived public Cult of Reason (1793) and Robespierre's Cult of the Supreme Being (1794). A prime example is the *Église Johannite des Chrétiens Primitifs* founded by the chiropodist and Templar revivalist Dr Bernard-Raymond Fabré-Palaprat (1777–1838). His was a heterodox Catholic cult based on alleged associations between Freemasonry and the Knights Templar, which practised occult rituals and seems to have attracted lapsed Catholic bishops and priests. It was one of many such sects that centred on the revival of heresy, particularly those linked with gnosis such as Catharism and the Templars, and sought to return to the simplicity of an imagined primitive Christianity.

Other schismatic churches were based on Gallicanism, a form of religious nationalism not dissimilar to that found in the Tudor reformations. Those involved believed French bishops and clergy had held the true doctrine of papal authority from as early as the fourth century, and had 'set a splendid example to the rest of the Catholic Church by their defence against the insidious encroachments of Rome' (Anson, 1964: 305). Four Gallican Articles, drawn up by French bishops, had been condemned by Pope Alexander VIII in 1690 and by Louis XIV in 1693, after which Gallicanism went underground; but it did not disappear. Though anti-clericalism against all Catholics – even those opposed to papal supremacy – had, 'eroded the power base of the national churches, thus opening the way to the ascendancy of Rome' (Blackbourn, 1991: 780), particularly after the proclamation of infallibility in 1870, projects to set up a national church in France continued to be encouraged in the early twentieth century. As mentioned in the previous chapter, Vilatte had taken advantage of new laws to form an *association culturelle catholique, apostolique et française* in 1907, giving legal status to a small group of clergy and laity of whom he was leader.

Despite irreligion and anti-clericalism, nineteenth century France witnessed a religious revival, though it has been characterised as 'a patchwork affair that took place alongside widespread dechristianization' (ibid.: 785).[3] As well as Gallicanism, Gnosticism and a yearning for a pure, primitive Christianity, it was characterised by the revelations of Joachim of Fiore (1132–1202) concerning the reign of the Paraclete[4] and by the associated cult of woman as redeemer.[5] In 1839, for example, an esoteric church called the *Œuvre de la Miséricorde* was founded by Pierre-Eugène-Michel Vintras (1807–75). He claimed visionary communications from the Archangel Michael, the Holy Ghost, the Virgin Mary and St Joseph, and believed himself to be the reincarnation of the prophet Elijah with a mission to proclaim the coming age of the Paraclete.[6] The 'Work of Mercy' spread rapidly, and was the home of alleged miracles such as bleeding hosts at Mass that appeared and disappeared. Condemned by the Bishop of Bordeaux, Vintras found himself in prison for six years on trumped-up charges of defrauding two women, during which time he founded the *Chevalerrie de Marie* (Knights of Mary) for an élite of his followers.

44

By 1848, Vintras was free and his movement declared heretical – his followers were no longer able to receive the sacraments from Catholic priests. In typical *episcopus vagans* style, Vintras responded by excommunicating the Pope and making himself pontiff. He claimed to have been consecrated *Pontife Adorateur*, *Pontife d'Amour* and *Pontife Provincial* by Christ himself, who had also shown him how to celebrate a new liturgy, at which he presided on 10 May. Ten days later, he consecrated seven Roman Catholic priests as *pontifes divins*; they then reciprocated by re-consecrating Vintras. All were condemned and excommunicated by the Catholic Church, and in 1852 the *Œuvre* was dissolved by Louis-Napoléon. Vintras fled to Belgium and then England, returning again to France in 1863 and eventually founding the *Carmel blanc* at Florence. After his death, Joseph-Antoine Boullan (1824–93) took control and 'transformed the *Église vintrasisanne* into a thoroughly occultist and spiritualist body' (Anson, 1964: 304) which nevertheless preached the imminent arrival of the Paraclete (Gould and Reeves, 2001: 208). Boullan claimed to be the reincarnation of St John the Baptist,[7] and constructed rituals which blended Catholicism, sex magic and occultism, which are alleged to have formed the basis of J.-K. Huysman's novel of satanism, *Là Bas* (1891).[8]

Along with Jews and witches, the Templars, Cathars and other gnostic groups had been accused of child sacrifice, satanic worship and, of course, orgies and sexual depravity in general. The neo-gnostic churches of the nineteenth and twentieth centuries were no strangers to accusations of sexual impropriety either. In some of the churches, sexual intercourse was an integral part of their teachings and practices which, alongside a preoccupation with the feminine both as divine and as manifest in post-revolutionary socialist feminism, may go some way to explaining the reasons why these secret societies and churches were open to women as well as men.[9] Vintras, for example, was alleged to have sanctioned forms of sex magic which included naked celebrations of the Mass, homosexuality, and magical prayers accompanied by masturbation. However, these allegations came from an ex-disciple named Gozzoli, who had been expelled from the movement in 1851. According to Christopher McIntosh (1975: 64), investigations by the police and the Bishop of Bayeux apparently found Vintras innocent, yet he is still cited as an early advocate of sex magic.[10]

Boullan, though, was a different matter. In his secret rites called 'Unions of Life', open to only an élite of his disciples, he taught a form of sex magic which was alleged to aid in the spiritual evolution of all beings and reverse the Fall. Boullan taught that 'since the fall of our first parents was the result of an act of culpable love, it is through acts of love accomplished in a religious spirit that the Redemption of humanity could and should be achieved' (Baldick, cited in McIntosh, 1975: 181).[11] In the 'ladder of life',[12] sexual intercourse with the higher spirit world (angels and other heavenly beings, plus the spirits of great humans)[13] would speed the redemption of humans, whilst sexual intercourse with the lower and elemental spirit

world and animals would help them to evolve spiritually. The neo-gnostic churches of the *episcopi vagantes* thus played upon the accusations levelled against earlier gnostic sects by orthodox Christianity, claiming them as true but, contrary to the persecutors, perceiving such practices to be spiritually beneficial. This was to be taken further by Aleister Crowley and the OTO, both influenced by the *Église Gnostique* founded by a librarian, Jules-Benoît Stanislas Doinel du Val-Michel (1842–1903), in 1890.[14]

Doinel was a spiritualist and Freemason who, like Éliphas Lévi, had visions of the divine feminine which he felt called to restore to its proper place in religion. He became fascinated with the history of the Cathars and their resistance against the papacy. In a vision in 1888, Doinel claimed that Jesus had consecrated him as Bishop of Montségur and Primate of the Albigenses, as a result of which he attempted to contact Cathar and Gnostic spirits during séances at Lady Caithness'[15] salons. In a séance held in September 1889, the spirit of Guilhabert de Castres, former Bishop of Montségur, was alleged to have manifested. He charged Doinel with establishing an Assembly of the Paraclete, called the Gnostic Church, through which the gnostic doctrines could be taught. Its holy book was the Gospel of John, and theological doctrines were drawn from Simon Magus,[16] Origen, Appolonius of Tyana, and Valentinus.[17] Sacraments were derived from the Cathars – the *consolamentum* and *appareillamentum* – conferred via rituals that drew heavily on those of the Roman Catholic Church. The Church included both male bishops and female 'sophias', working in pairs and, under their direction, pairs of deaconesses and deacons. It was also a system of spiritual and elitist Freemasonry, linked to the Scottish Rite through *the Ordre des chevaliers faydits*[18] *de la Colombe du Paraclet*, an imitation of the Strict Observance.[19]

Doinel proclaimed 1890 to be the beginning of the Era of Gnosis Restored, and assumed the office of Patriarch of the Gnostic Church, titling himself Valentin II. Valentin consecrated bishops who took names prefixed by the Greek letter Tau, representing the Tau cross and Egyptian ankh. One of the first to be raised to the episcopate was Gérard Encausse, better known as 'Papus' (1865–1916), who took the name Tau Vincent, Bishop of Toulouse. Doinel later joined Papus' 're-awakened' Martinist Order,[20] before converting to Roman Catholicism and abdicating his position as Patriarch of the Gnostic Church in 1895 (he was readmitted as a bishop five years later, in 1900). Close links developed between French gnostic churches and Martinism, which were formalised in 1911 when Papus signed a treaty with Jean Bricaud making the latter's break-away Gnostic Church the official church of the Martinist Order, along with the Gallican Church of France.

Jean 'Joanny' Bricaud (1881–1934) had been consecrated as Tau Johannes, Bishop of Lyon, in 1901, having previously been involved with Vintras' *Eliate Church of Carmel* and with the *Église Johannite des Chrétiens Primitifs* of Fabré-Palaprat. He had also joined the Martinist Order, after meeting Papus in 1899. Six years after his consecration, in 1907, Bricaud broke away from the *Église Gnostique* and founded his own schismatic branch of the Gnostic Church. It combined the Carmelite Church of Vintras, Fabré-Palaprat's Johannite Church, and Doinel's Gnostic Church; as stated above, it was closely tied to the Martinist Order. Bricaud became patriarch of this *Église Gnostique*, as Tau Jean II, which in 1908 was renamed *l'Église Gnostique Universelle* (EGU). The same year, on 24 June, Papus and Bricaud met Theodor Reuss, head of the Ordo Templi Orientis (OTO), at an international Masonic and Spiritualist Conference organised by Papus and held in Paris. It appears that Reuss was consecrated, probably by Papus, for he founded a German branch of the EGU, *Die Gnostische Katholische Kirche* (GKK), which he brought under the auspices of the OTO.

Bricaud later met the ex-Trappist monk Louis-Marie-François Giraud, and was consecrated into the Vilatte succession by him on 21 July 1913.[21] He seems to have believed that this episcopal consecration provided the EGU with a valid, if irregular, apostolic succession which would both allow Christian sacraments to be administered to the Catholic members of the Martinist Order[22] and, supposedly, make their magical rites more effective.[23] Reuss was conditionally re-consecrated at the hands of Bricaud on 18 September 1919, at which point he was appointed Gnostic Legate of the EGU to Switzerland;[24] the supposed apostolic succession from Antioch via Vilatte was thus passed to the OTO. By this time, Aleister Crowley (1875–1947) had already joined Reuss' OTO (1910) and been appointed National Grand Master for Ireland, Iona and all the Britains[25] (1912). He had also written *Liber XV*, the Gnostic Mass, whilst in Moscow in 1913, and come up with the Latin name *Ecclesiæ Gnosticæ Catholicæ* (EGC). Conceived as a public ceremony[26] corresponding to the mass of the Roman Catholic Church, the Gnostic Mass was published in 1918 in *The International*, and in *The Equinox*, vol. III (1) (the 'Blue Equinox') in 1919; Reuss published a German version in 1918. At this point, the EGC became independent from the EGU[27] and the Mass became its central ceremony; Reuss became 'Sovereign Patriarch and Primate of the *Ecclesiæ Gnosticæ Catholicæ*'.

According to Tau Apiryon's 'History of the Gnostic Catholic Church', claims were made in the late 1980s that Crowley received the apostolic succession of the Vilatte line via Reuss, and other lines of succession were introduced[28] in an attempt to gain recognition from civil authorities.[29] The claim regarding Crowley's ordination or consecration[30] seems to have now been dropped, as the conversion of the EGC to Crowley's system of Thelema removed the need for Christian apostolic succession. Nevertheless, the succession is valued 'as an aspect of the traditions inherited from the pre-Thelemic French Gnostic Church, and as a form of symbolic successorship to the great Christian, Hebraic and Pagan religious systems of the past'.[31] Thus, whilst the more relevant succession is seen to be that derived from Crowley himself, as the Prophet of Thelema, there is a willingness to accept the inheritance of heterodox Christianity through the French line of the Vilatte succession within the EGC and the OTO.

The English lines of succession from Vilatte came via Gulotti, mentioned in the previous chapter, and via Churchill Sibley, an Englishman consecrated by Lloyd on 8 September 1929 as 'Missionary Archbishop and Vicar-General of the Order of Antioch in England'. Sibley consecrated Ebenezer Johnson Anderson, a member of the Gold Coast Fanti tribe, as Mar Kwamin, Primate of the 'Autonomous African Universal Church and other Unifications of West African Churches in Africa and Florida of the Orthodox Faith'. Six months later, on 1 September 1935, Anderson consecrated Frederick Charles Aloysius Harrington as Primate of the 'Orthodox Keltic Church of the British Commonwealth of Nations', who has already been mentioned in Chapter 2, in the Ferrette succession. A few weeks later, on 6 October 1935, Sibley consecrated John Sebastian Marlow Ward.

Ward was born in Honduras in 1895 to a former Anglo-Catholic priest. He read history at Cambridge and went on to become head of the Diocesan Boys' School in Rangoon, and then Director of the Intelligence Department of the Federation of British Industries, from 1918–30. In October 1928, Ward and his second wife, Jessica Page, claimed to have visions of the Second Coming of Christ, which would bring with it a new revelation for a new age. A month later, they received visions telling them to found a mixed community of men and women to prepare for Christ's return. On 13 May 1929, Ward recorded, they were 'led by the Angelic Guardian of the work into the presence of Christ the King, and by Him solemnly consecrated for the task and given the requisite authority to organize the work and to found the Abbey' (Ward, *The Confraternity of Christ the King*, n.p. or d., cited in Anson, 1964: 283). Ward resigned the Directorship of the Intelligence Department in January 1930 in order to devote himself to the work he believed himself called to, and began to search for a suitable place and building for the abbey. They were guided by more visions to buy a plot of land at New Barnet, and found a fifteenth-century half-timbered tithe-barn which they re-erected on the site and transformed into a chapel. On the feast of St John the Baptist (24 June) 1930, The Confraternity of Christ the King[32] came into being, and the chapel was dedicated with Anglican rites on St Valentine's Day 1931 by the Anglo-Catholic Bishop of St Albans, Dr Michael Furse.[33] The bishop also appointed the parish vicar as chaplain to the community.

Members of the community gave up all personal possessions, taking life vows of obedience, poverty and self-sacrifice, and a new name, after a novitiate of three years. They also ran a school, St Michael's College, which taught the Wards' version of the Christian religion. This included reincarnation, the feminine nature of the Holy Spirit, and the gnostic teaching that Christ is the offspring of God the Father and God the Mother.[34] That this type of Christianity was incompatible with the Anglican version became clear at the end of 1934, when Ward submitted a constitution for the Confraternity to Bishop Furse, who not only felt unable to approve it, but decided not to renew the chaplain's licence. This seems to have been because the activities of the community were attracting local inhabitants and so were no longer limited to the members – Ward 'had no authority to Minister the Word and yet had done so by opening the Abbey Church to outsiders' (Ward, 1944: 38 cited in Anson, 1964: 285 and Heselton, 2003: 137). As far as Ward was concerned, he and his community had tried to retain a link to the Anglican Church, but the latter had broken this, attacking the work of the Abbey in a similar way to the manner in which it had treated Fr Ignatius at Llanthony.[35] In response, Ward questioned the validity of Anglican orders and the authority of Anglican bishops, concluding that,

> ... in the ecclesiastical sense the Anglican Church has no valid Orders, and therefore no Priests and no Bishops, and that the gentleman who calls himself a Bishop is only a layman given the name of Bishop by Act of Parliament, and appointed by the State like any other State Official.
>
> (Ward, 1944: 39)

This was an attitude shared by others, including Church of England clergy, some of whom continued in their work, which they saw as a state appointment, whilst regarding their ordinations by *episcopi vagantes* as their true priesthood.[36] Similarly, Ward now sought a Church with, as he saw it, valid orders and was ordained deacon and priest (12 September 1935) and consecrated bishop (15 September 1935) by Mar Kwamin (Anderson). On 24 September, Ward informed the Bishop of St Albans that the Abbey had severed its relations with the Church of England. Ward quickly found out, however, that Kwamin's consecration documents had been withheld as the latter had broken his agreement with Sibley not to operate in England. Ward therefore sought advice from Sibley himself, who offered to re-ordain and re-consecrate him. As mentioned above, this took place in October 1935 – Ward was re-baptised, confirmed and re-ordained on 5 October, and re-consecrated on the following day. He was also given the degree of DD from the Intercollegiate University, of which Sibley was Chancellor, and Jessica Ward was re-ordained to the diaconate. The Abbey thus became part of Sibley's Orthodox Catholic Church, which until that point had existed only on paper; in fact, it seems that the Abbey of Christ the King was one of the few churches that actually had its own dedicated place of worship and a membership. At this point, Ward closed St Michael's College and opened the Abbey Folk Park.[37]

Ward seems to have followed Harrington's earlier aim of uniting the Vilatte and Ferrette successions, for on 25 August 1945 he was consecrated a third time, by Mar Georgius, Patriarch of Glastonbury and Catholicos of the West (de Willmott Newman), after which Ward styled himself 'Mar John, Titular Archbishop of Olivet'. At the same time, the Orthodox Catholic Church, of which Ward was now Archbishop following Sibley's death in 1938, was received into full communion with the Catholicate of the West, and Mar Georgius made good use of what was now the Cathedral of Christ the King as a venue for performing consecrations. Ward, of course, was also performing consecrations and ordinations, but contrary to claims made by Davis,[38] he did not ordain Gardner.[39] Ward certainly seems to have been a heavy influence on Gardner, and they were friends enough by 1945 for Gardner to give Ward his land in Cyprus; but Gardner's ordination did not take place until a month after Ward had departed England for Cyprus on 13 July 1946, and the name on his certificate is that of Bishop Dorian, not Archbishop Olivet.

During a visit to the community in Cyprus in 1949, after Ward's death, Gardner was allegedly re-ordained by Colin Mackenzie Chamberlain (Fr Filius Domini), who had been consecrated as Gregory, Titular Archbishop of Bethany, by Mar Georgius, Ward, and four other prelates in a ceremony at the Cathedral of Christ the King on 6 June 1946, some two months before Gardner's initial ordination. After Ward's death on 2 July 1949, Chamberlain assumed the Primacy of the Orthodox Church in England, though he remained in Limasol. He did, however, consecrate a fellow priest of the community in March 1951, Fr William Martin Andrew, who, having been suspended by Mar Georgius (de Willmott Newman), went to Cyprus for the purpose of being raised to the episcopy and, on his return to England, founded the Church of Christ the King in Bournemouth.[40] The remnant of the Confraternity in Cyprus, under Mrs Ward as Reverend Mother, left for Australia. The Church, now known as Saint Cecilia's Orthodox Catholic Church of the New Age, is still in existence in Queensland, Australia, under the leadership of Bishop John Cuffe, who claims to be Ward's illegitimate son by one of the members of the community.[41]

The Cathedral of Christ the King continued to be used for worship by the Orthodox Catholic Church,[42] though the Abbey Folk Park had closed on the departure of Ward and his Confraternity. It was therefore perfectly possible for Gardner to be 'a regular visitor to the Abbey wearing a dog-collar' (Heselton, 2003: 144), a fact which Heselton finds to be inconsistent with the closure of the Abbey. Consequently, Heselton wonders whether Gardner was ordained into another such church, at an earlier date, but this is both unlikely and unnecessary given the continued use of Ward's old barn.[43] Gardner was in fact ordained into the Ancient British Church on 29 August 1946, by Frederic 'Dorian' Herbert. Herbert was consecrated as Bishop of Caerleon on 24 October 1937 by Mar Frederic (Harrington), Primate of the Orthodox Keltic Church, and later re-consecrated by Mar Georgius (de Willmott Newman) on 3 December 1944. Prior to either of these consecrations, however, he had already founded a church known variously as the Jesuene Church or as the Free Orthodox-Catholic Church.

Unlike most irregular bishops, who tended to lay claim to orthodoxy, Herbert unhesitatingly declared himself a heretic, proclaiming his church to be 'rationalistic in interpretation, unorthodox and heretical', aiming to 'free Christian interpretation from intellectual bondage, and to abolish the commercialization of the Christian religion' (cited in Anson, 1964: 294).[44] He explained the use of 'Agnostic' as follows:

I do not subscribe to modern interpretations of conventional Christianity. The original British Church ... existed before the creeds and theological dogmas were formulated. ... The Agnostic Christian is one who openly admits that he does not know, and rejects the fanciful notion that certain privileged ecclesiastical authoritarians, or any others, have any more real knowledge than he has. His Christian fellowship is based upon loyalty to identity of purpose – and not upon fear, or the promise of reward here or hereafter. Real nobility of character is in doing good for it own sake.

(cited in Anson, 1964: 298)[45]

With no creed, and disregarding belief as a criterion for membership, Herbert invited anyone to receive communion and, like many of the gnostic churches, regarded women as an essential part of the future church. In *Women Priesthood*, a pamphlet published in 1943, he declared that he would be delighted to ordain women and have them minister at his altars. Later, styling himself Mar Doreos and regarding himself as the successor of Mar Pelagius (Morgan), he revived the dormant Ancient British Church,[46] which he believed to be the only Christian Church to have existed in Britain for the first five centuries CE, eventually suppressed by the ascendancy of Canterbury.[47] Under the auspices of this revived Britonnic Church, Mar Doreos established the 'Holy Grail Christian Crusade against Brutality to Animals and all Wild Creatures', which he claimed had the patronage of King Arthur and the Knights of the Round Table. As Prior of this Order, he campaigned against gin-traps and marched through Liverpool in an attempt to save three police horses about to be shot, thus putting into practice his teaching that actions emulating Christ's were more important than beliefs.

Mar Doreos' vegetarianism and pro-Celticism were shared by another priest ordained in a heterodox church, Gardner's friend, fellow naturist and Druid Ross Nichols (1902–75). This chapter would be incomplete without a brief look at *Sainte Église celtique en Bretagne*, in which Nichols was ordained 'Archdeacon of the Isles' during a trip with the Chief of the Ancient Druid Order, Robert MacGregor Reid, to the *Goursez Breizh* (Breton Gorsedd)[48] of 1963. *Sainte Église* was founded by Jean-Pierre (Clodoald) Danyel (1917–68), a Frenchman who wanted initially to establish a vernacular Byzantine Rite parish in France but failed to obtain ordination from any Romanian, Russian or Greek Orthodox bishop. He was eventually ordained on 15 July 1951 by the Mariavite[49] Bishop of France, to whom he had been referred by the Liberal Catholic Church. Danyel, however, seems to have been quite particular that his orders should be recognised by Rome and by the Orthodox Church, but should not be given by a priest of either church, for he believed that neither Roman Catholicism nor Orthodoxy understood the needs of the modern world. Doubting the validity of his first ordination in the eyes of these Churches,[50] he received all the orders again on 1 March 1953. This time, he chose Mgr Lutgen, Archbishop of Antwerp, who was Metropolitan of the *Église catholique du rite dominicain*. Lutgen had been consecrated by Mar Georgius (de Willmott Newman), and thus was able to lay claim to at least fifteen lines of apostolic succession.

Danyel now felt secure that his orders would be recognised as valid, and set out to meet the needs of the times as he saw them. These needs were not, he decided, to be met by the Byzantine Rite after all, but by the revival of the ancient Celtic Church of Brittany.[51] Choosing the name of one of the seven founding saints of Brittany, Tugdual,[52] he founded the *Abbaye de la Sainte Présence* at Bois-Juhel, near Saint-Dolay where he lived as a hermit in emulation of the ancient Celtic monks. He soon attracted disciples from among the Breton people, and was elected as the first bishop of the revived (new) Celtic Church. He was consecrated on 5 May 1957 by Mgr Ireneaus, Archbishop of Arles (Comte Charles Borromée d'Eschevannes), Primate of the *Sainte Église catholique Gallicane autocéphale*. Tugdual (Danyel) now assumed the title 'Bishop of Redon', and claimed sixteen lines of succession, which he had printed in an eighteen-page pamphlet.[53] Convinced of the future growth of his Celtic Church, which he believed far more suited to the strongly Catholic Brittany, he proclaimed himself a metropolitan bishop on 19 December 1959, with the title Tugdual I, Archbishop of Dôl. As part of his attempt to re-convert the people of Brittany to the church of their ancestors, he revived Druidic rites[54] and customs and added the title '*Sa Blancheur l'Humble*' ('His Whiteness the Humble') which he claimed was of Druid origin.[55] His full title thus became 'His Whiteness the Humble Tugdual I, Archbishop of Dôl, Abbot of Saint-Dolay, Kayermo and Keroussek, Primate of the Holy Celtic Church, President of the Union of all the non-Roman Christian and Apostolic Churches'.[56]

At the time Anson was writing, four or five years before Tugdual's death on 11 August 1968, the church consisted of 'ten bishops[57] and two or three layfolk' (Anson, 1964: 318, n. 4). On his death, the hermitage was abandoned, but Tugdual had predicted that, ten years after his death, monks would return to inhabit the hermitage and to found a monastery which would continue his mission. On 4 October 1977 three monks from a monastery in Montpellier, founded in 1973 by a Celtic Orthodox priest, Paul-Edouard de Fournier de Brescia, settled at the dilapidated hermitage and began to build a wooden church on the site, which was dedicated to Notre-Dame du Signe in 1984. Tugdual was canonised by the church he founded in 1996 – as this implies, the church is still in existence and has grown significantly, though it is now called *l'Église Orthodoxe Celtique*. It is presently headed by Mäel Bliss (de Brescia),[58] Primate of the Celtic Orthodox Church, Archbishop of Dôl and titular Bishop of Iona.

L'Église Orthodoxe Celtique claims to be a native, Western, and autocephalous Orthodox Church,[59] established by Mar Julius (Ferrette), Bishop of Iona, the alleged Patriarchal Legate of the Syrian Jacobite Church for Western Europe. As explained in Chapter 2, Ferrette claimed to have been dispatched with authority to erect an indigenous Orthodox Church in Western Europe which would not be subject to Antioch. Following the official version of history outlined in Chapter 1, and that of Mar Pelagius (Morgan) (Chapter 2) and the Gallicans (above), the Celtic Orthodox Church reiterates the founding of the early British Church by Joseph of Arimathea, maintaining the traditions of Christianity untainted by later alterations and thus able to claim 'Orthodoxy': 'Of apostolic succession, she owed nothing to Rome, nor to any other historic Church of the East. During nearly 12 centuries, she guarded her sovereignty and resisted the hegemony of the Roman Church'.[60]

The Orthodox Church of the British Isles split from the French in 1995 under Mar Seraphim (William Henry Hugo Newman-Norton),[61] Metropolitan of Glastonbury, changing its name to the British Orthodox Church.[62] It became part of the Egyptian (Coptic) Orthodox Church through which the British Orthodox Church claims apostolic succession from the Syrian Orthodox Church.[63] As with all the other churches stemming from Ferrette, however, such claims rest on a 'history' written by Mar Georgius (de Willmott Newman) some eighty years later which tells of consecrations for which there is no documentary evidence and which bypasses the canon law of the Orthodox Church as regards autonomous patriarchates.[64]

Like Mar Pelagius (Morgan) in the 1870s, Tugdual seems to have believed, or at least found useful, the legend that the Druids and Christians merged their religions harmoniously during the period of 'pure and ancient' Christianity which existed before what they considered to be the encroachments of Rome changed the situation. Also like Morgan, he was able to ride on a wave of Celtic nationalism that included revived Druidry as part of its identity. Brittany had been independent until the defeat of the Breton army in 1488 forced a treaty giving the King of France the right to arrange the marriage of the Duke of Brittany's daughter and heir, Anne. She married Charles VIII and then Louis XII of France, and was the last independent ruler of the duchy. After her death, it passed to her daughter Claude, whose husband, François I, incorporated it into the Kingdom of France in 1532. The Bretons kept specific laws and taxes until the Revolution of 1789 removed all privileges, as well as suppressing Catholicism, as discussed earlier in this chapter. From that time on, the devoutly Catholic and royalist Breton region was a hotbed of insurrection, in which arose long-running uprisings such as that of the Chouans[65]against the revolution and the Republic.

The rebirth of Brittany began with the Breton folklorist and antiquarian Hersart de la Villemarque at the end of the 1830s. A collector of Breton folk songs, Villemarque was initiated at the Welsh Eisteddfod at Abergavenny in 1838, and established the first Bardic group in Brittany, *Breuriez Barzed Breiz* ('The Fraternity of Bards in Brittany'), in 1855. In 1885, Henri Lizeray, a writer on astrology, founded *l'Église Druidique et Nationale* in Paris, as a 'provocation rather than a possible indication of Christian affiliation' according to Michel Raoult (1996: 117).[66] However, in light of the nineteenth-century interest in national churches of a heterodox nature, and the ongoing appeal of myths relating Druidry to early Christianity, this is by no means certain.

From the foundation of the regionalist Breton Association in 1898 and the establishment of the Gorsedd of Bards in 1900, links between the Bretons and the Welsh increased and Breton nationalism grew ever more active: the Breton flag, *Gwenn ha Du* ('white and black'), was created in 1923, the Breton National Party was founded in 1930, and in July 1932 the Breton terrorist group (also called *Gwenn ha Du*) blew up a statue depicting the submission of Duchess Anne, kneeling before the King of France, in Rennes. Further attacks followed, in 1936, 1938 and 1939. Also in 1936, a new Celtic journal *Kad* was published, announcing the formation of a *Breuriez Spered Adnevezi* (a 'Fraternity of Regenerating Belief'). It called on the Bretons to 'renounce the authority of the [French] State and of the Christian Church simultaneously in order to encourage a return to Celtic roots' (Raoult, 1996: 115). It published articles on the druidic traditions in a journal called *Nemeton* which was edited by the designer of the Breton flag, Morvan Marchal, Druid Artonovios (ibid.: 115). After the war, the name of the group was changed to *Kredenn Geltiek* ('Celtic Belief'), and it claimed adherence to neo-Pagan Druidism.

As with the Welsh and Cornish gorsedds, the Breton gorsedd was largely focused on the promotion of Celtic languages and culture, in opposition to attempts by the government to stamp out the Breton language. Many bardic and druidic groups have sprung from it, though some survived only as long as their founders, including that of Villemarque (d. 1895) and the *Collège Bardique des Gaules* (1933–58) of Phileas Lebesque (1869–1958) though it had already spawned the *Collège Druidique des Gaules* in 1942. According to Nichols ([1975] 1992: 118), Lebesque, like Tugdual, felt that 'after the abrupt transition of the revolution, [France] should link with her earlier traditions', and that Druidry 'had much to say to the spiritual basis of modern France'. In 1950 Goff ar Steredennou created the Great Oak Forest Celtic College of Broceliande, which still exists, and the Great Oak, which had lasted until 1943, was reactivated in 1960 by Mic Goban. It was in this context of revived Druidry and the promotion of the Breton language and culture that Tugdual decided, in the 1950s, to focus his church on the ancient Celtic beliefs of the region.[67] Since he ordained Ross Nichols and made him Archdeacon at the Gorsedd of 1963, and given that he used Druidic titles, it seems Tugdual must himself have been a member of the Breton Gorsedd and a Druid, as well as Archbishop, Abbot and Primate of his various heterodox groups by this time.

So what was the attraction of heterodox Christianity for Ross Nichols and Gerald Gardner? Though neither of them saw either Druidry or Wicca as exclusive religious systems,[68] Nichols is perhaps the easier of the two to explain both because Druidry has a long history of friendly links with Christianity, unlike Wicca, and because Nichols' own attitude towards Christianity is well recorded and less ambivalent. In his foreword to Nichols'

The Book of Druidry, Philip Carr-Gomm, present Chief of the Order of Bards, Ovates and Druids, repeats the story of early links between Celtic Christianity and the Druids, suggesting that the priests of the Celtic Church 'had often been Druids' (Carr-Gomm, Foreword, in Nichols, [1975]1992: 14) who maintained a close relationship with nature. He states that 'Druidry is a way of working with the natural world, and is not a dogma or a religion. It can be combined with Buddhism or Christianity, Wiccan practice or Judaism, or it can be practised on its own' (ibid.: 14); but it is the supposed links with early Christianity[69] which have encouraged the Order to work towards a revival of the Celtic Church, meeting with representatives of various forms of Christianity at conferences held at Prinknash Grange in 1989, 1990 and 1991, and at Oxford and Lewes in 1996, for example. Again, the myth of an early pure and untainted Christianity is utilised, as all those involved in the first of these conferences apparently felt that a revival of the Celtic Church could help the church 'throw off its accretions of millennia and return to the practice of a simple and pure spirituality which is in tune with Nature' (ibid.: 14).

According to Carr-Gomm, Nichols 'had always been a practising Christian, and worked for the Church in boys' clubs in the East End of London' (ibid.: 5). He was also a member of the Martinist Order (re)founded by Papus,[70] and a friend of Paul Bouchet (Bod Koad), founder of the *Collège Druidique des Gaules*, whom he visited on several occasions (ibid.: 16). Interestingly, Nichols reports in his *Book of Druidry* (Nichols, [1975] 1992: 118) that Bouchet's Pendragon is none other than Paul de Brescia, who as Mäel Bliss heads the Celtic Orthodox Church at Saint-Présence, and whose Druid name is Ker Peoc'h. Clearly, there is some degree of overlap between French Druidy and the Celtic Orthodox Church which has continued and developed the vision shared by Tugdual and others over the past century, continuing the spiritual legacy of Mar Pelagius (Morgan). It is perhaps not surprising then that Nichols should have been attracted to the French, or specifically Breton forms of heterodoxy, given that reciprocal visits were being made between Chiefs and Pendragons of the English Ancient Druid Order and members of the Breton Gorsedd from the mid twentieth century on.[71]

An ordination into a heterodox church would also be in keeping with Gardner's predilections for joining little-known or secret societies, especially one that proudly proclaimed itself heretical and agnostic and claimed to be a revival of that ancient British Christianity that was so linked with Druidry in the minds of Gardner, Nichols and others, both at this time and before. Gardner's attitude towards Christianity is, however, more ambivalent than that of Nichols, which may be part of the reason for the latter's attraction to Druidry with its supposed links to that religion, whilst Gardner, though also a Druid, was drawn to the world of witchcraft, with all its attendant antagonism towards the Church. According to what is, for all practical purposes, Gardner's autobiography[72] his Uncle Joe, who lived just across the road from young Gerald, had something of an anti-Catholic attitude, accusing the local curate of 'Popish tendencies' (Bracelin, [1960] 1999: 14). He voted with his feet and with his purse, becoming a Methodist and building them a chapel until he fell out with them for reasons which are not disclosed. Ignoring the 'Popish' Anglican church, he returned to the Church of England by simply building another church. These are only Gardner's memories, but it is perhaps significant that he remembers this aspect of his uncle's character; it would be an early lesson in jumping from one type of Christianity to another. Uncle Joe was not the biggest influence on Gerald's childhood, however; the dominant personality was that of his nanny, Josephine McCombie ('Com'). Little is known of her life apart from Gerald's memories, but she was Irish and, with a name such as Josephine, she was quite probably a Catholic.[73] This is pure speculation, however. What we do know is that Gerald came under her 'care' from the age of four, travelling with her extensively, and that she was quite a different character once they were away from the control of his family; Gerald, it seems, grew to dislike her intensely.[74]

Between them, Uncle Joe and Com could very likely have stirred at least ambivalent feelings towards Catholicism, if not a fully-fledged hatred of Catholic doctrines.[75] Certainly, in later life Gerald made distinctions between the Roman Church and the Celtic, which fits with Dorian Herbert's brand of Christianity and that of Ross Nichols but could also have roots in earlier reactions to childhood influences. Throughout his work, Gardner draws a distinction between the Celtic Christianity of the pre-Augustinian mission and the Church of Rome, the same tactic used by many of the heterodox churches of the wandering bishops and by the Church of England at the time of its formation.[76] He repeats the story of Christianity arriving in Britain from two sources. The first is from Joseph of Arimathea, the nature-loving, tolerant Celtic Christianity of which the forerunners were the Druids. The second dates from the mission of St Augustine in 597, and is an invading force of Roman intolerance. Gardner therefore suggests that the witches of old were well disposed towards, 'the early Celtic Christians and the Culdees, the Druids who had become Christians', but disliked the invading Saxons and 'their type of Christianity, which derived from Rome and denounced witch rites with puritanical fervour' (Gardner, [1959] 2004: 20). Persecution, torture and horror stem from the orthodox Christianity brought by Augustine, which not only crushed 'the true Christianity, the faith which Jesus himself preached', followed by the witches, the Templars, and the Albigenses, but also provided a blueprint for all the 'crimes against humanity committed by the jackbooted louts of Hitler and Stalin' (ibid.: 26; 237–8).[77] 'With all the history of persecution', he asks,

> Can anyone wonder that members of the witch cult are not particularly fond of the orthodox Church, or that they distrust a faith which can take the teachings of its Master, who never persecuted anyone, and turn them into a frenzy of torture and horror?
>
> (Gardner, [1959] 2004: 26)

In addition to the persecutions perpetrated by the Church, he denounces it for its attitude towards sex (which will be discussed in Chapter 5) and for providing whist-drives, outings, and 'wonderful white weddings' rather than a faith in which people can believe (ibid.: 242). But it is orthodox, institutionalised Christianity that he is criticising.

Gardner is clearly following in the footsteps of Dorian Herbert and Richard Williams Morgan. Dorian's Ancient British Church was centred upon an emulation of the life of Jesus as a basis for human conduct, rather than on creeds and beliefs, whilst much of Gardner's history of Christianity in Britain comes straight from the pages of Morgan's *St Paul in Britain, or The Origin of British as Opposed to Papal Christianity*, a copy of which was in Gardner's library.[78] However, despite the savage persecutions perpetrated by the institutionalised orthodox forms of Christianity, heterodox forms are not so tainted, and in Gardner's view are not inimical to Wicca. He states, in *The Meaning of Witchcraft*,

> [i]t is usually said that to be made a witch one must abjure Christianity; this is not true; but they would naturally not receive into their ranks anyone who was a very narrow Christian.
>
> (Gardner, [1959] 2004: 18)

Wicca is not, in his mind, an exclusive religion. Like Nichols' ideas regarding Druidry, Gardner insists 'that a person can be a witch and a follower of another religion at the same time. ... The mystical nature of the Wica ... transcends the superficialities of ordinary religious worship' (Bracelin, [1960] 1999: 185). On the surface, then, Gardner's attitude towards Christianity appears to be ambivalent: the Church is at once responsible for all sorts of horrors, which he lists at length in *The Meaning of Witchcraft*,[79] and at the same time Christians are not to be excluded from one of the cults they persecuted, that of the witches. But Gardner is well aware that Christianity is no more a monolith than any other religion, and in his books he tries always to ensure it is understood to which type of Christianity he is referring. He labels them 'Celtic', 'Puritan', 'Church of England' and 'Roman', the last three being part of the problematic orthodox Church, the first being the one which he regards as the original early form of British Christianity, true to the teachings of Jesus. In a similar way, the Church of England under Elizabeth steered clear of both Rome and the Puritans whilst attempting to link itself with the 'original' British church. Gardner may not have written about his ordination or the Ancient British Church, but he retained a belief in its myth of Christian history and an appreciation for heterodoxy, just as he retained his certificate of ordination.[80] Nevertheless, the type of Christianity to which he was attracted was explicitly heterodox, the least like conventional Christianity, and consciously organised as the revival of Morgan's Ancient British Church, with all its attendant myths and associations.

Wicca may have come a long way in re-assessing its history and recognising the influences brought to bear on its development but whilst it has acknowledged its inheritance of Judaeo-Christian concepts and practices via the magical systems of, primarily, the Golden Dawn and its offshoots, it has continued to present itself as a religious system far removed from Christianity, and anathema to it. In this, it differs from Druidry – which can be seen as having close links with Christianity – and the *Ecclesiæ Gnosticæ Catholicæ* of the OTO – which whilst acknowledging its heritage sees itself as going beyond Christianity. By ignoring its inheritance from Christianity, Wicca can continue to claim a place on the margins of society, represented by those physical borderlands that Michelet regarded as so intrinsic to witchcraft's survival. In such marginality, it can exist beyond orthodoxy, in a place from which society, culture and religion can be critiqued. But this assumes Christianity to be homogeneous (which it is not) and overlooks the marginality of the heterodox Christianities discussed in this and the previous chapter. In failing to understand heterodox forms of Christianity, Wicca not only throws out, but completely fails to recognise, the proverbial baby in an ocean of bath water.

The heterodox churches outlined in the last two chapters exist beyond or behind orthodoxy, offering the potential for subversion, the chance to dream up new visions of society and religion, and an avenue for cultural criticism. Thus, even if Wicca did recognise its debt to heterodox Christianity, neither would be any less marginal. Gardner's interests in subversion were not just about naturism and witchcraft; they were also about heterodoxy in its radical forms, forms which go back to the roots of a church, of a religion, of a mythic ancient Britain. Thus, rather than dismissing his ordination as meeting a need for status,[81] claiming that he was never active in the church,[82] or suggesting he dropped all interest once Wicca had been formulated,[83] it is perhaps more constructive and illuminating to consider the attitudes towards Christianity revealed in Gardner's writings. These first three chapters have examined the heterodox Christianities that not only had a direct influence on Gardner and Wicca, but also on other systems on which Gardner drew – specifically ritual magic, the EGC associated with the OTO, and Druidry. However, Wicca has of course progressed since Gardner's time, and the second half of the book is more concerned with Wicca as practised today. The remaining three chapters therefore trace the influence on Wicca of Christian heterodoxy and the Catholic revival in England through the themes of ritual, sexuality and magic.

4

REDISCOVERING RITUAL

The heterodox churches by and large adopted and adapted the rich ceremonial of Eastern Orthodox liturgy, providing one alternative for those who desired the experience of ritual and were prepared to abandon orthodox Christianity. Similarly, one of the main concerns of the Catholic wing of the Church of England, whether among the sixteenth-century and Caroline Divines, Non-Jurors, Tractarians of the Oxford Movement or Anglo-Catholics, was the issue of ceremonial in worship. Indeed, it is one of the themes that links all of the above. The rise of what was to become known as the Ritualist Movement within Anglo-Catholicism after 1850 was to push the issue of ritual into the public arena, to the extent that the Evangelical wing argued for legislation against the activities of the Ritualists, which they eventually obtained in the Public Worship Regulation Act of 1874, of which more later.

The debate over ritual took place in the context of continued anti-Catholic feeling, exacerbated by the activities of Rome and the influx of Irish immigrants to Britain. One of the foremost characteristics of intolerance was that aimed at Catholic liturgy,[1] or 'ritual'. Thus, on the one hand, the idea that the Church of England *shouldn't* 'do' ritual stemmed from the Protestant, specifically Evangelical and anti-Catholic faction. On the other, the idea that the Church of England *doesn't* 'do' ritual, but should, had existed throughout its history, finding expression in the work of those mentioned in earlier chapters – Lancelot Andrewes and William Laud, Thomas Ken and other Non-Jurors, John Henry Newman, Pusey, and John Mason Neale, the last of whom is discussed below. The consequences of this are of vital importance to our understanding of the legacy of Christian traditions for Wicca, and it is this apparent lack of ritual that Vivianne Crowley[2] points to in her suggestion that Wicca's rich ritual system may make it particularly attractive to those of a Protestant background.[3] This dearth of ritual may be a characteristic of those reformed churches that are explicitly Protestant. As should now be clear, however, the situation is a little more complex in the case of the Church of England.

Such a stress on ritual, whether in orthodox or heterodox forms of Christianity, or in Wicca, can be seen as both unusual and subversive, given the connotations that have adhered to the word since the sixteenth century.

One of the issues central to the debates of the various Protestant reformations and the Catholic Counter Reformation focused on the real presence: was God physically present in the elements of bread and wine at the Eucharist, or were these elements simply representations of the body and blood of Christ? Presence, on the one hand, and representation, on the other, were the two extreme positions, as Catholics and Protestants began to develop divergent languages of ritual. It was as a result of this debate that the very concept of ritual emerged, as a means of denoting an activity distinct from the rites that had always been a part of Western culture. In reality, it was used as a pejorative word imposed on the other: 'what I do is ordained by God and is "true religion"; what you do is "mere ritual", at best useless, at worst profoundly evil' (Muir, 1997: 7). According to the OED, it first appeared in 1570 with the meaning ascribed to it as follows: 'contayning no manner of doctrine ... but only certain ritual decrees to no purpose'. The sensitivity surrounding the debate about presence and representation brought ritual behaviour under close scrutiny.

Prior to the era of the reformations, ritual was a highly sensual activity, centred on the body. The body of God was celebrated in the daily Mass and the annual Corpus Christi liturgy;[4] the bodies of the saints retained power which could be accessed through touching their physical relics; the human bodily processes of ingestion (Eucharist) and procreation (baptism), and the senses of sight, hearing, touch, taste, and smell were all employed. As Edward Muir has pointed out,

> medieval Christians *expected* to find the sacred manifest itself in material objects that could be seen, touched, smelled, tasted and ingested ....
> Christian ritual demanded the presence of human and divine bodies to work its wonders.
>
> (Muir, 1997: 157)

Of the senses, sight was perhaps the most important. Since taking communion at Mass was usually only an annual occasion for most laity, gazing upon the elevated host formed a fundamental part of their spiritual life. In addition, the pre-Kepler[5] theories of vision,[6] particularly that of intromission in which objects were believed to produce rays which then travelled through intervening space to the eye, partially explain the reverence for sacred images. As a result, sight was essential to spiritual insight, 'connecting mortal viewers to spiritual forces through the power of the gaze' (Muir, 1997: 193).[7] The power of the gaze was, however, problematic to the reformers who stressed the centrality of the Word, thus elevating hearing as the primary sense. Scripture was now to be at the heart of Christianity, rather than the liturgical rites, and the focus was to be on the 'Word that assumed meaning through study rather than flesh through ritual' (Muir, 1997: 165). Rituals now needed to be explained, interpreted, given meaning, but no consensus emerged as to what this meaning was to be.[8] For the German reformer Martin Luther

(1483–1546), ritual remained a necessary element of reformed Christianity. The central mystery of the presence in the elements of the Eucharist was to be experienced rather than understood, and it enabled God to reach people's bodies as well as their souls. For the Swiss radical Ulrich Zwingli (1484–1531), however, the mystery of the bodily presence produced only harmful misunderstandings rather than any spiritual benefits. To some reformers, ritual observance was regarded as a diversion from true spiritual concerns. To others, it was priestcraft's most manipulative fraud.

Humanism also contributed to the degradation of ritual, through its emphasis on personal responsibility for individual morality and an associated work ethic over collective ritual observance and sacramental mediations. Hence, Catholics – and anyone else who practised ritual observance – were associated with moral laxity, and the excessive number of saints' days, on which Catholics did not work, led to complaints that they were less economically effective members of society.[9] Thus was conceived the association of Protestantism with progress and Catholicism with degenerate backwardness, and the idea of Protestant north-western Europe as economically and morally superior to Ireland and the Catholic countries of the Mediterranean. Humanism also valued interpretation over experience and meaning over the presentation of the mysteries (Muir, 1997: 168).[10] Luther had been aware that mysteries, by their very nature, cannot be explained, and understood meaning to be *in* the presentation, but as the sixteenth century wore on rituals came increasingly to be seen as fraudulent, emotionally manipulative and ineffective rather than as points of access to divine mysteries. They were also a little too magical.

As early as 1395, the Lollards had dismissed the, 'material implements of liturgical ritual – the "wine, bread, and wax, water, salt and oil and incense" – [as] the tools of wizards' (cited in Muir, 1997: 166), whilst in the minds of some people, priestcraft and witchcraft were separated only by intent. Indeed, the attribution of the words 'hocus pocus' to magicians was directly derived from the 'magical' words of the priest that effected the miracle of transubstantiation – *hoc est enim corpus meum*.[11] The concern with ritual contributed to the allegations of anti-Christian ritual practised by Jews and supposed witches,[12] and stimulated fantasies about demonic rituals at which the power of the Eucharistic liturgy was inverted to become *maleficia*. The power of ritual was not in doubt; but such power was not to be trusted. As representation won out over presence, and the Word assumed meaning rather than flesh, the quasi-magical sacerdotalism of the Catholic Church was replaced with the pastors and ministers of the various Protestant churches, and Catholic liturgy became fixed in an obsessive ritual rigidity.

Wrapped up as it was in the bundle of fears outlined in Chapter 1, 'what had been a path to God in the medieval period had for many people become a pernicious form of deception by the early modern period' (Muir, 1997: 269). Carried on the continued wave of anti-Catholicism, ritual became by the eighteenth century 'a dirty word [implying] insincerity and empty formality' (ibid.). The shift in attention from the emotive power of rituals to their interpretation and meaning, brought about by the ritual revolution of the sixteenth century, has had a lasting effect on both popular perceptions of ritual and on its academic study. The revival and rediscovery of ritual practice in the nineteenth and twentieth centuries in reaction to the perceived dearth of ritual in an overly-rational Protestantism[13] is only now beginning to change the way in which ritual is studied.

At the beginning of the twentieth century, in *The Varieties of Religious Experience* (1902), William James suggested that

> [r]itual worship in general appears to the modern transcendentalist, as well as to the ultra-puritanic type of mind, as if addressed to a deity of an almost absurdly childish character, taking delight in toy-shop furniture, tapers and tinsel, costume and mumbling and mummery, and finding his 'glory' incomprehensibly enhanced thereby; – just as on the other hand the formless speciousness of pantheism appears quite empty to ritualistic natures, and the gaunt theism of evangelical sects seems intolerably bald and chalky and bleak.
>
> (James, [1902] 1985: 330)

In this short quotation is contained the spectrum of attitudes towards ritual held in the latter decades of the nineteenth century. The extreme Ritualism of Anglo-Catholicism that had grown out of the Oxford Movement would be characterised by its opponents as overly concerned with the tapers, tinsel, and costume of empty ritual,[14] imitating Roman Catholic 'mumbling and mummery'. On the other hand, the extreme austerity of the Puritan evangelicals, to the Anglo-Catholics would indeed appear bleak, offering, as James later argues, 'an almshouse for a palace' and pauperising 'the monarchical imagination' (James, [1902] 1985: 458–60). The varieties of religious experience that James explored did not, however, include experiences of ritual. Ritual was still very much a 'dirty word', far removed from Protestant experience by James' time and safely confined to either the 'primitive' societies being studied in the new discipline of anthropology, or to 'pagano-popery'. Ritual was still one of the chief dividing lines between Protestants and Catholics, and had become more suspect as the repeated persecutions of Catholics and laws against Catholic worship had transformed the latter into a practice carried out in private homes under conditions of strictest secrecy. The entrenched distrust of ritual and Catholicism meant that, even once measures were relaxed, the Anglo-Catholics and even the Old Catholics – whose attitude towards governance from Rome had led to their very existence – were subjected to anti-Catholic assaults.

'Ritualist', then, was a label introduced by detractors as a term of abuse.[15] Those Anglo-Catholics so labelled seemed, to their opponents, to be concerned only with outward form, and to dismiss doctrine as unimportant. Such allegations were, of course, more true of some Anglo-Catholic priests than others, but the label indicates the emptiness, insincerity and ineffectiveness still associated with ritual. That those who were excessively concerned with 'tapers and tinsel' were happy to be labelled as 'ritualists', however, also indicates changes in attitudes towards ritual. Such changes were in tune with the late nineteenth-century aesthetic movement, represented by the pre-Raphaelites[16] and Walter Pater (1839–94),[17] the adaptation of the rich orthodox liturgies adopted by the heterodox churches of the *episcopi vagantes*[18] and with the revival of ritual within a magical framework in the occult societies from the 1890s on.[19] Of these, Anglo-Catholicism, aestheticism and occultism were believed to be a hotbed of effeminacy.[20]

'Unnatural vice', along with ritual, magic and 'unEnglishness', formed part of the subtext of anti-Catholic feeling, and the activities of Leadbeater[21] 'did nothing to quell persistent rumours that the Theosophical Society and similar organizations were havens for homosexual men' (Owen, 2004: 107). Such speculations were exacerbated by the pathologization of homosexuality which drew on, but somewhat inverted, the work of sexual progressives like Krafft-Ebing[22] and Havelock Ellis, the 'Apostle of Love'. In *Sexual Inversion*[23] (1897), the latter had sought to 'absolve homosexuality of its association with vice-ridden degeneracy', noting instead 'the intellectual and artistic propensities, high ethical tone, and sometimes refined religious sensibilities of many "inverts"' (ibid.: 108).[24] Such 'refined religious sensibilities' may have found expression in ritualism, as well as in the arts and in occult magical orders. As David Hilliard has observed,

> it is possible that Anglo-Catholic ritualism provided a way of escape from the problems of sexual tension and forbidden love into a make-believe world of religious pageantry, ancient titles and ranks, exotic symbolism, and endless chatter about copes and candles, the apostolic succession, and the triumphs of the 'true faith'.
>
> (Hilliard, 2006: 8)

'Effeminate' men were thought to be just as susceptible to empty, outward show as women,[25] and so the sacerdotalism and ritualism of high Anglo-Catholicism was deemed to be not only 'unEnglish', but also 'unmanly'.[26] Secret societies and semi-secret churches 'provided an environment in which homosexual men could express … their dissent from heterosexual orthodoxy and from the Protestant values of those who wielded repressive power in church and state' (Hilliard, 2006: 24).

The Anglo-Catholic Ritualists were to be affected by this 'repressive power' through a piece of legislation designed to suppress ritual, the Public Worship Regulation Act of 1874, which *The Times* of 1 May 1874 characterised as 'protecting the sober majority of the Church from a medieval delirium'. Introduced by the Prime Minister, Benjamin Disraeli, the bill was supported by the Archbishop of Canterbury, William Howley (1868–83) and by Queen Victoria. In the period during which ritual was illegal, proceedings were initiated against Anglo-Catholic priests and bishops, but as soon as intransigent clergy began to be imprisoned, refusing to give up the illegal elements of their rituals,[27] public opinion turned and the law fell into disrepute. Charges could be brought by any three aggrieved parishioners, whether they attended church or not, but bishops had right of veto over proceedings brought against their diocesan clergy. Indeed, most cases were resolved by a process of negotiation between bishop and cleric, and as time went on the bishops increasingly used their right of veto to prevent proceedings. A few cases did go as far as imprisonment for contempt of court, for periods of between sixteen days and eighteen months. Imprisonment for contempt of court, however, looked to the average lay person like persecution for religious opinion, and support for the Act diminished. By 1892, at the close of proceedings against Edward King, Bishop of Lincoln, the struggle was over and the Ritualists had won the right to worship as they pleased. Toleration and an increasingly secular public meant that most people were simply bored by the controversy. As one anonymous author proclaimed in *Bombastes Religioso or The Protestant Pope of 1899*,

> an overwhelming majority of the English people are perfectly well satisfied to live and let live, and they care no more what amount of ritual is permitted in any given place of worship within the Queen's dominions than they care how many times the Sultan of Turkey prostrates himself next Friday.
>
> (cited in Reed, 1998: 256)

In a twist to the commonly-held attitude of Catholic political subversion, the author also argued that British dignity and independence was undermined by the absurd notion that the Pope was a threat to England. However, in supporting the Act at its inception Queen Victoria certainly believed that 'the defiance shown by the Clergy of the High Church and Ritualistic party is so great that something must be done to check it and prevent its continuation' (cited in Simpson, 1932: 142). The outrage at such defiance of monarch and state was a continuation of the fear at the root of anti-Catholicism: Roman Catholics might be the enemy, but Anglo-Catholics were traitors, and Ritualism was the Romish wolf disguised in the sheep's clothing of the established, national church.

In fact, like the 'wandering bishops', the Tractarians regarded authority as resting in the undivided church that had existed before the schism of East and West, and they thus rejected both papal claims to authority and those of Protestantism which was, so far as they were concerned, something of an over-reaction to the errors of Rome. The desire for a return to an undivided church led to the establishment of associations whose goal was just that. In 1864, for example, the Cambridge theologian John Mason Neale had helped to establish the Eastern Churches Association in an attempt to promote greater understanding and closer ties. Prior to that, the Association for the Promotion of the Unity of Christendom (APUC) had been founded in 1857. One of its founders, F. G. Lee, was irregularly consecrated in Italy in 1877,[28] after which he secretly re-ordained Anglican clergy concerned about the validity of their orders. Lee was also one of those responsible for the revival of the Order of Corporate Reunion, which regarded the Pope as the visible head of the Church on earth. Lee's pro-Rome activities got him thrown out of the APUC and expelled from the English Church Union; even the Society of the Holy Cross (*Societas Sanctae Crucis*, SSC) condemned the Order of Corporate Reunion as schismatic, defying the true Catholic Church of England.[29] But the fact that few Anglo-Catholics modelled themselves or their worship on contemporary Roman Catholic practices, and even those who did so rarely accepted the authority of the Pope,[30] did nothing to change the minds of those who saw little difference between an English Catholicism and that of Rome.

Like the Roman Catholics before them, the Anglo-Catholic Ritualists had been forced into practising in secret by riots and persecution, fuelled by suspected conspiracies with Catholic Irish immigrants and the Pope. Guilds, brotherhoods and religious communities had started to be established as early as the 1840s,[31] the latter enabling Anglo-Catholic ritualism to be practised away from the oversight of bishops and unobserved by scurrilous journalists. As a result, they were suspected of all sorts of improprieties, since secrecy was associated in the public mind with Roman Catholic 'monkish' practices. As Petà Dunstan (2004: 1) notes, '[t]he traditions of Religious Life were associated closely with Roman Catholicism, the deep-seated fear of which – as much political as theological – dominated much of the early reaction to the revival [of religious communities]'. The most secret organisation was solely for clergy. This was the Society of the Holy Cross, established in 1857, the existence of which was not publicly known for over a decade.[32] Its members were bound by vows of secrecy and absolute obedience, and secret greetings and symbolic rings were employed. For the laity, too, secrecy had its allure. Confession, one of the 'secret privileges' of young Anglo-Catholics (Harris, 1847: 227),[33] arcane ritual knowledge, and services held behind locked doors, sometimes at night, all served to heighten the feeling that one was participating in something avant-garde, *risqué* and a little bit 'naughty'.[34]

The secular avant-garde and advanced Anglo-Catholics overlapped significantly, with 'Pater, those under his spell, and other, similar young men float[ing] in and out of the Ritualist orbit' (Anson, 1955: 218). As far as the anti-Catholic faction was concerned, Ritualists and Papists were one and the same, and neither was far removed from Paganism.[35] To aesthetes such as Walter Pater and his circle, this was an added attraction. Pater had been an ardent Ritualist as a youth and even as an anti-Christian, 'when he was something of a high priest himself in his own cult of beauty' (Reed, 1998: 217), he regularly attended Fr Alexander Heriot Mackonochie's services at St Alban's, Holborn and Fr George Nugees's at St Austin's Priory, South

London. Both were infamous centres of advanced Ritualism. Along with fellow aesthetes such as Oscar Wilde (1854–1900), Edward Burne-Jones (1833–98) and Dante Gabriel Rossetti[36] (1828–82), Pater had developed the cult of beauty,[37] which considered beauty to be the basic factor in art that life should copy. It was characterised by a valuing of sensuality, symbols, and synaesthetic correspondences between words, colours and music, all of which could be found in the Ritualist churches. As 'high priest' of this 'cult of beauty', Pater argued that 'curiosity and the love of beauty' are the essential elements of the romantic spirit, illustrated by the Medieval period which he believed contained 'unworked sources of romantic effect, of a strange beauty, to be won, by strong imagination, out of things unlikely or remote'.[38] Such Medievalism was a contemporary obsession, as the Middle Ages suppressed by the Tudor reformations were rediscovered and romanticised as the ideal ages.

This fixation, growing out of earlier antiquarian research, could be clearly seen in the Gothic revival in art, architecture[39] and literature, renewed interest in ruins and historical preservation,[40] and the Pre-Raphaelite Brotherhood, who looked back to Raphael (Rafaello Sanzio, 1483–1520) and his Medieval precursors for their artistic inspiration. As Sir Roy Strong, ex-director of the Victoria and Albert Museum in London (1974–87) observes,

> [t]hanks to Scott's *Ivanhoe* (1819) the Middle Ages entered the Victorian age as an epoch when democratic liberties had been asserted against the yoke of Norman autocratic rule. ... At the same time they could be used to justify aristocratic rule as was done during the 1830s and 1840s.
>
> (Strong, 1999: 519)

The Arthurian romance had also become popular in the mid-nineteenth century, largely through Alfred, Lord Tennyson's version *Idylls of the King*, the first four of which were published in 1859. They were used by Prince Albert to shore up the monarchy,[41] and the government utilised ideas of chivalric Medievalism as historical and moral legitimation for imperialism. As part of this project, the Catholic Augustus Welby Pugin, favoured architect of the Anglo-Catholics, was commissioned to aid Sir Charles Barry in the re-building of the Palace of Westminster in the Gothic revival style, between 1837 and 1860, decorated with images of the imagined Middle Ages.[42] But Medievalism was also present in the revival of ritual, both Catholic and Anglican. Since 1832, the French Benedictine Abbey of Solesmes under Dom Prosper Guéranger had been dedicated to the study and recovery of Medieval Gregorian Chant and the liturgical heritage of Roman Catholicism. Likewise, the Tractarians of the Oxford Movement, J. M. Neale's Ecclesiological Society,[43] and the Ritualists, all looked back to the Middle Ages as a time when the Church met aesthetic needs through ritual and church decoration. Ecclesiology, Tractarianism, and the Aesthetic Movement were thus intertwined in their pursuit of the Medieval ideal.

As well as Medievalism, the Aesthetic Movement advocated a return to Hellenic Paganism[44] as a protest against the 'mechanical and graceless formalism of the modern era' (Morley, 1873, cited in Uglow, 1990: ix). To the Catholic Cambridge historian Lord Acton (1834–1902),

> [t]wo great principles divide the world, and contend for the mastery, antiquity and the middle ages. These are the two civilizations that have preceded us, the two elements of which ours is composed. All political as well as religious questions reduce themselves practically to this. This is the great dualism that runs through our society.[45]

According to Pater and Matthew Arnold (1822–88), the imbalance caused by the Hebraic values embedded in Christianity, 'where all sides of one's being were sacrificed to the religious side, and where systems of conduct and moral codes threatened to become more important than the spirit which originally inspired them',[46] needed to be redressed by a return to Hellenism and Medievalism. As a result of his studies, Pater maintained that the value of religion lay in the states of mind that worship induced rather than in any doctrinal element, and that these mental states could be maintained without the dogma which hitherto accompanied them.[47] Religion, he argued, should not be informed by profound ideals imposed by the intellect, but by those things which 'arise gradually and directly from concrete experience, from a sensory and spiritual appreciation of nature and harmony' (Pater, 1867, cited in Uglow, 1990: xiii). Whilst William James was advocating the 'fruits' of experience, Pater simply valued experience itself. As he proclaimed in the subversive 'Conclusion' to his 1873 work *Studies in the History of the Renaissance*,

> [n]ot the fruit of experience, but experience itself, is the end. A counted number of pulses only is given to us of a variegated, dramatic life. How may we see in them all that is to be seen in them by the finest senses …. To burn always with this hard, gem-like flame, to maintain this ecstasy, is success in life.
>
> (Pater, 1873: 152)

To some, then, the Ritualists represented a 'miserable resuscitation of effete Medievalism',[48] lacking in the Gospel; to others it provided that which the sixteenth century thought it had done away with: ritual that spoke to experience and the emotions rather than dogma and meaning. In many respects, contemporary Wicca can be regarded as a later manifestation of the rediscovery and revaluation of ritual after three centuries of Protestantism. By the time of Gardner's return to England, important themes identified above had become more widespread, partly due to the popularity of the art and literature produced prior to the Great War, and partly in response to the horrors of the latter. Thus, Medievalism had provided a form of escapism through a return to an idealised, pre-Reformation Church,[49] whilst reaction against evangelical Protestant perceptions of rituals had led to the subversive celebration of 'naughtiness' as a protest against (sexual) moralising and the abusiveness of detractors. Against the Puritan destruction of beauty that Gardner perceived,[50] the Aesthetic Movement had elevated beauty, which he regarded as an essential element of the witch cult he was later to formulate.[51]

Prior to the nineteenth-century romantic notions of Medievalism, however, the Middle Ages had been associated with 'centuries of dirt and darkness' during the Reformation period. In this dark and corrupt world, witchcraft and Roman Catholicism were the arch-heresies in the Protestant imagination. As Hugh Trevor-Roper pointed out (1969: 118), '"the Devil, the Mass, and witches" were lumped together by John Knox' and Lancashire was characterised as 'a nest of both Papists and witches'. In turn, Protestant 'heresy' and witchcraft were linked in the Catholic mind. Comparison, and even conflation between the two has continued into the present century, in both positive and negative forms. On the positive side, Aidan Kelly (1991: 4), for example, cites his Lady Epona, '"If the Roman Catholic church were actually as Greeley describes it, there would be no need for the Craft"', implying that Wicca is in some way a compensation for the failings of Catholicism. And with the emergence of witchcraft and Paganism in Catholic countries such as Italy and Malta, scholars have begun to note that 'Paganism and Catholicism may have more in common than evangelical Protestantism and Catholicism'.[52] On the negative side, as was noted in Chapter 1, there remain conflated portrayals of Roman Catholicism and witchcraft as evil.[53]

The link between the two is largely made via ritual, with suppositions being made that Catholics, because of their love of ritual, make good Pagans. Such an idea is refuted by Kelly,[54] who claims that witches are more likely to be Jewish than Catholic in religious background, stating that 6 per cent of Pagans are Jewish.[55] He does not produce any data to back this up, however. The supposition probably derives from early American studies, which do show a preponderance of people with Roman Catholic backgrounds in general Paganism.[56] In studies of Wicca, however, the situation is reversed. In 1990, Loretta Orion reported that 58.8 per cent of the Gardnerian witches in her US study had a Protestant background, 24.5 per cent were Roman Catholic, and 9.1 per cent were Jewish. Jone Salomonsen's portrait of the religious background of Reclaiming witches in the USA shows Catholic and Protestant roughly equal in representation (35 per cent and 32 per cent respectively), and 21 per cent from a Jewish background. Wiccans in Britain are overwhelmingly of Protestant religious background (62 per cent), with only 14 per cent having a Catholic background, and 21 per cent stating no religious background at all. Only one of the respondents to my 1996 survey (Pearson 1999) of Wiccans in the UK indicated that she had a Jewish cultural background, but added that she was brought up with no religion.

It seems, then, that Vivianne Crowley may have been correct in her comment that the experience of ritual is part of the attraction of Wicca to those brought up in countries where various forms of Protestantism provide the cultural, if not the religious background of Wiccans. However, this ignores the continued attraction of ritual for those brought up Catholics. It also fails to understand the revival of ritual within Anglicanism outlined above.[57] It thus seems a more useful exercise to trace the elements of Wiccan ritual that have been borrowed from the variant streams of Christianity, and the Protestant/Catholic diversity within nineteenth-century British Anglicanism, rather than attempt to account for Wiccan initiations on the basis of religion of upbringing, against which initiates might be perceived to be rebelling.[58] The following section therefore outlines Wiccan ritual, considers the traces of Christian influence in Wiccan ritual, and then returns to the theme of experience revived as an essential ingredient of religion.

As an orthopraxic religion, Wicca operates around a rich ritual system which incorporates four categories recognised in analyses of ritual. First, rites of passage are celebrated, including Wiccanings for the birth of a new child, handfastings,[59] and funeral rites. Second, and essential to Wicca as an initiatory mystery religion, initiation rituals are performed, marking the individual as a first, second or third degree Wiccan. Such initiation rituals can also be termed rites of passage, with the emphasis being on spiritual and psychological growth rather than physical maturation or change in social status. Third, worship and training rituals, known as esbats, are traditionally held at each full moon, though in practice they are usually held every two to three weeks at a date convenient for all involved. Fourth, eight celebrations known as Sabbats[60] are held to mark the changing seasons of the year. The Sabbats comprise the ritual sequence that is the experiential expression of the underlying mythic cycle of Wicca, the Wheel of the Year. The basic *modus operandi* of Wicca is, then, ritualistic, expressed through small group communities known as covens, which emphasise an experiential dimension and innovative practice. According to Wiccans, the true meaning of their religion can *only* be expressed and experienced through direct participation in its rituals.

The basic Western ritual framework used by Wicca is adapted from a ritual magic that contains Judaeo-Christian elements. The implements used within Wiccan ritual are predominantly Catholic, being the Lollardian 'tools of wizards' referred to earlier: wine, bread, and wax (candles), water, salt and oil and incense, plus bells, asperges, and scourge.[61] Wicca has no churches or cathedrals, but sacred space and people are consecrated with the four elements: earth (salt), water, fire and air (incense). A candle, symbolising light, represents the fifth element of ether, or spirit. There is also often a shared proliferation of statuary, dressing of the altar, and flowers.[62] The generic framework in which these are utilised has been adopted from The Hermetic Order of the Golden Dawn, and involves the casting of a circle to create sacred space, its consecration as mentioned above, and the calling of the four quarters (east, south, west and north) to guard and protect the circle, an obvious departure from Catholic liturgy. The circle is cast using a sword or black-handled ritual knife, called an athame, which is taken from the *Key of Solomon* rather than being derived from the Golden Dawn. Whilst knives are not present in Roman Catholic liturgy, knives retained for solely ritual purposes are used in the Divine Liturgy of the Orthodox Church, in the *Prothesis* or *Proskomide*.[63] Lastly, whilst in orthodox Eucharistic liturgies, communion wafers/bread and wine are given to each individual by a priest, deacon or steward, in Wicca the cakes and wine are blessed and then passed from person to person. This is the exact form taken in the Plymouth Brethren sect, the sect in which Aleister Crowley was brought up. Given that the Wiccan ceremony of cakes and wine is taken directly from Crowley's Gnostic Mass,[64] it is quite possible that this form of administering consecrated food and drink derives ultimately from the Brethren.

This, then, is the extent to which Wicca has borrowed from Christian liturgical traditions, and many Wiccans would claim that Christianity itself first borrowed many of them from the Paganism of the ancient world. The four elements, for example, existed long before the birth of Christianity, as did the use of incense and shared meals of communion. Apart from this latter, what has been described above is only the framework of Wiccan ritual, and whilst this is important in establishing the space within which the main body of the rituals takes place, it should not be taken as the ritual in its entirety. At the same time, this is not to relegate it to a marginal position, for it is an essential component that enables the experiential dimension of Wiccan ritual by providing a liminal space described as 'a time that is not a time and a place that is not a place',[65] a phrase used by Wiccans within ritual while making the 'location' of the circle quite specific.[66] Starhawk describes it as existing

> on the boundaries of ordinary space and time; it is 'between the world' of the seen and unseen, of flashlight and starlight consciousness, a space in which alternate realities meet, in which the past and future are open to us.
>
> (Starhawk, 1989: 72)

The words used in casting the circle are an obvious expression of the intent to place a boundary between the physical, everyday reality of life and the magical, otherworldly reality that the Wiccans perceive themselves to be entering:

> *We conjure thee, O Circle of Power,*
> *that thou beist a boundary*
> *between the world of men and the realms of the Mighty Ones,*
> *a Guardian and a Protection*
> *that shall preserve and contain*
> *the power which we shall raise within thee;*

wherefore do we bless thee, and consecrate thee
in the most sacred and powerful names
of (the God) and (the Goddess).

(Crowley, Vivianne, 1996: 61)

Formalised words and gesture are, then, used by Wiccans to communicate the stages of removal from the everyday into the ritual working space,[67] from the consecration of the space and people, to the casting of the circle. This is then often immediately followed by the Witches' Rune,[68] a dance and chant in which formalisation gives way to movement controlled only by the rhythm of the chant and the holding of hands in a circle. From the slow circumambulations which constitute the building up of the circle, the Wiccans join together in a faster, smaller circular movement, in which they feel the power produced by their dancing creating what the Wiccans call the 'cone of power' in the centre of the circle. This dance operates as a bridging mechanism between the formalised framework of the ritual construction of sacred space and entering into a liminal space. The hypnotic rhythms of dancing and chanting help Wiccans 'to enter into a deeper state of consciousness ... [where] we are both separate and joined, individual yet one' (Crowley, Vivianne, 1996: 86).

Rather than implying something rigid, then, a constraint within which ritual *must* be performed, the framework operates as a mechanism used to build ritual space and time – it *frames* liminality. The framework provides Wiccan ritual with a recognisable format, but the nature of the rituals performed within that framework is of a different character, as might be expected of something taking place beyond the 'threshold' or 'limen'. The energy raised by the dance is focused in the invocation of the Divine, which forms the central part of the ritual. This may be spontaneous and unwritten, the fundamental framework having created the liminal dimension in which such an experience can occur. The spiritual force of the Goddess and God are believed to be drawn into the body of a Priestess and Priest, in a process known as 'Drawing down the Moon/Sun' or, more commonly, as 'invocation'. The Priest or Priestess who is to be invoked stands before the altar and empties their mind, becoming still, becoming an empty vessel that the Divine can enter. The invoker kneels before the Priest or Priestess and uses the words of an invocation to imagine an image of the deity, visualising the image forming behind the body of the Priest/Priestess and then merging into his or her aura. The energy of the Divine is held within the body of the Priestess/Priest who, for the duration of this time, is considered to *be* the Goddess or God invoked. Vivianne Crowley describes her experience of the process as follows:

'I invoke thee and call upon thee
O Mighty Mother of us all ...'

71

I was standing with my back to the altar, my feet were a little apart, my arms outstretched to the heavens to form the symbol of the Star Goddess. The Priest was invoking the Goddess, calling her to enter the body of her Priestess.

'By seed and root and bud and stem ...'

My awareness of the people around me faded, I felt my body grow taller. The voice of the Priest was becoming distant. The circle seemed far below.

'By leaf and flower and fruit ...'

I was becoming the World Tree. My feet were rooted in the Earth, my arms were branches that touched the arch of heaven and around my head swirled the stars. I lost all sense of self – my body was empty, a vacuum waiting to be filled.

> *'By life and love*
> *I do invoke thee and call upon thee*
> *To descend upon the body of thy servant and Priestess.'*

I felt the power – Her power – flow through me and out into the circle. My consciousness was dissolving into unity. There was no longer any 'I' and 'other' – only 'She'. Words came unbidden from a place deep within me:

> *'I am thy Goddess*
> *High-born full-blooded and lusting free am I*
> *The wind is my voice and my song ...'*

After a while it came to an end. The Priest kissed my feet bringing my consciousness down to Earth once more. I looked at the circle of people around me. I did not need to ask. I could see from their faces that the invocation had worked. Together we had touched that other realm and crossed the boundaries between the self and the infinite.

(Crowley, Vivianne, 1990a: 60–1)

What is described here is the invocation of the Divine, in this case the Goddess, into the body of the practitioner. Aidan Kelly notes that

> [w]hat the priestess does internally during this process is – either purposely or 'instinctively' – to alter her state of consciousness, to take on the persona of the Goddess, whom she will represent (or even, in some senses, be) for the working part of the ritual.

(cited in Adler, 1986: 168)

In the centre of the ritual, the Priestess *experiences* the Goddess, a process which Jane Ellen Harrison observes in her *Epilogomena to the Study of Greek Religion*. Harrison (1962: xliv–xlvi) writes that the dancer who plays a god in a sacred rite 'cannot be said to worship his god, he lives him, experiences him'. The Protestant theologian Friedrich Schleiermacher (1768–1834) defined the experience of the Divine, or the infinite, as the essence of religion. This experience, says Peter Berger (1979: 130) in his commentary on Schleiermacher, is 'what religion is all about – *not* theoretical speculation, *nor* moral preachings. ... The underlying experience of all religion, its essence, is one of encountering the infinite within the finite phenomena of human life'. Such an affective and imaginative engagement with holy mystery is characteristic of Anglo-Catholic and Wiccan ritual, as well as echoing Pater's notion of the pre-eminence of experience over doctrinal formulations.

This 'encountering the infinite within the finite phenomena of human life' is particularly marked when the latter is represented by the naked body,[69] which, through the process of invocation, incarnates or embodies, rather than ingests, the Divine. But there is also a sense in which the Priestess is 'grasped and held by a superior power' (Roof and Taylor, 1995: 201). However, it is not necessarily the case that communion with the Divine will occur at every ritual, or that, if it does occur, it will always be a powerful, 'mind-blowing' experience for all concerned. Undoubtedly, some rituals can be particularly powerful in their effects, but at other times it is clear that the Priest or Priestess has not, for a variety of reasons, made contact with the Divine. As Adler recounts,

> I have seen priestesses who simply recited lines and priestesses who went through genuinely transforming experiences. I have seen a young woman, with little education or verbal expertise, come forth with inspired words of poetry during a state of deep trance. I have heard messages of wisdom and intuition from the mouths of those who, in their ordinary lives, often seem superficial and without insight.
>
> (Adler, 1986: 168–9)

This uncertainty principle, at least partly, prevents the routinisation of religious experience in Wicca. The operation of covens in which Priests and Priestesses work spontaneously and innovatively as well as according to format, and are not 'routinely' invoked, prevents the sacred from becoming an 'habitual experience' (Berger, 1979: 47). Certain techniques can be used, however, to facilitate such experiences, aside from the sense of being in a sacred space 'between the worlds'.

William James referred to these techniques as 'transports', 'mechanism[s] by which an individual achieves a mystical state – that is, some sort of action, practice, or exercise that "brings you there". To get "there" involves mental and bodily exercises that trigger the experience, a catalyst for the emotion' (Roof and Taylor, 1995: 201). In Wicca, these 'transports' include what are known as the 'eight paths to realisation' or the 'eight paths of magic'. They are blood control through binding; scourging; rites, chants and spells; dance; sex (the Great Rite); incense, drugs and wine; meditation/concentration; and trance.[70] Fasting before a rite is also commonly practised. But transports are also used in the generic ritual framework, and these are shared by Wicca and both Roman and Anglo-Catholicism. They include candles, music, incense, decorated altars, statuary, water and oil, all of which engage the five senses.

All involve the body[71] and are not far removed from the transports named by James ([1902] 1985: 314), which he takes from Yoga: diet, posture, breathing, intellectual concentration, and moral discipline – preliminary voluntary operations which facilitate the oncoming of the mystical state (ibid.: 300). In the excerpt on invocation, Crowley uses the Sanskrit term 'samadhi'[72] to describe this state (Crowley, Vivianne, 1990a: 60–1). Attaining such alterations of consciousness necessitates some training – learning and methodical practice that allows the practitioner to consciously manipulate the senses in order to achieve this state. And this, as Roof and Taylor (1995: 202) point out, means that 'religious experience can arise out of practice and that people have the capacity to learn to have religious experiences', whilst continuing to value those transports that 'get you there'.

This ability comes gradually from the practice of ritual, and the experience enabled by it must be distinguished from the preliminary efforts by which it is preceded.[73] Such learning does not mean that the experience itself is forced or controlled – it is often powerful and manifests in unexpected ways, for 'beyond the threshold of waking consciousness, we have dimensions of experience not readily understood by the normal self' (Taylor, 1996: 85). Ritual is clearly one of the mechanisms by which consciousness beyond the margins might be tapped, but it is learned by *doing*, by opening oneself to the religious experience which ritual facilitates. Ritual thus becomes a legitimate means of 'knowing', an embodied, incarnate means of knowing. It is not empty, or simply a reinforcing interpretation of something else, nor is it 'simply an alternative way to express certain things … [for] certain things can be expressed *only* in ritual' (Rappaport, 1979: 174, emphasis added).

This is largely because ritual inverts the quotidian contexts in which thoughts dominate experience, exchanging 'cognitive tyranny' for 'actual experience' (Napier, 1992: 181). This 'cognitive tyranny' can be seen in traditional understandings of ritual, in which beliefs are regarded as primary and rites as secondary, the function of ritual being to legitimise and reinforce beliefs. It can also be seen in the Protestant attitudes towards ritual as 'empty ceremonial', devoid of doctrine and therefore of meaning. Wicca, however, is self-consciously resistant to dogma, doctrine and creed, and belief is not a prerequisite either for initiation or for ritual work. Wiccan rituals instead stress personal input, invention and experience, in which an overly analytical approach would miss the *experience* of ritual. As Edmund Leach (1976: 41) has argued, the act of scholarly interpretation of ritual necessitates a deconstructive technique which removes from the ritual experience the

74

sense of synchronous expression and transmission of combined messages; the flow of the dance of ritual is lost.

In insisting on translating the experience of ritual into words, '[t]he Reformation altered the institutional and ideological framework of rituals, making ritual a highly problematic form of behaviour in the modern world and intensifying the crusade against magical rituals and superstitious beliefs' (Muir, 1997: 149). The meaning of ritual replaced the evocation of emotions as the central question, leading to an inability to value ritual. The end result has been that

> [p]sychologists have treated private ritual as synonymous with neurosis... [t]heologians have regarded self-generated rites as lacking in moral character ... [a]nd anthropologists have thought of ritual as traditional, collective representation, implying that the notion of individual or invented ritual was a contradiction in terms.
>
> (Grimes, cited in Bell, 1997: 223)

For scholars researching ritual practised by contemporary, literate, post-industrial Western religions such as Wicca, however, it has been necessary to develop methods of interpreting just such private, self-generated, invented rituals. New developments in interpretation stand in contrast to '[t]he tendency to think of ritual as essentially unchanging ... that effective rituals cannot be invented' (ibid.: 223). Instead, scholars have begun exploring ritual through such concepts as 'self-conscious ritual entrepreneurship' or 'postmodern ritual'. In the former, groups and individuals

> plan their rites step by step, watch themselves perform them, and are quite likely to sit down afterward and analyse what worked and what didn't, both in terms of the ritual dynamics themselves and in terms of the effects the ritual was expected to produce.
>
> (Bell, 1997: 224–5)

In the latter, rituals are characterised as reflexive, fluid, playful, indeterminate, expressing intimate community, critiques of knowledge and ways of knowing, and celebrating private and collective (as opposed to hierarchically structured) experience.[74] Given the reflexive attitude of Wiccans towards their rituals, which tend to be partially constructed in reference to a common, generic framework, and partially innovative and spontaneous, Bell's 'self-conscious ritual entrepreneurship' is more appropriate to an exploration of Wiccan ritual experience than earlier ideas of ritual. Similarly, Wiccan rituals *are* always partly being made up as they are carried out, and contain evidence of all the hallmarks of Grimes' postmodern ritual. Thus, although Wiccans adopt a somewhat mechanical, repetitive ritual framework which aids them to bypass the 'rational' mind and enter into a state of consciousness beyond that of daily experience, the recycling and simulation of ritual *content* is minimal. Rather, spontaneity, innovation, experimentation and individual experience are emphasised.[75] Wiccan ritual space can, then, be considered an 'arena of contradictory and contestable perspectives – participants having their own reasons, viewpoints, and motives', which Gerholm regards as postmodernist ritual,[76] contrary to Victor Turner's (1969: 9) view that 'rituals cannot constitute ... the free associations or eccentric views of individuals'.

Whilst interpretation of rituals remains very different to the individual experience of them, then, new methods of scholarship have emerged alongside the revival of ritual. In terms of its focus on ritual, Wicca makes use of earlier rediscoveries of ritual in response to what were perceived as the excesses of Protestant reactions to Catholic liturgy. This liturgy seemed to facilitate an experience of the Divine that Protestantism sought to control through emphasis on the Word which assumed meaning through rationality rather than flesh through ritual, and that was revived by Anglo-Catholic Ritualists and heterodox churches. Wicca differs, however, in that it stresses individual responsibility rather than any collective ritual observance, for although ritual is predominantly a group activity, Wiccan groups are far too small to be compared with the mass observance associated with Christian rites. In addition, there is no mediation by priests to a congregation, since in Wicca all are initiated as Priests and Priestesses.[77] The vestiges of Catholic ceremonial that are present in Wiccan ritual are, in a sense, conducted by people who have taken the Protestant doctrine of the priesthood of all believers to its logical conclusion. In this respect, Wicca subverts both the (male) sacerdotalism of the Roman Catholic Church and the anti-ritualism generally associated with Protestantism. A further disruption emerges in a practice that has only been hinted at in this chapter. That is the sacredness of the body, articulated by expressions of sexuality and the practice of ritual nudity within Wiccan ritual.

5

SEX AND THE SACRED

The neo-gnostic churches of the *episcopi vagantes* discussed in Chapter 3 played upon the accusations of sexual licentiousness and/or deviance levelled against earlier gnostic sects by orthodox Christianity. They accepted the claims as true but, contrary to orthodoxy, perceived sexual practices to be spiritually beneficial. This was to be taken further by the Ordo Templi Orientis (OTO) and, in particular, Aleister Crowley (1875–1947). Given the latter's influence on Wicca's sex-magical practices, it makes sense to begin this chapter with an assessment of Crowley, sex magic and Thelema.

Crowley was raised in the Plymouth Brethren sect, a highly puritanical form of Christianity[1] against which he increasingly rebelled after his father's death in 1887. Attracted to occultism, Crowley was initiated into the London temple of the Hermetic Order of the Golden Dawn in November 1898 at the age of 23, and quickly rose through the initiatory grades of the Order. Having been initially friendly, and later intensely competitive with the Chief, Samuel Liddell 'MacGregor' Mathers, he was subsequently expelled from the Order. Confident of his own abilities, however, Crowley awarded himself the highest grade of Ipsissimus,[2] and went on to found the Argenteum Astrum (AA), or Order of the Silver Star, through whose journal, *The Equinox*, he published many of the Golden Dawn's secret rituals between 1909 and 1913. In 1910, Crowley became involved in the OTO, after Theodor Reuss accused him of revealing the secret sexual magic of the Order in his *Book of Lies* (1913). Accepting that he had come to these 'great truths' independently, and therefore had revealed them unintentionally, Reuss apparently insisted that Crowley be initiated into the seventh degree of the order. As mentioned in Chapter 3, Crowley was named Sovereign Grand Master General of Ireland, Iona and all the Britains. In 1922, Crowley became head of the OTO, and expanded its original nine degrees to eleven, revising them to include what were, at the time, explicitly transgressive sexual acts – masturbation and homosexual intercourse.

As outlined in Chapter 3, the OTO under Reuss was influenced by the heterodox neo-gnostic French churches established by, and attractive to, many of the leading European occultists of the time. The overlapping memberships of various Masonic rites, heterodox churches, Martinism etc.

enabled certain teachings to gain a wide airing. A prime example was the sexual magic teaching of the Hermetic Brotherhood of Luxor (HB of L), of which Papus was a member. Papus, as previously mentioned, was head of various occult orders and 'the best publicist that occultism ever had' (Godwin, 1994: 361). He used the groups and orders that he founded as recruiting grounds for the Brotherhood, drawing people from the Gnostic Church, the Martinists, the Kabbalistic Order of the Rosy Cross, and the French Theosophical Society, among others. The magical practices of the HB of L were based almost exclusively on the sexual magical teachings of the American Paschal Beverley Randolph (1825–75). Randolph believed that, at its highest level, sex was a sacrament and therefore needed to be guarded by taboos: it should not be enjoyed frequently or promiscuously, contraception should not be used, and it should never be performed alone or with a partner of the same sex. Via the HB of L, Randolph's teachings entered the OTO but, as Godwin points out, they were then developed in a very different direction, eventually ignoring all taboos in Crowley's expanded system.[3]

For Crowley, sex, particularly in what the Victorians saw as its most deviant extremes of homosexuality and masturbation,[4] was the most obvious weapon to hurl against Christianity, especially its puritanical forms. It was, in Godwin's term (1994: 66), a form of 'therapeutic blasphemy',[5] in which calculated acts of transgression violated and inverted the moral laws and sexual codes of both Christianity and the larger social order.[6] Randolph had claimed that 'true Sex-power is God-power', and stressed orgasm as 'the most intense and powerful experience in human life, for it is the moment when the soul is suddenly opened to the divine realm and the breath of God infuses life into this world' (Urban, 2003: 23, n. 21).[7] Similarly, Crowley 'identifi[ed] sex as the most central aspect of the human being and the most profound source of magical power' (ibid.: 11), stressing the experience of sexual orgasm as the key to magical power, when one's soul is open to cosmic powers to such an extent that whatever one wills becomes manifest. In such powerful moments of sexual liberation, so the argument goes, lies true freedom.

Crowley's mission, taken straight from Nietzsche, was to 'burst the boundaries of conventional Christian morality in order to liberate the supreme freedom of the individual self' (ibid.: 14), replacing it with the higher morality and phallic power of the Will.[8] Sin and guilt are swept aside with the sheer affirmation of the Will and the fullest enjoyment of the flesh. In 'The Law of Liberty',[9] he writes:

> Then comes the first call of the Great Goddess Nuit, Lady of the Starry Heaven ... 'Come forth, O children, under the stars, and take your fill of love! I am above you and in you. My ecstasy is in yours. My joy is to see your joy' ...
>
> And what are the conditions of this joy, and peace, and glory? Is ours the gloomy asceticism of the Christian, and the Buddhist, and the

Hindu? Are we walking in eternal fear lest some 'sin' should cut us off from 'grace'? By no means.

'Be goodly therefore: dress ye all in fine apparel; eat rich foods and drink sweet wines and wines that foam! Also, take your fill of love as ye will, when, where, and with whom ye will! But always unto me' ...

For hear, how gracious is the Goddess; 'I give unimaginable joys on earth: certainty, not faith, while in life, upon death; peace unutterable, rest, ecstasy; nor do I demand aught in sacrifice.'

Is this not better than the death-in-life of the slaves of the Slave-Gods, as they go oppressed by consciousness of 'sin', wearily seeking or simulating wearisome and tedious 'virtues'?

Such liberation and affirmation of the sexual instinct was central to Crowley's Thelema. Thelema was revealed in the *Book of the Law*, dictated, so Crowley claimed, by the manifested presence of a discarnate presence called Aiwass, on three consecutive afternoons between noon and 1 pm in April 1904. The most important and most remembered of these laws is the Law of Thelema – 'Do what thou wilt shall be the whole of the law; love is the law, love under will' (Crowley, 1904, 1: 40 and 1: 57). In 1920 he founded the Abbey of Thelema to explore this law in Cefalu, Sicily.[10] The protoype Thelemite Abbey was already in existence, albeit in fictional form. In 1534, a former Franciscan friar turned Benedictine monk, François Rabelais (*c*.1494–1553), had set out the guidelines for the Abbey of Thélème in his novel *Gargantua*. The Abbey was to be set up in distinct contrast to usual monastic communities, with all the restrictions normally found in the religious life inverted. Thus, there were to be no walls, women and men should both be admitted, vows of chastity, poverty and obedience would be dismissed so that members could be married, become rich, or live at liberty, and whereas the Christian monastic novitiate was followed by an expectation of life-long residency, those at Thélème could come and go as they pleased.[11] Regarding Rabelais as an earlier prophet of the new aeon,[12] Crowley saw himself as fulfilling the 'prophecy' set out in the former's fictional abbey, and took his rule directly from it:

All their life was regulated not by laws, statutes, or rules, but according to their free will and pleasure. ... In their rules there was only one clause:

DO WHAT YOU WILL.

(Rabelais, [1534] 1985: 150–1)

Rabelais was highly critical of the priesthood in general, and monastic orders in particular. As far as he was concerned, when people are allowed to be free they 'have a natural spur and instinct which drives them to virtuous deeds and deflects them from vice' (ibid.: 159). However, if they are enslaved and constrained, they strive after forbidden things and invert their noble qualities in order to throw off the yoke of slavery. Crowley would of course fit into this second category. He agreed with Shelley and Nietzsche in defining Christianity as 'the religious expression of the slave spirit in man' (Crowley, (1910) 1985 : xxix) in the preface to his poem *The World's Tragedy*. Christianity was, to him, an 'awful fear of nature and God ... twisted into an engine of oppression and torture against anyone who declines to grovel and cringe before their filthy fetish' (ibid.: xxxi). Crowley does, however, absolve the figure of Jesus from responsibility, for he sees the problems as arising from within a church, a religion, which has forgotten and deliberately misread the teachings of its founder. What he fights so bitterly against is

> the religion which makes England today a hell for any man who cares at all for freedom. That religion they call Christianity; the devil they honour they call God ... and it is their God and their religion that I hate and will destroy.
>
> (Ibid.)

Clearly, his own 'natural spur and instinct which drives [him] to virtuous deeds' was redirected to the breaking of the Christian yoke of slavery via the pursuit of that which is forbidden and denied.

This church that has perverted the teachings of its founder is populated by those 'Priests in black gowns ... walking their rounds,/And binding with briars my joys and desires' who inhabit Blake's Garden of Love.[13] Yet Crowley's alternative was, of course, heavily influenced by St Augustine of Hippo who, although regarded as 'spiritually adolescent' by Crowley (1978: 529), authored the famous precept, 'Love, and do what you will'.[14] As a Latin scholar and lover of learning, Rabelais would have had a sound knowledge of Augustine's works, and his *Fay ce que voudras* is most likely to have derived from the second part of the precept. But whilst Rabelais' fictional use is satirical, mocking the Church to which he belonged all his life, Crowley takes the precept and develops it into a doctrine of the Will which is central to his understanding of magic.[15] He may shake off the shackles of (Christian and Victorian) restraint, but he does so by adaptation of a Christian framework. Augustine's precept that desire (love of God) should order what we will is inverted in the Law of Thelema, in which love is under Will, and is stripped of all reference to an external deity and oriented towards the Self. As Crowley described it, '[t]he sexual act is a sacrament of Will. To profane it is the great offence. All true expression of it is lawful; all suppression or distortion of it is contrary to the Law of Liberty'[16] (Crowley, 1996: 42). Sex was not utilised solely for operative magic however; it was also an essential part of the central rite of the *Ecclesiæ Gnosticæ Catholicæ*, the Gnostic Mass, which Crowley had written in Moscow in 1913.[17] It is in the Gnostic Mass that it is possible to trace the type of sex magic bequeathed to Wicca, and this predominantly symbolic form will be discussed later in this chapter.

80

Like Crowley, Gardner found the attitude of orthodox Christianity towards sexuality and the body somewhat problematic. He criticised the attitude of institutional Christianity towards sexuality and the body, claiming that the witches of old practised nudity in their rites which 'to their Christian opponents was mere shamelessness' (Gardner, [1959] 2004: 9), and claiming that the Church was 'always forbidding anything nice' (ibid.: 22). Puritanism in particular is at fault because of its destruction of beauty, whether in churches, sex, or nature, as a result of which the Puritans, in Gardner's eyes, 'made such a desert of England, and from whose excesses we still suffer' (ibid.: 115). As far as he is concerned, if marriage is solely for the purpose of procreation, then human love is no better than cattle breeding.[18] Agreeing with Swinburne's *Hymn to Proserpine (after the Proclamation in Rome of the Christian Faith)*,[19] he states that, 'the Church has taken all the pleasures out of our lives, and has done this simply to enforce their dictum that "Love is Shame"' (ibid.: 125). To Gardner, this is rather ridiculous as it discredits the 'Great Architect of the Universe', who surely knew what 'He' was doing when he made humans as sexual beings (ibid.: 133). As he understood them, the teachings of orthodox Christianity on sex are at once against beauty, against nature, and against women. Little wonder, then, that Gardner's imagined witch cult – a cult that worships beauty (ibid.: 116) and nature, a 'Horned and Phallic God and His Moon Goddess consort' (ibid.: 133) – regards sex as something sacred, which unsurprisingly attracted the projections of Christian repression.

These projections are well documented through the heresy trials of the Middle Ages and, as was mentioned in Chapter 3, there is a long history of sexual transgression in esoteric orders, even if only in the imaginations of the accusers.[20] Such alleged transgressions commonly included devil worship, orgies, incest, child sacrifice/cannibalism and, occasionally, nudity.[21] The early accusations give a clear indication of the importance of an imaginary alterity in defining the borders of the emerging Christian orthodoxy; attitudes towards sexuality and the body can be read through the registers of what is rejected and condemned. They may also show the existence of alternative approaches to sexuality, the body, and the divine, at least in the imagination, and even if condemned;[22] but there is no proof that any of the heretical sects actually practised the things of which they were accused. From the alleged sexual licentiousness of gnostic sects such as the Carpocratians,[23] to the supposed sodomy of the Knights Templar,[24] to the perversions of Cathars, Jews and witches, sex, magic and secrecy have been associated with esoteric and heretical groups in the western religious imagination. But, as Gardner asks, what is this sexual perversion?

The worship of 'the divine spirit of Creation, which is the Life-spring of the world, and without which the world would perish'? Is that 'sexual perversion'?

The worship of the witch cult is, and always has been, that of the principle of Life itself. It has made of that principle, as manifested in sex, something sacred. *Which is the perversion?* This, or the outlook which seeks to make humans ashamed of their naked bodies, and fearful of sex and 'original sin' and something unclean? ...

... the witch cult does not hold sex sacred as an end in itself, but as a living symbol and manifestation of the Great Source of All Things which men call God.

(Gardner, [1959] 2004: 210)

The so-called black magic of which witches were accused, he argues, has done very little damage compared to the psychological damage done by the Church's doctrine of original sin and its attendant teachings on sexuality, which pervert nature. Theirs, he argues, is the dangerous, unhealthy perversion; the nudity and sexuality of the witches is healthy and natural, but it has been portrayed as deviant. Accusations of moral – especially sexual – licentiousness have been a long-standing technique of bringing opponents into disrepute, whether they be opponents in US political elections, rival religious sects in the early days of Christianity, or witches. And of course, such representations continue to this day. The following is a parody of the astonishing array of images that can still be found in tabloid reports of witchcraft:

Sado-Masochistic Black Magic Satanic Witch Coven in Suburbia. Last Saturday, on the night of the grand witch's sabbat of Beltane, I infiltrated a coven on the night of an initiation. 13 people gathered in a suburban terrace in Manchester, had a few drinks, and then proceeded to get their kit off! Before I knew what was happening, my field of vision was full of tits! Black candles were lit, incense burned, doors locked (no way of escape then!) and all kinds of paraphernalia laid out: knives, a sword, phallic wands, cords, inverted pentagrams, a great chalice of wine, and a bloody great scourge! I listened hard for the bleating of a goat! The poor guy was led in, bound, blindfold and naked, only to be confronted with a sword blade pressed against his chest, and that was nothing! Within minutes, he was on his knees, head down, and the so-called High Priestess was beating the shit out of him with the scourge! And then she kissed him – all over his body – before pricking his finger and squeezing till the blood flowed!!! 'We adore the body as sacred', the High Priestess later told me, 'and use sexual energy for our magic'. Yeah right – perverted sex if you ask me, or maybe they're just a bunch of Christians pissed off that flagellation's died out. I left before the orgy started.

(Pearson, 2005: 31–2)

Tabloid sensationalism has dogged Wicca from its early days in the 1950s,[25] and the ritual abuse cases of the late 1980s/early 1990s exacerbated the threat posed by such reporting. The power of the imagery contained in the above pastiche is that (apart from the goat!) it is based on fact rather than rumour – scourging and binding, ritual nudity and symbolic sexual expression do have a place within Wiccan ritual. But although all of these elements of ritual have deeply symbolic meanings ascribed to them which allow for a very different interpretation from that of the sensationalist tabloid reports, the prevalence of such sensationalist interpretations has led to a tendency among some Wiccans to excise the sexual elements of their rituals, at least publicly. Since the mid-1980s, Wicca has to an extent portrayed itself as the inverse of the popular image of witchcraft: light, rather than dark; liking babies rather than sacrificing them; practising sacred sex rather than engaging in orgies; healing rather than harmful; and definitely far removed from anything remotely satanic. Thus, whilst a view of sex as sacred has been retained, the role of sex magic has been played down and 'spirituality' emphasised over sexuality, rather than a fusion of the two. The now very evident commercialisation and commodification of Wicca has come about partly because of this desire on the part of Wiccans some fifteen years ago to present Wicca as an 'acceptable' religion for the post/modern world. Many practitioners, however, have reacted to what they consider to be the development of a 'fluffy', white-washed Wicca. They prefer instead to invoke the allure of witchcraft, retaining its dark and sexual connotations and, importantly, its aura of power, elements of the Western Christian stereotype of the witch constructed in the fourteenth century and embellished ever since.[26]

In twenty-first century Wicca, these dark and sexual connotations include sex magic (both symbolic and in physical actuality), S/M techniques, and ritual nudity. Each shall be considered in turn. Sex magic as a symbolic thread runs through most Wiccan rituals, whether they be initiations, esbats or sabbats. Gardner's library holdings suggest an interest in sex magic. He owned the classics by Randolph (1874) and Jennings (1887), as well as a number of volumes produced in the 1930s.[27] As stated above, however, Crowley's Gnostic Mass is a major influence on the sexual symbolism of Wiccan ritual, particularly that contained in the act of communion, the blessing of cakes and wine.

In this ceremony, which takes place towards the end of each ritual, a Priest takes the cakes, and offers them to the invoked Priestess/Goddess:

> O Queen most secret, bless this food unto our bodies, bestowing health, wealth, strength, joy and peace, and that fulfilment of love which is perpetual happiness.[28]

The Priestess blesses them, the purpose being to imbue the food with the remaining power of the Goddess previously invoked into her.[29] Breaking off a piece for herself and the Priest, the cakes are then passed to the other coveners. The Priest then holds the chalice before the Priestess, who plunges her athame into the wine saying,

As the athame is male, so the cup is female, and conjoined they bring forth blessedness.

This ceremony is regarded as one of the symbolic forms of the Great Rite; it can be performed 'in token', i.e. symbolically, as part of the third degree initiation. If the third degree Great Rite is being performed 'in true', i.e. as full sexual intercourse, it is usually though not always the preserve of established couples, and is done in private. Aidan Kelly (1991: 67) notes that 'the concern here is the positive one of emphasizing the similar and inherent goodness of wine, cake and sex ... sex glorified as the greatest sacrament', and the sexual symbolism, according to Vivianne Crowley, contains 'the relationship between the God and the Goddess: the two Divine forces ultimately reconciled in One' (Crowley, Vivianne, 1996: 188).[30]

Similar symbolism is used at initiations, where the besom is laid across the threshold of the doorway. The besom, or broomstick, is considered to be a further symbol of the male and female conjoined, '*the rod which penetrates the bush*, and it is via this symbol of sexual union that the candidate enters the circle of rebirth' (Crowley, Vivianne, 1996: 111). The initiate is bound, blindfold and naked, purified with scourging, and then consecrated with oil, wine and lips.[31] It is this apparent use of S/M techniques[32] – binding, blindfolding and scourging – that has become problematic for some Wiccans, even on a symbolic level, whilst for others they are an inherent part of Wiccan ritual and their removal signifies a 'white-washing' of Wicca. The practice of scourging and binding, according to Aidan Kelly, came from Gerald Gardner's own sexual predilections.[33] Blindfolding and binding are, however, common practices in initiatory, secret societies, stemming ultimately from Freemasonry, whilst scourging and blood-control via binding are well-known techniques for changing consciousness. In Wicca, 'the cords are used to apply a gentle restriction of the blood circulation to produce dizziness, and the scourge is applied very lightly and steadily to induce a rhythmical tingling sensation' (Hutton, 1999: 235), drawing the blood away from the brain and into the body, thus enabling the person being scourged to enter a more 'pure' state of consciousness. Scourging, of course, has a long history as a method of purification and discipline, and in Wicca the scourge itself is 'the sign of power and dominance' and the ritual agent of 'suffering and purification' used to administer initiatory ordeals (ibid.: 229).[34] In many covens, scourging is practised only as part of initiation rituals (where a prescribed number of strokes are administered), as Vivianne Crowley explains:

> Once the measure has been taken, the initiate is symbolically scourged. This is not designed to cause pain. This is not because of Western squeamishness. Most people are prepared to suffer in order to be worthy of initiation. [But] today ... physical endurance is a minor part of our lives and the gifts of initiation are not won by undergoing a small amount

of physical discomfort. It is an effort of the mind, soul and spirit which is required to achieve the goal of initiation – higher consciousness.

(Crowley, Vivianne, 1996: 116)

The scourging is, then, symbolic and the scourge itself may even consist of pieces of cotton thread rather than anything more substantial. Whilst infliction of pain is not the aim, one might wonder whether such a scourge could aid the attainment of a trance state or act as an effective means of purification. However, as Paul Huson comments,

> many traditional-minded witches feel that this [scourging] ... though peculiar to certain aspects of later Roman versions of the Greek mysteries, seems to be more bound up with English 'public school' and 'spankers' club' traditions than any inherent in the craft itself. To be beaten, whether symbolically or in actuality, does not by any means arouse in everyone the same feelings of glowing inner cleanliness or spiritual tone-up that it apparently did for a Nordic warrior, cloistered medieval monk, English public school boy, or sky-clad witch.
>
> (Huson, 1970: 214–15)

Thus, whilst binding and blindfolding can be accepted as practices with a long pedigree in Masonic circles, scourging tends to be associated with S/M and with Christianity, in the monastic use of 'the discipline', for example. As might be expected, reactions vary. On the one hand, there are Wiccans with an interest in S/M who make greater use of bondage and flagellation, and experiment with pain, drawing S/M techniques into the rituals of Wicca physically as opposed to the abstract or symbolic appreciation of scourge and cords found in most covens. On the other hand, there are those, particularly women, to whom the use of scourging, blood control through bondage, or sex as magical techniques are inappropriate, even dangerous forms of sexuality. As a result, some Wiccan covens no longer consider the scourge an appropriate magical weapon,[35] and have removed it from their altars; they have also discontinued scourging, binding, and explicit forms of sex magic. They may find other ways of appropriating the Wiccan magic circle as a space of resistance, in which the sexual morals of Christianity and patriarchy can be subverted. One means of doing so is by embracing the witch as identificatory image, becoming the witch – *because of*, rather than in spite of, its stereotypical connotations.

As has previously been noted, although the ghost of a direct historical link to the witches and witchcraft of early modern Europe was laid to rest by historians in the 1970s, in the same decade feminist consciousness, particularly in the USA, re-forged those links on a psychological, spiritual and political level. 'Witch' was rendered 'Women's International Terrorist Conspiracy from Hell';[36] every woman was a witch; witchcraft was 'wimmin's religion' and would remain so until true equality was a reality. The witch of early modern Europe was 'constantly cast and recast as the late twentieth century's idea of a proto-feminist, a sister from the past' (Purkiss, 1996: x). She was a powerful and liberated woman who used her sexuality according to her own dictates – to emasculate as well as to empower, rather than to bow down to horny old men who used religion and/or magic as an excuse for sexual voyeurism, or even abuse.

Since the Christian stereotype of the witch was strongly associated with the embodiment of female sexuality and the negation of male (sexual) potency, the sexual power of the witch was harnessed as a positive force. As Jane Ussher has pointed out, 'the witch is portrayed in myth as having ferocious sexual energy ... she is impelled by sexual envy; and she seeks power. She is a "woman" so imbued with sexuality that her very existence stands as a threat to "man"' (Ussher, 1997: 118).[37] Being a witch was seen as a way in which to play with the male fear of female sexuality. It was argued that this fear had led to the Great Witch Hunt in the first place, a witch hunt which, according to feminist writers such as Mary Daly,[38] Andrea Dworkin and Merlin Stone, had never really ended but had mutated into myriad forms. The witch as a symbol of female sexuality and power was thus as firmly entrenched as ever,[39] but women were now adapting the image to reflect their own interests and concerns.[40] The interpretation of the stereotype may thus be inverted, but there is a great deal of resistance to its potential collapse in a white-washed Wicca. Wiccans do not necessarily want to move 'from the Devil's gateway to the Goddess within' (Hanegraaff, 1995b) unless, of course, the Goddess within is the devil herself.

For those who value the dark allure of Wicca, the divine feminine is not limited to the Great Mother, who is 'the beauty of the green earth and the white moon among the stars and the mystery of the waters' depicted in the Wiccan Charge of the Goddess,[41] though she may well be 'the desire in the heart of man'. She is, more often than not, the witch-goddess – represented by the great Greek sorceresses Circe, Medea, and Hecate, or by Adam's first wife Lilith, or by the Mesopotamian Anaïtis. These goddesses express themselves in powerful and sexual terms during the ritual process of invocation, a process which is itself extremely sexual. As an example, following is an invocation of Anaïtis, which evokes a sense of the level of empowerment possible through this practice. A priestess stands, naked, in candlelight, wreathed in heady incense smoke, towering above the man or woman who kneels before her, head at her feet, the energy of adoration spiralling through her body. She smiles cruelly, and the words come:[42]

> For I, and none but I, can waken that desire which uses all of a man, and so wastes nothing, even though it leave that favored man forever after like wan ashes in the sunlight. And with you I have no more concern, for it is I that am leaving you forever. Join with your graying fellows, then! and help them to affront the clean sane sunlight, by making guilds and

laws and solemn phrases wherewith to rid the world of me. I, Anaïtis, laugh, and my heart is a wave in the sunlight. For there is no power like my power, and no living thing which can withstand my power; and those who deride me, as I well know, are but the dead dry husks that a wind moves, with hissing noises, while I harvest in open sunlight. For I am the desire that uses all of a man: and it is I that am leaving you forever.

(Cabell, [1921] 1984: 269)

Sexual energy permeates the room – you can smell it and see its effects. So is this where the orgy begins? Well, no. The witch as pervert and sexual deviant exists mainly in the imagination. The delay and postponement of a sexual act which never actually happens but which is at the same time always happening leads to a heightening of sexual energy and thus, according to Wiccans, to more effective magic. In addition to the ambience of ritual, the techniques discussed above and practices such as invocation, such effectiveness is facilitated by ritual nudity.

The practice of ritual nudity in Wicca stems in part from Leland's *Aradia*, picked up by Gardner, 'a convinced naturist, with an ardent belief in the physical, moral, and magical benefits of nudity' (Hutton, 2003d: 194).[43] Doreen Valiente (1989: 98) notes, '[i]t may well be that Gerald Gardner's naturist beliefs coloured his ideas about witchcraft; because he maintained that witches *always* worked in the nude, and in the climate of the British Isles this is just not a practical possibility'. We may also note as influential those paintings portraying witches as female and nude.[44] Yet Wiccans have sought to legitimate and explain ritual nudity with a variety of provenances and explanations.[45]

Wiccans argue that magic is specifically facilitated through sexual energy released through the body, and through the practising of techniques which have long been understood to effect a change of consciousness. The practice of ritual nudity is considered to be an important part of this. It tends to be the main source of salacious tabloid articles, because at least on a superficial level it is easily 'understood' by the British public, the suggestion being that people getting together naked in private houses and performing rituals must at best be engaging in orgies, and at worst be dangerous perverts who indulge in ritual abuse. Thus, whilst naturist resorts are now more or less perfectly acceptable, private gatherings of naked people for religious ceremonies remain deviant and suspect. The accusations against Vintras mentioned in Chapter 3, for example, were not simply concerned with the allegations that he and his followers were naked, but that the Mass was being celebrated in such a context. Prior to nineteenth-century heterodoxy, Christian dissenters such as the Ranters and Quakers of the first half of the seventeenth century had 'stripped to nakedness in church as a symbol of resurrection' (Merchant, 1982: 124),[46] a reminder, perhaps, of the older practice of regeneration through the initiatory rite of nude baptism.[47] If Wicca's use of ritual nudity is therefore seen as 'investing the whole of its workings with the intensity and transformative effect of rites of passage', as Hutton (2003d: 207) claims, then they are certainly not the first to do so. That others have been Christian somewhat undermines Hutton's assertion that 'Wicca boldly goes where no religions have gone before' (ibid.).[48]

Quite the opposite point of view to that of deviance is stressed by Wiccans, who argue that one very quickly becomes immune to the naked bodies surrounding one: if familiarity doesn't breed contempt, it at least frees one's mind from moral struggles and allows one to focus on 'higher things'.[49] Anticipating Foucault,[50] Aleister Crowley noted at his Abbey of Thelema in Cefalu,

> I had rather expected that by releasing and encouraging the [sexual] instinct it would loom larger in our lives. The exact contrary was the case.[51] ... The importance of the subject, its omnipresence, is due to the constant irritation set up by its suppression. ... In the Abbey we removed the sources of irritation, with the result that it slipped back into its proper physiological proportion, into serenity and silence. *We almost forgot its existence.* It began to surprise us when the sexual symbols which we had exhibited in the abbey, so that familiarity might breed forgetfulness, excited strangers.
>
> (Crowley, 1978: 852, emphasis added)

To many, being naked, or 'skyclad', is a means of allowing power to flow from the body unimpeded,[52] and when robes are worn, natural fabrics such as cotton, silk or wool are preferred, as natural fibres are thought to allow magical energy to pass through them. The problem with this interpretation, as Hutton has noted, is that it implies the failure of clothed magicians. In doing so, it

> consigns to this inferior category the most famous and sophisticated societies for the practice of ritual magic which are known to history, including the Golden Dawn, the Stella Matutina, and the Ordo Templi Orientis.
>
> (Hutton, 2003d: 194)

It also undermines the efficacy of famous fictional and legendary magicians and sorceresses beloved of Wiccans, such as Merlin, Vivianne, Morgan le Fay, Circe, Hecate and Medea.

A more acceptable explanation for ritual nudity is that shedding clothes is a symbolic gesture of removing the last vestiges of the everyday world. Prior to Wiccan rituals, if space allows, men and women will often undress separately. [ba] Separating men and women at this point helps to differentiate ritual nudity from that which may be experienced in other settings, such as unisex changing rooms at a swimming pool or gym, at a naturist resort, or simply between two people who are in a relationship and are used to seeing each other naked, and it is a reminder that working skyclad is not done for titillation or eroticism. As Luhrmann points out, in her experience,

> [t]here are no orgies, little eroticism, and in fact little behaviour that would be different if clothes were being worn. That witches dance around in the nude probably is part of the attractive fantasy that draws outsiders into the practice,[54] but the fantasy is a piece with the paganism and not the source of salacious sexuality.
>
> (Luhrmann, 1994: 51)

In addition, for new coven members who are not used to getting undressed in the company of others and may not feel comfortable with their bodies, it is far gentler to be with members of one's own gender and to enter the temple surrounded by them.

Ritual nudity thus reinforces the mutuality of the Wiccan circle; as Salomonsen (2002: 225) notes, '[r]itual nudity symbolizes that the participants, at a deep level, are one body, one being, one member …'. Entering the circle naked is a sign of vulnerability and trust, representing the mutual dependency and feeling of well-being which Victor Turner links to the experience of communitas.[55] He cites Martin Buber as an aid to explaining his concept of communitas:

> Community is the being no longer side by side (and, one might add, above and below) but *with* one another of a multitude of persons. And this multitude, though it moves towards one goal, yet experiences everywhere a turning to, a dynamic facing of, the others, a flowing from I to *Thou*.
>
> (Buber, 1961: 51 in Turner, 1969: 127)

Ritual nudity may well offer a very real example of communitas in which there occurs a 'direct, immediate, and total confrontation of human identities' (Turner, 1969: 132), 'a transformative experience that goes to the root of each person's being and finds in that root something profoundly communal and shared' (ibid.: 138). And nakedness, says Turner, is 'the master symbol of emancipation from structural and economic bondage'.[56] The contrast with social norms is, indeed, radical, and nudity most obviously discards as inappropriate the 'canons of reality which guide everyday behaviour' (Rappaport, 1979: 213). The practice of ritual nudity in Wicca can be regarded as a symbol of freedom, after part of the Great Charge of the Goddess derived from Leland (Crowley, Vivianne, 1996: 189; cf. Leland [1890], 1990: 6–7) which exhorts Wiccans to be 'free from slavery, and as a sign that ye be really free, ye shall be naked in your rites'.

Removing the last vestiges of the everyday world through undressing thus aids entry into the extraordinary space of ritual; it marks a movement from what Peter Berger (1979) has called paramount reality, into the spiritual realm. Valiente writes (1989: 99), '[a]s a room in an ordinary house becomes a different place by the light of the candles around the magic circle, so the naked witch dancing by the light of those candles is a different person from the usual inhabitant of that room'. As an inversion of social norms, ritual nudity proclaims a levelling of status, a denial of social distinctions, a uniformity – a process by which the coveners become equal. The body thus becomes a symbol in itself, a symbol of trust and intimacy. But nakedness also

> dramatises the paradox of exclusion and inclusion, and is connected to the secrecy. In our society some level of trust among a group of people is usually necessary for nakedness: those among whom one would be naked is usually a relatively exclusive group. Nakedness also necessitates extra care to keep outsiders away.
>
> (Neitz, 1994: 147, n. 14)

Wiccans regard themselves as going before their Gods in ritual, and baring their souls, represented by being naked. But they not only regard themselves as naked before their Gods, but as 'open' to each other and to themselves. Because Wicca is concerned with personal spiritual growth, initiates learn to look at the good and the bad, acknowledging what they do not like about themselves – 'we must see our souls naked and unveiled' (Crowley, Vivianne, 1996: 108). In today's body-conscious world, where the media pressure to be ever thinner can be unbearable, it is important to Wiccans that they feel comfortable with their bodies and are accepted by others *as they are* rather than feeling they would be acceptable if only they could lose half a stone. An American witch, Laura Wildman, reported[57] on the Nature Religion Scholars List in May 1999 her experience of her first Wiccan gathering: 'for the first time in my life, after years of trying to force my body to fit the conventions of the time and failing, I FELT beautiful. It changed my life forever'. Yet ritual nudity can also have the opposite effect, adding to the pressure to conform to the image of the perfect body in Western society.[58]

Set apart from the exoteric world of the everyday, however, acceptance of the body as sacred can be interpreted within an esoteric framework. In the Western Esoteric Tradition, the Divine is experienced in the things of earth according to the Hermetic maxim, 'As Above, So Below'. Thus, as Antoine Faivre has pointed out,

> if they [esotericists] see the body as a magical object, mystically linked to the planets and to the elements of nature, it is because they find sense everywhere in things and transcend the illusion of banality, a poetic task par excellence. This path is certainly more poetic than ascetic, but if asceticism is the source of technological progress, it is not necessarily a model to follow to experience totality.
>
> (Faivre, 1988: 434)

Here Faivre indicates a point vital to understanding the Wiccan practice of ritual nudity. The body is the most obvious indication of human corporeal existence, as spiritual beings in the physical world. Thus, by working nude, the presence of the physical within the spiritual and sacred space of the circle is made explicit. In his introduction to *Modern Esoteric Spirituality*, Jacob Needleman (1992: xxviii) writes of the esoteric acceptance of a harmonious relationship between all things, in which the unity of heaven and earth constitutes a, 'deeply natural and mutually fecundating relationship'. He explains further that

> the aim of unity refers to a circulating exchange of force among parts that are, up to a very considerable degree, ineluctably independent as well as being ultimately one in the service of the Absolute or God-principle. ... It is when the levels and separateness of principal forms within reality are clearly seen and diligently maintained that the divine mutual organic exchange of universal conscious energy can flow. When this flows, then *all is one.*
>
> (Needleman and Faivre, 1992: xxviii, emphasis in original)

The spiritual and the physical, heaven and earth, are thus analogous to two poles of a battery which are necessary for energy to flow. Given the Wiccan proclivity for engaging in spiritual development whilst fully engaging in everyday life and society, negating dualities, and stepping 'between the worlds' to contact the Divine, the Wiccan practice of ritual nudity can be perceived as an obvious manifestation of the separateness between heaven and earth which allows the development of a 'deeply natural and mutually fecundating relationship' between the human (Wiccans) and the Divine. It may also echo the Hermetic idea of ascension where, upon death, the spiritual 'man' ascends through the spheres, leaving a part of his mortal nature at each one until, entirely denuded of all that the spheres had imprinted on him, he becomes one with the universe.[59]

The 'shamelessness' which Gardner perceived nudity to represent to orthodox Christianity is therefore subverted in Wiccan ritual, where it becomes a symbol of confidence, power and community. To Hutton (2003d: 195), its 'blatant presence in ritual was just one example of the way in which, during the middle decades of the twentieth century, Wicca crashed the barriers of convention'. If nudity is shameless and offensive, then adopting it can be seen as a proclamation of exemption from normal controls and conventions. This is certainly one of the reasons why heresiologists accused gnostic sects of nudity, reading into claims to be the elect, predestined to gnosis, and no longer under the thrall of evil, inferences to moral autonomy. Claims to magical efficacy, however, relate more to the feelings of communitas engendered by ritual nudity rather than to nakedness as a prerequisite for the flowing of magical power. In taking an orthodox Christian stereotype of moral and sexual disorder, in its practice of nudity Wicca disrupts normal

SEX AND THE SACRED

Western conventions, but it does so only within the limitations and privacy of the Wiccan circle. Whilst it can therefore operate as an aid to shifts in consciousness recognised as necessary for both ritual and magical efficacy, the practice of ritual nudity can hardly be regarded as particularly subversive in the wider cultural context. Its critique is wholly contained and, like tantra, remains a conservative force that effects no change external to the practitioners themselves.[60]

The Wiccan circle, then, can be used as a space in which to play with the expression of sexuality, confronting the limits and boundaries of what constitutes acceptable sexuality in sacred spaces. The construction and performance of bodily ritual facilitate a flirtation with the power of sexuality. That such constructions are constrained within a voyeuristic rather than 'real' sex environment does not lessen the *potential* to disrupt. However, unless the third degree Great Rite is being performed, which usually, though not always, is the preserve of established couples, it seems that Crowley's transgressive sex magic has been transformed in Wicca into the channelling of creative energy, a sublimation or transfiguration rather than repression or expression.[61] Within the constructed magic circle, (dangerous) sexual energy is neutralised through controlling mechanisms that facilitate its transformation into (safe) magical energy.[62] Attitudes to sexuality expressed through nudity are one thing, but when taken out of the symbolic realm – when the energy is not constrained, transformed, and 'earthed' through a magical act – terrible things might happen: people might actually have sex!

Despite its often fervent claims to radicalism, openness and maturity, then, Wicca attempts to invoke an aura of danger and perversity whilst still embracing accepted norms of appropriate sexual behaviour,[63] articulating a rather complex attitude towards sexuality. In its use of ritual nudity, sex magic (invocation, Great Rite, raising energy), and S/M techniques such as scourging and binding, Wicca claims to subvert accepted codes of (religious) behaviour. However, for all this vaunted disruption, S/M concepts in particular have been largely abstracted into symbolic forms which strongly deny the 'inappropriate' sexuality embedded in Wiccan initiation rituals (specifically) and formative ideologies (generally).[64] Thus, whilst the similarities between some Wiccan and S/M practices suggests a common conceptual ground, the physical actuality expressed and embraced in S/M is rarely found in Wicca except in cases where a genuine combination of S/M and Wicca exists for individuals. A rhetoric of disruptive sexuality may be retained in Wicca, but the emphasis tends to lie firmly in its symbolic value: inappropriate, dangerous sexuality is largely forbidden. Outside the magic circle, Wiccans claim to challenge concepts of and attitudes towards sexuality in their celebration of sex as something at once both sacred and wholly natural. In the end, however, the emphasis is firmly embedded in perceived magical efficacy rather than a challenge to social norms, which is regarded largely as a by-product. What does challenge social norms is the practice of ritual nudity and treatment of the body as 'a shrine to be reverenced and not despised, to be honoured and not treated with shame' (Crowley, Vivianne, 1996: 115). It is a temple in which the human meets and blends with the Divine. As that other advocate of naturism and celebrant of the human body, William Blake, succinctly put it,

> ... Love's Temple that God dwelleth in,
> And his in secret hidden Shrine
> The Naked Human Form divine.
>> (Blake, *The Everlasting Gospel*, e: 64–6, Notebook, *c.*1818,
>> cited in Howard, 1982: 125)

Naturism, pioneered by Gardner and Nichols, among many in the 1940s and 1950s, may now be an accepted part of modern Western culture. But among groups of people gathered together in private homes for the purposes of religious observance, nudity remains suspect and unusual, 'defined by its transgressive repudiation of normative religious models' (Verter, 2002: 8). This is especially so when combined not only with religious ritual, but with that other theme long associated with witchcraft, Catholicism and heterodoxy: magic.

6

THE MAGIC OF THE MARGINS

Magic is a word to conjure with. It confuses, and evades constraint, so that it is configured in contradictory ways. To some theorists, it is anti-social, even anarchistic. To others, it is socially conservative and authoritarian. As such, it offers the potential for disruption, resisting, critiquing, overturning constructed social norms, or it can constrain a society, keeping it attached to the past and stultifying change and innovation. It has become a privileged category, one that is imposed by white, Western, Protestant, male, imperial academics onto the 'other'. Likewise, the concept of religion taught in the academy rests on the same privileged platform. As noted in Chapter 4, ritual became a dirty word as attention shifted to religion as an internal state of mind, concerned with ideas and beliefs, becoming orthodoxic rather than orthopraxic. This change began during the various Protestant and Catholic reformations of the sixteenth century, and became embedded in the theories of religion and magic that emerged with the new disciplines of anthropology and sociology at the end of the nineteenth century.

The revival of interest in magic in the heart of Europe from the late nineteenth century on, in the secret occult societies of London and Paris, remained hidden and unstudied by anthropologists at that time. Magic was firmly associated with the so-called 'primitive', with non-Western, non-modern peoples existing on what were perceived to be the margins of civilisation. Thus, theories of magic both reflected, and helped to legitimate, the imperial expansion begun in the sixteenth century which reached its zenith in the nineteenth. This necessarily influenced the study of modern Western practitioners of magic from the 1970s on, treating them as deviant, irrational, and locked in the past. But increasingly, the colonialist tone in such assumptions about both magic and religion has begun to be noted, opening the way for more nuanced accounts of contemporary magical practice. However, this also requires a reassessment of the relations between religion and magic if their combination in Wicca is to be understood.

As Randall Styers comments, these themes of the Protestant and Catholic reformations were amplified in the Enlightenment, which

disparaged all visible manifestations of religious life and practice –
communities, institutions, rituals ... – as dubious encrustations. ... true
religion was localized within the private intellect as a matter of properly
warranted cognition.

(Styers, 2004: 5)

Such dubious encrustations, as already noted, provided a focus for opponents
to the Catholic revival in England in both its Roman and Anglican forms,
but particularly the latter which brought 'popish' practices into the bosom of
the Church of England and thus the state itself. At the same time, 'a "new"
occultism underpinned by a magical heritage emerged around the time that
religion and magic became accepted analytical categories and the subjects of
intellectual inquiry in the developing fields of anthropology and the study
of comparative religions' (Owen, 2004: 7–8). Early theories of magic, from
anthropologists such as Edward Tylor (1832–1917)[1] and Sir James Frazer
(1854–1941) consigned magic, like ritual, to a marginal existence in popish
enclaves or in the pre-modern, non-western societies with which these early
anthropologists were concerned. Evidence of magical practice within the
domestic population of Britain was largely ignored, and elsewhere in Europe
it was easily dismissed. Thus Tylor, raised a Quaker, was 'dismayed by the
persistence of magic within the heart of Europe' (ibid.: 17), among marginal
peoples such as the 'German cottager', the 'Hessian lad', sailors, and the
'Cornishman' (Tylor, 1889: 116–19, 123–33, 156, cited in Styers, 2004:
16). Regarding magic as 'one of the most pernicious delusions that ever
vexed mankind', belonging to the 'lowest known stages of civilisation', Tylor
deplored the fact that it had 'lasted on more or less among modern cultured
nations' (Tylor, 1929: 72, 112).

The presence of magic in Tylor's 'modern cultured nations' in fact
'muddie[d] the contemporaneous picture formulated by James Frazer and
the Victorian evolutionists of a straightforward magic-religion-science
march of cultural evolution' (Owen, 2004: 8). Influenced by Tylor's
notion of survivals and the evolution from magic to religion to science,
the Presbyterian-raised Frazer saw magic as 'the bastard sister of science'
(Frazer, 1990: 50), wholly anachronistic in modern Western society. It was a
theme that would be echoed in later studies of magic, but by the middle of
the twentieth century magic could no longer be effectively confined to the
margins. Bronislaw Malinowski (1884–1942), for example, despaired at the
magic articulated via 'stale revivals of half-understood ancient creeds and
cults, dished up under the names of "theosophy", "spiritism", "spiritualism",
and various pseudo-"sciences", -ologies and -isms' (1948: 50). Malinowski
situates this magic in the slums of London, where Anglo-Catholic ritualism
was particularly strong, and among European peasantry; but theosophy,
spiritualism, phrenology and psychology were certainly not limited to
marginal groups in society – not even to women. Indeed, as Alex Owen has
argued (2004: 4, 5), 'fin de siècle occultism attracted an educated, usually

middle-class clientele', and 'had a distinctly bourgeois tone that smacked of the gentleman's private club'.[2]

For sociologists, the distinguishing features of magic and religion were somewhat different from those expounded by the anthropologists, being concerned with the well-being of the community. Thus, Durkheim ([1912] 1965) stressed the individuality of magic, distinguishing magical beliefs and rites from religion on the basis that religion unites people together in society whereas magic, as an individual rather than collective practice, does not. For Durkheim, magic falls outside the group dynamics necessary to religion as a social institution, a distinction pre-empted by his nephew Marcel Mauss ([1902] 2001) who considered magic to be any rite which plays no part in organised religion and which is therefore private, secret and mysterious. A. R. Radcliffe Brown (1948) introduced ritual and social value to theories of magic, and the anthropologist E. E. Evans-Pritchard[3] emphasised a sociological dimension in stressing the importance of networks of social links, tensions and conflicts to Zande magic, which is used not to change nature but to combat powers and events caused by other people.

Such distinctions, however, have not been without criticism. As H. S. Versnel (1991: 117) points out, the distinctions between magic, religion and science have been under attack since the 1940s, and earlier. As early as 1911 R. R. Marrett, for example, claimed that the distinctions between magic and religion are illusory, stemming from ethnocentric projection and the distortion of history, and coined the term 'magico-religious' in an attempt to bridge the division. Claude Lévi-Strauss (1966) saw magic as the naturalisation of human actions and religion as the humanisation of natural laws; consequently, both magic and religion imply each other and are complementary and inseparable. Taking the lack of distinction between magic and religion to its logical extreme, Lévi-Strauss suggested that magic as a concept is empty of meaning and should therefore not be used. As Versnel notes (1991: 181), however, the problem is that one 'cannot talk about magic without using the term magic'.

Max Weber's understanding of the decline of magic in the wake of the Protestant Reformation was followed in Keith Thomas' landmark study *Religion and the Decline of Magic* (1971). For Weber, whereas religion was rational, organised and functional, magic was primitive, the 'guardian of the irrational' (Wax and Wax, 1963: 501). He regarded magic as a widespread form of popular religion in pre-industrial society, recourse to which prevented the rationalisation of economic life. Keith Thomas provides historical evidence to suggest that religion and magic were indistinguishable before the seventeenth century, and that distinctions between religion and magic were the product of a specific epoch in European history, when the Protestant Reformation attempted to take the magic out of religion during the sixteenth century. Protestantism, according to Thomas, thus created the division of magic from religion, and the subsequent decline of magic allowed for the 'rationalisation of economic life'. Thomas concludes that the decline of magic was complete by the end of the seventeenth century, with the growth of urban living, the rise of science, and the ideology of self-help emancipating people from the need for magical beliefs.[4] Intellectual changes, new technology, and new aspirations thus replaced belief in magic with optimism in humankind's ability.

However, it was precisely the sixteenth century that produced the foundation of the Western Esoteric Tradition, as the Renaissance spread beyond Italy throughout Western Europe. Within Renaissance esotericism, magic was viewed as 'the circulation and transformation of universal pneuma by the force of love' (Orion, 1995: 93), a common cosmic spirit (*spiritus mundi*) which operated as a channel between the heavens and man, the macrocosm and the microcosm. This understanding of magic was by no means in conflict with religion,[5] for magic was not regarded as purely instrumental and pragmatic but, at its highest level, as mystical religion which has love as its foundation. The tension between various *uses* of magic, however, becomes evident in Cornelius Agrippa's *De occulta philosophia* of 1533, where pragmatic goals are superseded by religious goals such as prophecy and mystical experience. Nevertheless, as Hanegraaff points out,

> even in the explicitly 'magical' occult philosophy of Agrippa, the general framework is one of a spiritual path oriented towards the attainment of *gnosis*. The pragmatic aspect oriented towards short-term goals may get a lot of attention, but in the end it is always subordinate to the long-term goal of mystical attainment.
>
> (Hanegraaff, 1999: 21)

Thomas' ([1971] 1991: 800) rather limited definition of magic as 'the employment of ineffective techniques to allay anxiety when effective ones are not available' which have today 'either disappeared or [are] at least greatly decayed in prestige' thus needs to be questioned. Like so many scholars, Thomas fails to engage with the developing understanding of magic during the sixteenth century, preferring instead to confine his understanding to that articulated by the turn of the century scholars mentioned above, none of whom took note of the real hothouse of magic in the midst of the domestic population, the Hermetic Order of the Golden Dawn.[6] But it is this Order that had the strongest influence on the practice of magic in England and its subsequent development, for 'all modern thinking on occult matters has been profoundly influenced by these seminal systems ... there is hardly a legitimate occult order in Europe or America that has not borrowed directly or indirectly from the Golden Dawn' (Regardie, 1983: 7). And it is from the Golden Dawn that Wicca traces its magical heritage.

The key founders of the Golden Dawn were Master Masons Dr William Wynn Westcott, a London coroner, Dr William Robert Woodman, and Samuel Liddell MacGregor Mathers. In 1887, Westcott had obtained part of a manuscript from a fellow Freemason, Rev. A. F. A. Woodford. On deciphering the manuscript, Westcott claimed to have discovered that it contained fragments of rituals from the Golden Dawn, a previously unheard of German occult order that admitted women as well as men. Mathers developed the fragments into full scale rituals, which he based largely on Freemasonry, and papers were forged to give the Golden Dawn a history and authenticity. The original manuscript was later shown to be a forgery also, and it was on such dubious grounds that the Isis-Urania temple of the Hermetic Order of the Golden Dawn was established in London in 1888. The Golden Dawn was organised with a headquarters in London and lodges in Bristol, Weston-Super-Mare, Bradford, Edinburgh and Paris, where Mathers, its leader, based himself. An elaborate hierarchy was created consisting of Neophyte plus ten grades or degrees, which were divided into three orders – the Outer (Zelator, Theoricus, Practicus, Philosophus, Adeptus Minor), the Second (Adeptus Major, Adeptus Exemptus) and the Third Order (Magister Temple, Magus, Ipsissimus) made up of the astral chiefs with whom only Mathers could communicate. The secret society quickly caught on, with 315 initiations taking place during its heyday (1888–96) before, in 1897, members discovered Westcott's questionable role in 'discovering' the Golden Dawn, and irreparable schisms began to form. Hierarchy was inherent within the extensive grading system, competition between individuals was rife, and splinter groups proliferated. The eventual disintegration of the Golden Dawn in the early twentieth century has predominantly been interpreted as a natural consequence of the clash of egos between various people involved in the Order.[7]

From 1888–96, however, the Golden Dawn 'paved the way for people such as Aleister Crowley and Dion Fortune and the numerous magical and Pagan groups that have since set up shop to practise magic' (Butler, 2004: 213).[8] Members gathered together Western magical knowledge, including studies on the Kabbalistic Tree of Life, the Key of Solomon, Abra-Melin Magic, Enochian Magic, as well as material gleaned from the Egyptian Book of the Dead, William Blake's Prophetic Books, and the Chaldean Chronicles. In essence, the Golden Dawn established its own magical canon (Butler, 2004: 217). The legacy of the Golden Dawn for contemporary Wicca and magical groups is immense, for it quickly became 'the sole depository of magical knowledge, the only occult order of any real worth that the West in our time has known' (Regardie, 1989: 16), 'the order that would virtually redefine the British occult world for the Twentieth Century' (Godwin, 1994: 223). Though based on Rosicrucianism,[9] the Golden Dawn took no official stance either for or against establishment Christianity, though it did offer 'an alternative to the opposing camps of orthodox Christianity, scientific naturalism, and the mixed camp of theosophy, Rosicrucianism, Hermeticism and occultism' (Butler, 2004: 229). Like the Theosophical Society, the Spiritualist movement and Freemasonry, the Golden Dawn attracted many people who were at least uncomfortable with, if not in direct revolt against Christianity; but on the other hand, many Christian members made use of the pre-Christian and magical methods to facilitate their Christian spiritual development. For many members, there existed no abyss between Christianity and the occult, and they found no difficulty in neatly dovetailing their Christian faith with their occult interests and magical leanings.

Indeed, this was true of occultism in general. In France, Éliphas Lévi remained a Catholic throughout his life, as did the doyen of spiritualist circles, Lady Caithness. As previous chapters have shown, the membership of French occult societies, heterodox churches and esoteric Christian and druidic circles overlapped significantly. Likewise, in Britain Anna Kingsford (1846–88) converted to Roman Catholicism in 1870 and promoted a form of esoteric Christianity in her Hermetic Society. Arthur Edward Waite (1857–1942), raised a Roman Catholic, developed his own brand of mystical, sacramental Christianity, drawing on ideas of a secret or interior Church which were articulated in his writings and in his Orders, the Independent and Rectified Rite (1903–14) and the Fellowship of the Rosy Cross, founded in 1915.[10] Dion Fortune (Violet Mary Firth), a member of both the Theosophical Society and of a Golden Dawn offshoot, the Stella Matutina, formed her own Fraternity of the Inner Light in 1924. Her attention vacillated between Christianity and Paganism,[11] evidence of the dichotomy, described by her biographer Alan Richardson (1991: 42), 'which ran right through her life: between the Gods and the one God; between the Mystery at Bethlehem and those of Karnak, Atlantis, and Avalon'. In the end, Francis King (1989: 158) judged that '[t]oday the Inner Light can no longer be considered a magical fraternity, it rather more resembles a heterodox semi-Christian cult, rather like the Liberal Catholic Church of the Theosophists'. Such a judgement, however, belies the author's own attitude towards the relationship between magic and Christianity, for what is now the Society of the Inner Light does indeed practise ritual magic.[12]

The above are, then, a few examples of occultists who were comfortable inhabiting that borderland in which Christianity and magic could co-exist. Outside these margins, either magic was 'popish', to the Protestants still attempting to rid the world of Catholicism; or it was a ridiculous notion unsuitable for the modern West, to the academics theorising it in 'primitive' culture; or it was something completely separate from Christianity which should be removed from the tarnish of the latter, to anti-Christian occultists such as Crowley. It is, perhaps, this latter attitude that is more discernible in Wicca, but on closer inspection the influences of that borderland are clear to see. This requires, however, a brief explanation of the types of magic to be found practised in Wicca, and attitudes towards them that underline the location of Wicca on the borderlands between Paganism and occultism.

Ritual magic has been portrayed by some scholars as the central neopagan practice.[13] That this is not the case can be seen from a selection of examples from a debate that has been rumbling in the journal of the Pagan Federation, *Pagan Dawn*, since 1998. It began with a letter from one 'Jerry C' in the Samhain 1998 issue, asking,

Why is magic such a priority in Paganism? When I first came to the Goddess, magic had nothing to do with my beliefs. My spiritual path was and is to focus on the Earth and my relationship with it, not all this magic crap! Why do some Pagans seem to take as their reference source the grimoires[14] and other old magical texts? ... It seems to me they are following the path of hermetic occultism, not Paganism. And, so this might be the root of our problems: hermetic magic!

Paganism as I see it, has nothing to do with magic whatsoever. In my experience, to follow a path of hermetic magic causes no end of problems, such as feeding the little ego, self-empowerment over others, emotional and mental instability. In the final analysis, the point of the hermetic magician is to stand in the centre of the Cosmos with total power and total Will over everything. Erm, excuse me? This is not Paganism!

(Jerry C, 1998: 38–9)

The same issue of the journal contained an article by Heathen Pete Jennings on Norse Tradition Magic – which has nothing to do with Hermeticism – and both letter and article provoked debate. In the next issue, 'Sean' wrote the Star Letter in which he claimed magic was merely one more way of interacting with the Earth and spoke of those (indigenous) peoples who live close to the earth:

Okay, they don't wave bloody great ceremonial swords bathed in dragon's sweat at the hour of Mercury on the day of Mars with Saturn rising retrograde, but they still have ceremonial objects imbued with enormous magical significance. They don't perform scripted rituals in chalk and salt circles surrounded by anagrams in Hebrew, but they do magic! ... Are these people Pagans because they live in direct relationship with the Earth and commune with deities and spirits, or are they not Pagans because they do magic? ... The energy that is used in magic by everyone from the Arch High Mage with his robes and fancy equipment to the ancient village midwife using only skill and experience and wisdom is the same stuff. It is Earth energy; the spiritual magical energy that is inherent within all life on Earth. All you have to do is look at a dandelion struggling to grow through a crack in the pavement to know that. ... I don't think we're doomed because many of us choose to use magic at whatever level – I live in a magical world.

(Sean, 1999: 43)

John Davies then wrote an article on 'Paganism and Magical Ethics' for the Beltane issue, in which he says:

Wouldn't it be nice to have a purely religious paganism, free from all this magical nonsense? Maybe, but I don't see that it can work. We live in a magical universe. This morning the air was crisp and clean. Overhead the sky was a strong blue, with the finest of mares' tails. The trees are beginning to flame with the colours of autumn, and the land talks to me with every step. Abandon magic indeed! It would be as easy to stop breathing! ... The real question seems to be not whether magic should be a part of paganism, but rather what kind of magic? Should it be Celtic, Hermetic, Wiccan or some other synthesis?

(Davies, 1999: 28–9)

These extracts from letters and articles outline the confusion of conflicting ideas about magic and its place in contemporary Paganism, Wicca, and occultism. As Graham Harvey has pointed out:

[n]ot all Magicians are Pagans, but a significant number are. Not all Pagans engage in magic, but a significant number do. What Magicians and Pagans mean by magic varies greatly.

(Harvey 1997: 87)

It is clear that some practitioners are uneasy and unhappy about the inclusion of highly-structured ritual magic within Paganism, understanding magic as hermetic, as an occult branch of magic which is not particularly Pagan, as opposed to the 'ordinary magic' of everyday life identified by Van Baal (1963). This latter form of magic is seen as a method of interaction with other people or with the Earth, sometimes to the extent of seeing Paganism as magical because it is concerned with a connection to the Earth, which is in its turn seen as inherently magical. Thus, the feeling of connectedness with the sky, the trees, the soil becomes a part of magical practice; if Paganism is about being at one with the environment, and if magic is understood as a level of connection and interaction with the earth, then Paganism is essentially magical. If, however, magic is hermetic, occult or ceremonial, then this creates a distance from the Earth and thus cannot be part of Paganism. A distinction thus persists between not only perceptions of religion and magic, but between what Justin Woodman (2000) has called 'stellar-based occultist magic and earth-based pagan magic', and for some, never the twain shall meet. Thus, a diverse array of magical practices, from ceremonial magic to chaos magick, left-hand path to kitchen magic, 'natural' magic to eco-magic, are understood and practised in different ways. In Wicca, it is the inclusion of ritual magic adapted from the Golden Dawn, Aleister Crowley and Dion Fortune that takes Wicca from the margins of Paganism, into the occult domain.[15]

Wicca uses a blend of high ceremonial ritual magic, herbal magic, seership/divination, and eco-magic, and many Wiccans share with Pagans a conception of the natural world as magical. For American feminist witch and political activist Starhawk (1982: 99), magic is 'the art of turning negatives into positives, of spinning straw into gold'. Such a definition is not limited to either hermetic magic or earth magic, but is a flexible idea of magic which can be put to use in any magical practice which seeks to bring about a beneficial end (though who is to say that gold is more positive than straw?). Wiccans, however, tend to favour Aleister Crowley's definition of magick as 'the Science and Art of causing change to occur in conformity with Will' (Crowley, 1973: 131), or Dion Fortune's, 'Magic is the art and the science of changing consciousness according to the Will'.[16] Both of these definitions might usefully be compared with Jacob Böehme's vision of magic as 'in itself nothing but a will, and this will is the great mystery of all wonders and secrets. ... In sum: Magic is the activity of the Will-spirit' ([1620] 1989: 5: 2 and 24). Again, a different spin can be put on both Crowley and Fortune's definition, and although both were ceremonial magicians rather than Wiccans, their influence on Wicca has already been noted and their definitions of magic are not, in any case, regarded as limited to the type of magic with which they were engaged.

Unlike Starhawk, however, these two definitions do not anchor themselves in an idea of 'positive', 'beneficial' practice; as such, they contain within them the possibility of magic utilised for 'negative', 'malefic' ends dictated by the individual's Will, which brings in more obviously the question of ethics.[17] Wiccans share with Pagans the notion that everyday life is magical, in that consciousness can be changed in order that the quotidian becomes 'significant, imbued with value, sacred or paradoxically suffused with transcendence' (Harvey, 1997: 87). But they also use magic in ritual to change things or situations and, more importantly, to change themselves. Wicca thus operates with three distinct types of magic, two of which have traditionally been called 'low' and 'high' magic. In an attempt to get away from the implicit hierarchy of 'low' and 'high', Salomonsen (2002: 149–52) uses the idea of a horizontal and a vertical axis to describe, respectively, the 'magic of everyday life' and the 'magic of ritual'. To this can be added the third type of magic – that of 'spiritual alchemy' – a term borrowed from Dolores Ashcroft-Nowicki, Director of Studies of the Servants of the Light School of Occult Science.[18] Also used in the Hermetic Order of the Golden Dawn, this third idea of magic is imbued with notions derived from the hermetic, occultist magic and gnostic texts.

Briefly, 'horizontal' magic includes traditional concepts of spellcraft, for example herbs, chants, dances, and poppets.[19] This type of magic tends to consist of isolated, specific spells, and in Wicca they may be performed separately from ritual or at the end of ritual. They tend to be time and place specific, immediate rather than continuous, goal orientated and pragmatic, for example chanting a formula over a herb mixture to give to someone for healing purposes. In this sense, magic is partly concerned with the 'specific, concrete' problems referred to by Malinowski and are not necessarily related to 'religion' (Malinowski, 1948: 86–7). As Cornish village witch Cassandra Latham (2002) explains, 'I do not need a religion to do what I do. I could be a Christian and do what I do. I just happen to be a Pagan'. In this, we see the type of magic that Protestant reformers claimed Catholicism encouraged through the cult of the saints, relics, etc., the power that was immanent in material things.

Likewise, 'vertical' magic may not be concerned with 'religion'. In conceptual terms, it is more or less identical to the highly-structured ritual magic mentioned above. This type of magic tends to be performed as part of ritual (e.g. a ritual based on the Jewish mystical system of the Kabbalah, which might be used to empower planetary talismans) and may well be integrated into a whole system of correspondences. Such systems of magical correspondences form associative clusters of phenomena thought to share common affinities, the purpose of which is to link the microcosm with the macrocosm.[20] For example, in the Kabbalah, the lunar sphere of Yesod is associated with such things as: the Moon (planet), violet (colour), 9 (number), quartz (precious stone), mandrake (plant), jasmine (perfume). These are in turn associated with other phenomena: thus, the Moon relates to specific lunar deities such as Diana/Artemis, Selene, Hecate, Thoth, Astarte, and to water (the element which it rules), mirrors (due to its reflective nature), the sea, tides and flux, the colour silver as well as violet, and moonstone as well as quartz. In this way, huge systems of magical correspondences are built up such that the mention of 'Yesod' or 'the Moon' automatically sets off a chain of images, linked through association, which can be used in magical ritual. Though goal oriented, 'vertical' magic is less immediate and specific than 'horizontal' magic, tending towards the sequential and processual, magic performed as part of ongoing ritual continuity. A talisman for protection, for example, might be made, consecrated, charged and repeatedly re-charged over a series of rituals.

Spiritual alchemy, the third type of magic, is the magic of transmutation, one of the four fundamental characteristics of Western esotericism identified by Antoine Faivre.[21] The alchemical term 'transmutation' is used to define the initiatory path of development by which 'the esotericist gains insight into the hidden mysteries of cosmos, self and God' (Hanegraaff, 1995a: 112). As transmutation implies a change in the very substance of a thing or person[22] there is, according to Faivre (1994: 13), no separation between knowledge (gnosis) and inner experience, or intellectual activity and active imagination. In Wicca, the magic that brings about this experience of transmutation is termed the 'greater magic', or 'Great Work', and is both 'vertical' and 'horizontal' in nature, in the sense that it is integrated into both solemn ritual and the everyday world. This magic is journey-oriented, relating to an ongoing process of spiritual and personal growth that is seen as experiential, holistic and non-specific, not limited even to this life, but perceived as an eternal process. The means by which this is done is not the specificity of the spell or defined piece of magic, but the 'greater magic' which is forged within the ritual setting and which occurs as a gradual process marked, for example, by initiations or the effect of sequential ritual.[23] It is not, therefore, measurable scientifically as an effect brought about by a cause, as spellcraft may be, but rather by the noticeable experience of deep inner change. The efficacy of the greater magic, the Great Work, can only be measured in incomplete stages, for Wiccans believe it to take many lifetimes to come to fruition. Wicca is therefore a magical religion that weaves nature and astral magic into a continuation of the hermetic doctrine of spiritual progress.

What this all too brief synopsis shows is that Wiccan ideas about magic are suffused with notions drawn from understandings of magic prevalent in occultism and earlier Judaeo-Christian esoteric and heterodox currents, but also contain more commonly-held ideas about what is magical within the wider Pagan milieu. Drawing on Wicca, non-aligned expressions of Paganism generally do utilise basic elements of the Golden Dawn framework for the purposes of ritual,[24] and thus make use of ritual magic to this limited extent even if they then use no other forms of structured magic, preferring to focus on horizontal magic or simply a perception of something as 'magical'. Much Gardnerian magical practice was based on the popular magic associated with pre-Reformation folk practices, though the emphasis on vertical magic was evident in the ritual framework of Wicca adopted from the Golden Dawn by Gardner, via Crowley. The greater emphasis on ritual magic arrived with Alex Sanders in the 1960s, but the sacramental magic encountered in Orthodoxy and Roman Catholicism was already reflected in the magico-religious rites that Gardner took from Crowley's Gnostic Mass. The notion of spiritual alchemy is also present in the Golden Dawn, from which it entered Crowley's system, and in ideas articulated by Dion Fortune in a rather less shocking fashion, and all are infused with earlier gnostic influences.

None of it, of course, is the demonic magic of which witches were accused by both Protestants and Catholics in the early modern period, and with which Wicca is still associated in the minds of some detractors. Much of it draws on traditions of folk magic, practices associated with the lay piety and popular devotionalism of Catholicism, both past and present. Other practices draw on the sacramental magic of orthodox Christianity, though with the difference in intent that it was claimed separated priestcraft and witchcraft in the sixteenth century. But in spiritual alchemy, the third type of magic, Wicca uses magic for religious and spiritual purposes, and in so doing collapses the boundaries between priestcraft and witchcraft, between religion and magic. The process and experience of invocation outlined in Chapter 4 is a case in point. Is it supplication to (i.e. religious) or coercion of (i.e. magical) a deity? In terms of its similarities with Jane Ellen Harrison's characterisation of Greek worship, it is clearly religious. In terms of invoking and calling upon a god or goddess 'to descend into the body of [the] servant and priest/ess' (Crowley, Vivianne, 1990a: 61; see pp. 71–2), it might be deemed a magical coercion. In this sense, it could be compared with the 'magic' thought by some Protestant reformers to be used by Roman Catholic priests invoking the Spirit into a 'host', which then becomes the body of Christ. That the people performing the act of invocation in Wicca are initiated as priests and priestesses as well as witches collapses the boundaries still further. It is therefore necessary to question the constructed opposition of religion and magic, priestcraft and witchcraft.

In Medieval Europe, magic and religion were intertwined and boundaries between the two were fluid and permeable. This was so not just in the minds of the uneducated majority of the population, but also in the magico-religious practices of the clergy[25] and late medieval/early modern Christian ritual magicians such as Marsilio Ficino (1433–99),[26] Giovanni Pico della Mirandola (1463–94)[27] and Giordano Bruno (1548–1600).[28] In 1460, a Greek manuscript containing part of the *Corpus Hermeticum*[29] was brought to Cosimo de Medici in Florence by the monk Leonardo of Pistoia. Ficino, a physician and scholar and later to become a canon of Florence cathedral (1487), immediately interrupted his translation into Latin of all Plato's dialogues to begin translating the manuscript. Around the same time, refugees from the expulsion of the Jews from Spain in 1492 brought the Jewish Kabbalah to Florence. Ficino was able not only to translate the *Corpus Hermeticum* but to experiment with its contents, along with Kabbalah. Nevertheless, such heterodox 'dabbling in the occult' was a serious and dangerous business. Ficino's student, the Italian humanist Pico della Mirandola, earned the condemnation of Pope Innocent VIII for his use of the Kabbalah to support Christian theology, and was forced to seek the protection of Lorenzo de Medici in Florence. But the fertile marriage of Egyptian, Greek and Jewish thought had produced 'a practical, spiritual "way" – an attempt to understand the self, the world and the divine' (Fowden, 1986: xvi, cited in Orion, 1995: 80).

The Western Esoteric Tradition thus emerged in Renaissance Florence at the end of the fifteenth century, a time when the 'churning turbid flood of Hermetic, cabalistic, Gnostic, theurgic, Sabean, Pythagorean and generally mystical notions ... broke over Europe ... carrying everything before it' (de Santillana, 1965: 455, cited in Hudson, 1994: 9). In this crucible, ancient materials, Christianity, Judaism and Islam were regarded by men such as Ficino to be mutually complementary, perceiving that systems of thought could be combined together to form one homogeneous whole.[30] For example, in 1486 Pico della Mirandola offered to prove in public debate in Rome that his 900 theses drawn from all philosophies were reconcilable with one another. The debate never took place, but Pico's thoughts were obviously at home in the Renaissance climate which Faivre, in his introduction to Faivre and Needleman's *Modern Esoteric Spirituality* ([1992] 1993: xiii), describes as an 'illuminated atmosphere in which analogical thinking prevails and ... in which harmony was more or less universal'.

The will of people like Pico della Mirandola to seek common denominators within this corpus transformed the *prisca theologia* of the Middle Ages into the *philosophia perennis* and the *philosophia occulta*, terms which were (and are) not interchangeable, but which designated 'a relatively autonomous nebula in the mental universe of the time, one which was detached from theology per se' (Faivre and Voss, 1995: 50–1). Thus on the one hand, the *philosophia perennis* became 'Tradition', constituted by a chain of mythical or historical representatives including Zoroaster, Hermes Trismegistos, Moses, Orpheus, the Sibyls, Pythagoras and Plato.[31] The *philosophia occulta*, on the other hand, emerged in Hermeticism and Christian Kabbalah as an autonomous body of reference which came to be seen as 'esoteric' *vis-à-vis* the official 'exoteric' Christian religion, whether it be a variant of Protestantism or Catholicism. This, Faivre and Voss argue (1995: 51), is 'the true starting point for what we designate ... "esotericism"'. Such an esotericism had been unnecessary during the Middle Ages, when the paradigms of metaphysics and cosmology were embedded in theology,[32] but

> when the sciences of Nature freed themselves from theology, they began to be cultivated for themselves ... . Henceforth the esoteric field could be constituted, which in the Renaissance began to deal with the interface between metaphysics and cosmology, i.e., to function as an extratheological modality for linking the universal to the particular.
>
> (Faivre, 1994: 8)

But it was the apostate Dominican from Nola, near Naples, Giordano Bruno, who lived life most dangerously. Bruno was a magician who believed that the Egyptian 'religion of the world' was purer than either Catholicism or Protestantism, although he sought for its return within a reformed Catholicism. Egyptianism runs throughout Bruno's work, as he took magic back to its pagan source rather than attempting to reconcile it with Christianity. Bruno took the idea of divinity in nature and developed it into a 'nature religion' designed to replace the warring sects of Christians, and he portrayed the witch as transformer of society in *Cantus Circaeus* (1582) and *Spaccio della bestia trionfante* (1584), some 300 years before Michelet's 1862 rendition of the same theme in *La Sorcière*.[33] His visit to Oxford University in 1583, where he identified himself as a Ficinian magus and debated hermetic magic, was not well received. He bitterly complained of the Oxford doctors as humanist, 'grammarian pedants' who failed to understand philosophy and thought he was mad to suggest that the earth moves round the sun.[34] He was, according to Frances Yates, 'a Hermetic Magus of a most extreme kind with a magico-religious mission of which Copernicanism was a symbol. ... Madly impossible in a Protestant country ... [and bringing] him to the stake in Counter Reformation Rome' (Yates, 1991: 168).[35] These are just three well-known examples of Renaissance theologians who not only engaged with, but helped to formulate, learned magic – what Yates dubbed the 'hermetic-cabbalist tradition' of the Renaissance. And it was their Christianisation of older Greek, Egyptian, Gnostic and Jewish magical currents that provided the ritual framework for the Golden Dawn, Crowley, Fortune, and Wicca.

The obvious difference between the three magicians is that only Bruno lived in Europe as it underwent the various Protestant and Catholic reformations, and only he was executed for his beliefs and practices. As discussed in Chapter 4, Catholic sacramental ritual and devotional practices were denounced as magical by Protestant reformers. The differentiation between religion and magic had already begun. Indeed, as Keith Thomas noted,

> the conventional distinction between a prayer and a spell seems to have been first hammered out, not by the nineteenth-century anthropologists, with whom it is usually associated, but by sixteenth-century Protestant theologians.
>
> (Thomas, [1971] 1991: 69)

The initial focus of such theologians had been the Mass, but it soon widened to encompass the whole of Roman Catholicism. In 1591, the Puritan William Perkins was sure that 'if a man will but take a view of all Popery, he shall easily see that a great part of it is mere magic' (Perkins, 1591, cited in Thomas, [1971] 1991: 27). This 'mere magic', by the beginning of the eighteenth century, had become more specifically an 'entire system of anti-Christian magic' (Defoe, 1727: 352, cited in Thomas, [1971] 1991: 68–9) to Daniel Defoe, as 'Catholic miracles were confidently attributed to witchcraft' (Thomas, [1971] 1991: 68). But the Mass remained at the heart of Catholic magic. Developing the Protestant claims regarding the Eucharist to include twentieth century theories of magic, H. L. Mencken characterised the Mass as follows:

> [h]ere we have all the characteristics of a magical act, as experts set them forth: the suspension of natural laws, the transmutation of a material substance, the use of a puissant verbal formula, and the presence of an adept.
>
> (Mencken, 1930: 31)

The barely audible mumbling of this verbal formula was to be replaced by the Word of the gospel clearly preached by Protestant *ministers*, who were to replace the *priest* and his craft. The 'belief in the profound interconnectedness of supernatural forces and the body' (ibid.) which characterised pre-Reformation Catholic theology and folk magical practices was to be disrupted as the carnivalesque lower body gave way to the rational upper body[36] in 'a radical disjuncture between flesh and spirit' (Roper, 1994: 181). What was perceived as magic now had to be disentangled from religion, and there was to be no more of what Zwingli called 'bread worship'.[37] Magic was now seen as a coercive ritual, religion as intercessory; spells and prayers, magic and religion, were to be seen as distinct activities,[38] carried out by distinct groups of people. Magic had become something done by the 'Other' – the Jew, the witch, the woman, the foreigner, and now, the Catholic.

This 'othering' of the magical was not new. It had been associated with ignorance, irrationality, nomadic lifestyles, and 'the East' in ancient Greek thought, which sought to divorce conceptual doctrines such as the Platonic notion of the immortality of the soul from their possible origins.[39] Simon During has argued that '[t]he West's longstanding image of the East as a home of irrationality may be accounted for partly by the transmission of ancient magics westward' (During, 2002: 5), with Heraclitus (c.500 BCE) scorning it as exotic as early as the fifth century BCE. Magic was contrasted with philosophy and empiricism, and Plutarch (c.49–125) 'dismissed magical practices as symptoms of weakness' (During, 2002: 6). Magic, after all, hailed from 'the East'. It emerged in Chaldea (southern Babylonia) and its full flowering was, arguably, in Egypt, a land reputed to be a nest of magic. The representatives of the *philosophia perennis* were Zoroaster and Hermes Trismegistos before we get to Greeks such as Plato and Orpheus. Its name is that given to the Persian *magoi* by the ancient Greeks in the fifth and fourth centuries, though '*magos, mageia* and cognates never became really popular in later Greek culture.[40] The Romans ... used *magia, magicus* and *magus/maga* much more frequently than the Greeks ever did' (Bremmer, 2002: 11). Magic was linked, derogatively, with false healing, charlatanism and 'barbarous' songs, *magoi* being 'purifiers and begging priests and humbugs', in an anonymous treatise ascribed to Hippocrates (ibid.: 3–5).

In the context of late Medieval Catholicism, the 'theurgy' or white magic associated with Plato and Orpheus was acceptable, however, and indeed it developed in the Neoplatonic revival of the Renaissance. Practical magic was able to flourish within traditions in which 'the divine order is so disjunct from the human order that communication across the two can happen only as a mystery' (ibid.: 7), and where the living world is one soul, *anima mundi*, bound together by forces of sympathy and correspondence, manifestations of divine love. Thus, although magic was dangerous and open to abuse, it also existed as part of wisdom or mystery traditions and philosophies, infused with Christianity under the Renaissance scholars discussed above.

The so-called 'voyages of discovery' which began in the same era encouraged a related 'blackening' of the magical arts. As had been the case in ancient Greece, irrationality was regarded as the preserve of the outsider, the other, when compared with the 'rational' West. As During argues,

> European expansion, especially into Africa, perpetuated the old division between 'white' magic and pagan or diabolical magics. A patina of racism intruded into the 'blackness' of black magic, which now also connoted skin colour. The old terms 'necromancy' (literally, magic conjuring up the dead) and 'negromancy' (black or malevolent divination) had been used interchangeably in the medieval period, and the linguistic accident which tied death to blackness would be exploited, perhaps unknowingly, by colonialist discourse.
>
> (During, 2002: 10)

Later theories of magic and observations of its practitioners have been 'tinged by Orientalist scorn' (ibid.: 5). Since the rationalising critique of the Enlightenment – emerging from Protestant attacks on Catholicism – tended to see all magic as grounded in superstition and ignorance, it is not surprising that early academic engagements with magic continued in this vein. The budding discipline of anthropology repeated those very same arguments against magic as the Protestant reformers had repeated from Greek and Roman scorn: it is primitive, irrational, exotic, fascinating, ignorant, superstitious and 'other', and all have been discredited as projections of Western ethnocentrism.[41] Tylor, Frazer and, later, Marcel Mauss (1872–1950), in *A General Theory of Magic* (1905), 'systematized the magic/reason opposition and inserted it into an implicitly colonialist theory of history and society' (During, 2002: 16), in which the civilised and the primitive are as different from each other as reason is from magic. Science, after all, had replaced magic (and, arguably, religion) in the evolutionary scheme of things, becoming both its destroyer and, as 'magic which actually works', its substitute (ibid.: 20). Western magicians were effectively marginalised in the discourses of intellectual imperialism, which placed magic – the 'other' – in the past, ignoring its contemporaneity, as it sought to formulate authoritative knowledge. Only 'primitives' with no knowledge of the explanations of science could still believe in a unique and unfathomable magic.

The modern concept of magic thus evolved from antiquity, formulated as Christianity defined its boundaries in order to distinguish itself from its Jewish parent and from the influence of the pagan mystery religions. According to H. S. Versnel, it

> acquired its definitive Western connotations under the double influence of a comparable theological conflict between Protestants and Roman Catholics in the sixteenth century and the subsequent evolution of Western scientific ideas.
>
> (Versnel, 1991: 180)

Such a wholly Western, biased concept was always unsuitable for use in the study of non-Western cultures, 'where similar dichotomies cannot always be demonstrated, either terminologically or conceptually' (ibid.). This is not, however, the entire problem, for anthropological concepts of magic applied to the study of 'primitive' societies are equally unsuited to the interpretation of magical practices amongst contemporary Western people. Not only has magic as a phenomenon been dominated by orientalism throughout its history, but also the academic study of magic, when applied to 'primitive' societies, has been inherently colonial, and this colonialism has mutated into intellectual imperialism when magic in the contemporary West has come under academic scrutiny. Criticisms of evolutionary theories of magic have come predominantly from anthropologists and sociologists concerned with the applicability of Western concepts of magic to non-Western peoples, resulting in a 'confusing spectrum of divergent theories' (ibid.: 181). Anthropologists such as Stanley Tambiah and Tanya Luhrmann have concurred, becoming concerned not with the applicability of Western concepts of magic to non-Western peoples, but with the inadequacy of anthropological paradigms of magic applied to the study of 'primitive' societies for the interpretation of magical practices in literate, post-industrial Western societies. As Tambiah notes,

> [i]f the distinctions between religion and sacramental magic, between prayer and spell, between sovereign deity and manipulable divine being, were the product of a specific historical epoch in European history and its particular preoccupations stemming from Judaeo-Christian concepts and concerns, can these same categories (embedded in and stemming from an historical context) fruitfully serve as universal, analytical categories and illuminate the texture of other cultures and societies?[42]
>
> (Tambiah, 1999: 20–1)

Academia had essentialised the magic-religion opposition, and in so doing reified complex structures of ideas and practices,[43] ignoring or dismissing Western magic and denying its location in the history of Western discourses. Magic has been policed 'in the interests of maintaining religious or civic norms' (During, 2002: 27). It has been analysed in relation to religion and science/rationality, regarded as an indicator of deviance – particularly in its occult manifestations – or as a badge of resistance to rational culture, or regarded as purely psychological. Magic has been colonised – tamed, subsumed, demystified, normalised, 'rationalised'. It is not only the wisdom, learning, and cultures of subaltern peoples which have been ignored, dismissed, neglected, and looted by colonising powers – there has also been a suppression of certain types of Western knowledge/gnosis by the imperialists of the academy.

As a result, in academic disciplines such as anthropology, sociology and religious studies at the start of the twentieth century, magic was 'relegated' to the study of so-called 'primitive' peoples. This obtained until the 1960s, when attitudes towards so many assumptions were being challenged. Rosalie and Murray Wax, for example, proposed in 1963 that magic can best be understood as a worldview rather than as a rite or a cult, a worldview which is distinctive from the rational worldviews of Western science or Judaeo-Christian religion, but which is itself 'a sensible, coherent system of thought and action employed by practical and intelligent people' (1963: 502). Jan van Baal (1963) likewise placed an emphasis on magic as a participatory worldview, and urged a focus on what magic expresses rather than on its supposed results. Van Baal regarded magic as part of religion whilst maintaining manageable distinctions which he claimed were ideal-typical and pragmatic rather than absolute and rigid. More recently, the study of magic has become a necessary part of the study of modern witchcraft, Wicca,

Paganism, and magical practice in Western, post-industrial, literate societies. Contemporary researchers such as Wouter Hanegraaff (1998), Richard Sutcliffe (1996) and Sarah Pike (1996) have all written about magic as a participatory practice, Hanegraaff linking magic historically to esotericism and Sutcliffe regarding it as a form of gnostic spirituality within the broader spectrum of the Western Esoteric Tradition, a spirituality which is radically individualistic and aimed at self-transmutation.

'The true purpose of all magic', according to Vivianne Crowley (1996: 200), 'is transformation. This can be transformation of the outer world but, more importantly, it is transformation of the inner world that is the aim'. Sutcliffe (1996: 112) stresses this transformation, stating that 'the practice of ritual magick constitutes a specific and radical project of auto-poesis (self-creation), which has as its ultimate aim the transmutation of the self'. The goals of Wiccan magic, especially the third type – the Great Work or spiritual alchemy – can be conflated with those of Wiccan religious rituals which are themselves imbued with magic. Far from operating as 'the employment of ineffective techniques to allay anxiety when effective ones are not available' (Thomas, [1971] 1991: 800), magic in Wicca is understood in a similar way to that portrayed in the Renaissance. Magic is not set in opposition to religion, but rather is an important element of spiritual growth towards the mystical attainment of gnosis, with any short-term pragmatic goals being secondary to this end result, the experience of transmutation which, as noted earlier, produces 'insight into the hidden mysteries of cosmos, self and God' (Hanegraaff, 1995a: 112) and allows 'no separation between knowledge (gnosis) and inner experience, or intellectual activity and active imagination' (Faivre, 1994: 13). In terms of Wiccan understanding, magic has been transformed from a contra-religious, instrumental means of control practised by individuals, to a participative, group practice which forms an integral part of religion. In all its understandings of magic, Wicca thus draws on the spiritual legacy of such Christian mystics as Jacob Böehme (1575–1624), to whom is given the last word. In his 1620 work *Sex Puncta Mystica or A Short Explanation of Six Mystical Points*, Böehme's fifth point, 'On Magic', has words for both the academic and the theologian, and makes no distinction between magic and religion. Rather,

22. Magic is the book of all scholars. All that will learn must first learn Magic, be it a high or a lowly art. Even the peasant in the field must go to the magical school if he would cultivate his field.

23. Magic is the best theology, for in it true faith is both grounded and found. And he is a fool that reviles it; for he knows it not, and blasphemes against God and himself, and is more a juggler than a theologian of understanding.

(Böehme, [1620] 1989: www.facsicle.com/issue02/imagining-language/bohme3.html, accessed 4 January 2007)

AFTERWORD: THE
CHRISTIAN HERITAGE?

Wicca and the Christian Heritage has explored an aspect of Wicca's history that has been disregarded, unacknowledged or ignored. Its concern has been with those elements within marginal variants of Christianity on which Gardner may have drawn in his formulation of Wicca. It has detailed the little-known stories of the heterodox churches set up by *episcopi vagantes* in nineteenth- and twentieth-century England, Wales and France, as well as the more widely known developments of the Oxford Movement, Anglo-Catholicism and Ritualism. It has traced the influences of the terminology of 'the old religion', the emphasis on lines of succession, and the revival of ritual. Perhaps most clearly, the concentration of priests and bishops within the heterodox churches is reflected in the initiation of all Wiccans as priestesses and priests. That the notion of Wicca as a priesthood remains under-explored[1] is largely a result of the continuing over-emphasis on the concept of witchcraft, which itself is central to the idea of Wicca and Christianity as antithetical and mutually exclusive. In bringing the two together in order to explore a fraction of Wicca's heritage, this book may have come as a surprise to many Christians, as well as some Wiccans. Gardner himself, however, recognised a place in which the two could meet, and seems to have thought this to be impossible only with regard to institutionalised, orthodox versions of Christianity.

Orthodoxy, of course, is usually less about right belief than it is about winning, and then suppressing the loser.[2] The valuing of those ideas that did not win and which were assigned to the margins, suggests that a critical and alternative marginal identity might be attractive. This attraction may explain the overlapping membership of Christian heterodox churches and other groups marginalised according to the dictates of orthodox hegemony in Western Europe – the occult and esoteric subcurrents and, in England and France, Roman Catholicism. Masonic Lodges possibly provided the central meeting grounds. The use of ritual links them all, whether magical, religious or secular, and Wicca benefits from this inheritance. Wicca also shares with these marginalised Christian groups and other secret societies accusations of sexual impropriety and magical manipulation. The persecutions of the past on which rest continued pejorative perceptions were visited upon the heterodox and heretical as much as they were on those accused of witchcraft.

But if heresy and witchcraft are constructs of the Christian imagination, then a Christianity that has been constructed as 'other' by some Wiccans is also a product of imagination. At worst it is characterised as an evangelical, bible-bashing monolith, or a tyrannical orthodoxy suppressing the heterodox margins; at best as irrelevant to Wiccan history and contemporary life. In such constructions, Christianity derides ritual, hates sex, oppresses women, and is decidedly anti-magic. The antagonisms between Christianity and Wicca may centre on the identificatory label 'witch', but they belie a wider association with the borderlands of Christianity which few are happy to inhabit.

The argument of *Wicca and the Christian Heritage* has not been that Wicca and Christianity – whether heterodox, Roman Catholic or Anglo-Catholic – are somehow interchangeable. To argue such a conflation is, as Hutton (2003c: 15) has suggested, 'more than bad history; it is bad manners'. Neither has its aim been to suggest that Wicca is a bastardised version of Christianity, as Woodhead's (1996) notion of Wicca as a 'new reformation' rather than a 'new religion' seems to suggest. Historical contingencies in the nineteenth century – aestheticism, the Gothic revival, Medievalism – provided a cultural matrix in which Christianity was bound up and which influenced the development of Wicca. But cultural influences filtered through a Christian culture can only partly be understood as derivative of Christianity itself, for they belong to the wider society and the borderlands between them are nothing if not permeable. But this does not negate their place in the history of Wicca. The influence of radical heterodoxy and Anglo-Catholicism may constitute only the smallest ingredient in the cauldron of inspiration from which Wicca emerged, but it is an ingredient that enriches the mix and without it the result may well have been decidedly different.

NOTES

PREFACE

1 Luhrmann, 1989, 1994; Greenwood, 2000.
2 Harvey, 1997; Hume, 1997; Greenwood, 1996, 2000; Salomonsen, 2002.
3 Hutton, 1999.
4 Tiryakian, 1974; Truzzi, 1974.
5 Berger, 1999.
6 An exception to this is Salomonsen, 2002.
7 In particular, Éliphas Lévi, Papus, Arthur Edward Waite, Lady Caithness, Anna Kingsford, Annie Besant, W.B. Crow and Dion Fortune, of whom the first five were Roman Catholic, either lapsed or practising.
8 See Pearson, 2003a.
9 See, for example, Berman, 1990; Brown, 2001; Bruce, 2002; Dunstan, 2006; Owen, 2004; Weber, 1988; Wilson, 1999.
10 See, for example, Godwin, 1994; Hutton, 1999; Owen, 2004.
11 My concern here is with Catholicism in the era up to and preceding the emergence of Gardner's Wicca, rather than with studies of the tensions between Catholics and Protestants in Northern Ireland, for example.

INTRODUCTION

1 Scholarship on the history of Wicca has not yet identified its precise origins or the part played by Gerald Gardner in the process of its formulation (see Hutton, 1999 and Heselton, 2000, 2003). Nevertheless, it has been well-established that Gardner was the key figure in the appearance of Wicca.
2 'Wica' with one 'c' is the original spelling used by Gardner in *Witchcraft Today* and in *The Meaning of Witchcraft*. This may have been as a result of the dyslexia from which he allegedly suffered. In any case the more accurate spelling of Wicca has now been universally accepted.
3 See Chapter 1.
4 Sanders was regarded by many Gardnerians as something of a maverick, bringing Wicca into disrepute. Over time, however, it was recognised that the Alexandrian stream of Wicca was as valid as the Gardnerian, and the rifts started to heal. In 1989, nine months after the death of Alex Sanders, the editors of the Pagan Federation journal *The Wiccan* announced an end to hostilities:

> our members include not only 'Elders' ... from Gerald Gardner's original covens of the 1950s, their continuations and daughter covens, but Witches from other traditions, both newer and older; even, amazing as it may seem to original readers, many Alexandrians. Whoever is of good will, who loves

Nature, and who worships both the Goddess and the God, is welcome in our Federation, and the current started in the 1960s by that old ritual magician A. Sanders has stood the test of time.

(*The Wiccan*, 91, February 1989: 2)

5 In which, for a joke, Sanders and his coven staged a black mass.
6 The fact that it has spread in the far-northern and far-southern hemispheres perhaps indicates its relevance to those of a Protestant background.
7 The American Anglican Bishop, John Shelby Spong also argues for a reconsideration of the Christian liturgical year in the southern hemisphere in order to make it more appropriate to the seasons. He writes,

[p]erhaps the Christian part of the southern hemisphere will someday free itself from the European imposed liturgical connection of the birth of Jesus with December 25th ... and begin to celebrate his birth as light coming into the world's darkness in late June, which would be *its* winter solstice.

(Spong, 2002: 210)

8 See Rountree, 2004.
9 See Gallagher, 2000.
10 Orion (1995: 143) lists several differences, including a less formal and hierarchical ritual style which is more inventive and celebratory, Native American influences such as shamanism and drumming, the superimposition of psychotherapy onto Wicca, and the application of Wicca to political activism.
11 See Salomonsen, 2002: 7–8.
12 Hutton, 1999: 401.
13 See Hutton, 1999: 400.
14 See Crowley, 1994; Pengelly *et al.*, 1997: 23.
15 Such as when Frederic Lamond, a long-standing Wiccan priest, suggested that Wiccans should 'be available as priests to the Pagan community when needed' (Lamond, 1997). Wiccan priests and priestesses do not tend to consider themselves 'clergy' to a Pagan 'laity', but the perception that this is indeed how they think of themselves can create hostility.
16 This is well-documented – Doreen Valiente openly stated in *The Rebirth of Witchcraft* that she rewrote much of Gardner's material, replacing that which was obviously Crowley's with her own poetry (1989: 60–1). Gardner's Wiccan Rede is too similar to Crowley's Law of Thelema to be coincidental, and Crowley's blessing of the cakes from the Gnostic Mass has also been adopted (compare, for instance, Vivianne Crowley, 1996: 118 with Aleister Crowley, Liber XV). His invocation 'by seed and root and stem and bud and leaf and flower' has been incorporated verbatim (see Chapter 4), and Valiente's 'Charge of the Goddess' was rewritten from an earlier Charge contained in Crowley's Gnostic Mass, which he in turn took from Leland's *Aradia*. Hutton (2007) traces the influence of Crowley on Gardner's formulation of Wicca; my thanks to him for supplying me with a draft of this chapter prior to publication.
17 See, amongst others, Godwin, 1994; relevant entries in Hanegraaff *et al.*, 2005; Hutton, 1999; Pearson, 2002b.
18 See, for example, Rob Hardy (1997: 21) who would 'hope to see the Craft keep its individuality and not be swallowed up by general Paganism'. Also the (anonymous) comment published in the article entitled 'Defing Paganism and Wicca', *The Wiccan*, 94, p. 10, October 1989: 'All Wiccans are Pagans, but not all Pagans are Wiccans. Nor should they be, any more than all Xtians [sic] should be monks or nuns. The way of the mystic is not the way of everyday life, and to pretend otherwise is sloppy thinking and false psychology'.

19 Mary Daly (1981: 221) argued that, 'to limit the term [witch] only to those who have esoteric knowledge of and participation in "the Craft" is ... reductionism'. It is a fact that 'witch' and 'witchcraft' are not limited to those initiated into Wicca. However, Wicca does require initiation into, and the practice of, an esoteric mystery religion, and the two terms can and do refer to different entities.

20 No doubt figures will have diverged further during the past seven years.

21 See, for example, Telesco, 1994 and West, 2002; Ravenwolf, 2003 and Horne, 2002; La Vey, 2003 and Ford, 2005; Hardie and Morris, 1998 and Hardie, 1998a, 1998b.

22 Cyber witches, Jewitches and Christian witches could also be added to this list.

23 For analysis of witchcraft and consumerism see Ezzy, 2006, 2003, 2001.

24 An exception to this is the excellent study of feminist witches in New Zealand by Kathryn Rountree, 2004.

25 See Pearson, 2002a, 2007.

26 Thomas (1971) and Cohn (1975) fractured Murray's thesis, yet twenty years on, at a conference on the trials held at the University of Exeter in 1991, Sir Keith Thomas 'told participants that he despaired that the public would ever forsake the mythology which had grown out of the work of Murray and her predecessors and followers [and] [h]is statement met with widespread sympathy and assent' (Hutton, 1999: 362).

27 Also noted by Hutton, 1999: 361.

28 Prior to the 1990s, introductions to and chapters in books written by practitioners presented the accepted (and acceptable) mythic history, contrary to the claims that such histories had been disintegrating since the 1970s. This way of reading and writing the imagined past was repeated throughout the 1970s and 1980s – see for example Crowley, 1989; Farrar and Farrar, 1981 and Starhawk, 1989: 16–22. It continues in some more recent practitioner publications, for example Moura, 2000. Hutton (1999: 215) warns, '[t]here is a real danger that as modern witches acquire more knowledge of their history without all of them also acquiring a greater sense of historical relativism, then the misinformation is only going to become more sophisticated'.

29 This is certainly how Hutton perceived their reaction. He says (2003b: 281), 'they have tended to ignore my work completely and to carry on writing as though it had never appeared, as successive articles in recent issues of magazines such as *The Cauldron* evince'.

30 And reiterated in paraphrased form 2003b: 280, 284.

31 Hutton's comment follows from his anxiety that he has 'probably failed to include [aspects of nineteenth- and twentieth-century British culture] which will later prove to have significance' for the history of modern Pagan witchcraft (1999: xi). However, during the course of the book, Hutton does go on to discuss spiritualism in relation to Blavatsky, feminism, Dion Fortune and Alex Sanders. In my own work, I have previously stressed the importance of spiritualism in the repeal of the 1736 Witchcraft Act in 1951 (see Pearson, 2002a: 197), and the role of spiritualism in the occult revival of the *fin de siècle*, and the religious milieu of that period generally has certainly not been relegated to the realms of the 'invisible' (see Godwin, 1994; Webb, 1971, 1976; Adler, 1986).

32 Spiritualists and their supporters were seeking religious freedom to practice their beliefs, and this was noted by various Labour MPs. For example, Mr Monslow, Labour MP for Barrow-in-Furness argued, 'for over half a century the spiritualist movement had been seeking to have accorded to it what was accorded to other religious denominations – religious freedom', and the Labour MP for Normanton, Mr T. Brooks, firmly believed that the replacement of the 1736 Witchcraft Act with the Fraudulent Mediums Act 'would help to remove a

real grievance and indignity which the spiritualists had suffered for many years' (Rights of Spiritualists', *The Times*, 21 April 1951: 5).

33 See Gardner, (1959) 2004: 256.

34 Including the Liberal Catholic Church (see Chapter 2) and the Ordo Templi Orientis (see Chapter 3).

1 ENGLAND'S 'OLD RELIGIONS'

1 *c*.603, Augustine along with Ethelbert, King of Kent, sought to reach an agreement with representatives of the remnant of the ancient Celtic Church that had survived the incursions of the Saxons in the fifth century. Having been cut off from communications with Rome and the continent, they were at variance with Rome on points of discipline and practice, and Augustine's attempt at reconciliation failed. Agreement was not effected until the Synod of Whitby in 664.

2 For the myth of the English Reformation as portrayed by the nineteenth-century Tractarians, see MacCulloch, 1991.

3 Cranmer adopted an increasingly Protestant line, especially after Henry's death, adopting a Zwinglian standpoint on the Eucharist and seeking union with the reforming churches of Europe. He was largely responsible for the abolition of church ceremonial and the destruction of images and relics, as well as authoring the 1549 and 1552 Books of Common Prayer. Under Mary, Cranmer was tried for heresy and recanted, affirming belief in transubstantiation and Papal supremacy. On renouncing these recantations, he was burned at the stake in Oxford on 21 March 1556.

4 Cromwell served Cardinal Wolsey from 1514 and succeeded him as Henry VIII's chief adviser in 1531, presiding over the king's divorce from Catherine of Aragon and overseeing the break with Rome. Cromwell arranged the visitations and then dissolution of the monasteries, and attempted to ally England with the Protestant princes of Germany via the marriage of Henry to his fourth wife, Anne of Cleves. It was a marriage that so disgusted Henry – he referred to Anne as the 'Flanders mare' – however, that it was annulled within six months and Cromwell was tried for treason and beheaded on 28 July 1540. Henry had sought out Catholic nobles such as Marie de Guise and Christina of Milan, and indeed his fifth wife, Catherine Howard, was of one of the oldest English Catholic families. Cromwell's dream of a Protestant alliance was a total failure.

5 As Yates (2000: 11) asserts, the Elizabethan Acts of Supremacy and Uniformity (1559) 'disguised a good deal of religious confusion'.

6 It has often been noted how little opposition there was to the dissolution of the monasteries. In Glastonbury, for example, the dissolving of the Abbey was more a relief than a reason to riot, and the town subsequently became a hotbed of Protestant radicalism, the Abbey kitchen being preserved and used as a Quaker meeting house (see Hutton, 2003a: 62). Yet the Pilgrimage of Grace was a protest against the closure of the northern monasteries, for many were considered to be better landlords than the secular landowners.

7 Thomas Bell, *Thomas Bel's motives: ...*, London, 1593, STC.1830: 9, cited in Wiener, 1971: 49.

8 Though there is no doubt that this was the crunch. Until the question of his divorce, Henry VIII was a staunch and conservative Catholic, who had defended Catholic orthodoxy against Luther in his treatise on the seven sacraments, for which the title Defender of the Faith was conferred on him by Pope Leo X in 1521. Ironically, the title was recognised by Parliament as an official title of the English monarch in 1544, by which time the faith being defended, though

not Lutheran, was far from orthodox Catholic. The title has been borne by all subsequent – Protestant – monarchs.

9   This is not to suggest that it did so gently; undeniably, the English reformations were revolutionary in character. The point is, however, that they were not to be *seen* as revolutionary, but rather as a continuation of England's pure and untainted past which obtained until the corruption of the papacy during the Middle Ages.

10 As Carol Wiener points out:

> Outwardly given to mocking at Roman rites and ceremonies, many sensed the tremendous persuasive powers which these ancient traditions held for the majority of men ... awe created by the customs of the old Church – customs whose psychological efficacy Protestantism could not match.
>
> (Wiener, 1971: 44)

11 Hence the problems noted regarding the continued use of 'the new religion' as a label for Protestantism. See Barnett, 1999, 'Where was your church before Luther?'.

12 Without the 1533 Act, the monarch could not be supreme, absolute ruler. If appeals could be made to Rome from England, as elsewhere in Europe, then the law of the universal church retained jurisdiction and the Pope would still have supremacy in spiritual and ecclesiastical matters.

13 Act in Restraint of Appeals, 1533, 24 Henry VIII.c.12.3S.R.427.

14 Ibid. II.

15 Literally, the traditional, ancient church.

16 This being burned down in the fire of 1184, but the site of which was reputed to be where the remains of the Lady Chapel now stand.

17 According to Barnett (1999: 20), this legend was included in early drafts of the preamble to the 1533 Act in Restraint of Appeals.

18 This seems often to have been a causal factor. Lagorio (1971: 210) identifies 'certain constants' in the shaping of monastic legends: 'a period of crisis or rehabilitation, a desire to reflect glory on the monastery and also to promote pilgrimages, the borrowing of available materials to supplement pious belief, and monastic creativity coupled with opportunism'. These constants can also be seen in Cromwell: the crisis constituted by Henry's divorce and the resulting reformation; the desire to reflect glory on England and promote it as a nation; the borrowing of available materials to supplement claims for a continuation of England's Christian past and detract from the break with Catholic Europe, and Cromwell's own creativity.

19 Barnett, 1999: 16. Indeed, only those passages also occurring in the third recension of Malmesbury's *Gesta regum* are indisputably his. Hutton (2003a: 69) suggests that the tale of Joseph bringing the Holy Grail to the 'vaus d'Avaron' was told in Robert de Boron's *Joseph d'Arimathie* and was extant before 1200, was then identified with the Arthurian Avalon (which Glastonbury had claimed to be since 'finding' the tombs of Arthur and Guinevere in 1191), and by 1250 Joseph had been claimed as Glastonbury's apostolic founder by a series of interpolations in Malmesbury's *De Antiquitate* (Lagorio, 1971: 216). Such claims still exist: in its guidebook, the Abbey (under Church of England control since it bought the site in 1907) continues to claim a history from the first century CE, and the cross of oak situated in the grounds, presented to the Abbey by Queen Elizabeth II in 1965, is inscribed: 'A Christian sanctuary so ancient that only legend can record its origin'. Websites exist, such as Palden Jenkins' 'Of Nazareth and Arimathaea' on http://www.isleofavalon.co.uk/avalon-mysteries4.html (accessed January 2006 and 14 March 2006) which stretches the legend further with the claim that

Jesus visited Glastonbury as a boy with Joseph of Arimathea, and contains many historical inaccuracies, including the claim that Glastonbury Abbey was the last to be dissolved, some two years after all the others (in fact, Waltham Abbey was the last to be dissolved, in March 1549, four months after Glastonbury). See also Lagorio, 1971 and Crawford, 1993, 1994. The persistence of the legend and Glastonbury's claims to antiquity are also attested to by the Anglican and Roman Catholic pilgrimages to the Abbey, which were revived after the First World War and continue to be held each July.

20 Lagorio writes,

> According to traditional belief, from the earliest era of Christianity, Great Britain was a stronghold of the faith, with all of the myriad legends pointing to its origin in the land of the Britons, centuries before the coming of Augustine in 597.
>
> (Lagorio, 1971: 212–13)

21 Indeed, perhaps not until his lifetime. As Lagorio points out (1971: 217, 228), Joseph was a relatively unknown saint, appearing only briefly in the Bible and in the apocryphal *Gospel of Nicodemus*. In addition, the English people of the thirteenth century were largely unaware of the Grail romances, and therefore Joseph's connection with England and with Arthur was not made in their minds. It was not until William Caxton's printed version of Malory's *Morte d'Arthur* in 1485 that the combined legend of Glastonbury, Joseph and Arthur was widely disseminated throughout England, and a life of Joseph only appeared in the third edition of the *Nova Legenda Angliae* printed in 1516. It was with this last that 'Joseph and the Glastonbury legend received ecclesiastical and national recognition' (ibid.: 228).

22 Later accretions to the legend included the claim, by 1677, that the hawthorns which flowered at midwinter were brought by Joseph. This is despite the fact that the thorn was chopped down by an Elizabethan puritan, by which time it had plenty of offshoots. By 1715, the original tree was said to have sprouted miraculously from his staff. By 1886, the Chalice Well was owned by a Roman Catholic Seminary and it was claimed that Joseph had buried the cup used at the Last Supper there, causing a red spring to appear at the site. See Hutton, 2003a: 62–3.

23 He also had a new crypt built beneath the Lady Chapel as a shrine to Joseph of Arimathea.

24 Primarily due to the punitive taxation levied on the abbey as a result of the West Country rising against the Crown.

25 In November 1539.

26 This was particularly important in terms of Anglo-French apostolic rivalry. The French claimed conversion either by Mary Magdalene, Martha and Lazarus, or by Dionysus the Areopagite (St Denis); whilst Joseph had been closely associated with Christ himself, St Denis could only claim a discipleship with St Paul (Acts xvii.34), 'thereby advancing England over France in terms of the authority as well as the antiquity of its faith' (Lagorio, 1971: 222). Such precedence over Catholic France remained important for the new Anglican Church.

27 John Bale, *The first two partes of the Actes*, 1: sigs. A5 – verso – A6. Cited in Fairfield, 1976: 95. See his *Vocacyon of Johân Bale*:

> He [Joseph of Arimathea] published there [in Britain] amonge them that Gospell of saluacion whiche Christe first of all and afterwardes hys Apostles had taught at Jerusalem ... From the schole of Christe himselfe haue we receyued the documentes of oure fayth. From Jerusalem and not from Rome

whom both Peter and also Christe hath called Babylon for that she so aptely thervnto agreeth in ministrying confusion to the world'.

(Bale, 1553 sig.B4v, cited in Barnett, 1999: 16)

28 Ibid. 1: sig.C1, in Fairfield, 1976: 95.
29 First published as *Commentarii Rerum in Ecclesia Gestarum* in Strasbourg, 1554, dealing almost entirely with English Lollards. An expanded version was published in Basle in 1559 as *Rerum in Ecclesia Gestarum*, listing recent victims in Mary's England.
30 Mark Greengrass, www.hrionline.ac.uk/foxe/foxe_project/Wx2/aim.html, accessed 13 March 2006.
31 Further editions continued to be published throughout the seventeenth century, rewritten to suit new agendas, 'and during the eighteenth century bowdlerised and adapted versions maintained the popular appeal of anticatholicism throughout the Enlightenment' (ibid.). In the nineteenth century, it became a focus in the conflict between the Evangelical revival and the Oxford Movement, the latter regarding Foxe as 'a malign influence who had poisoned the Catholic roots of English religion' (ibid.).
32 'While Foxe found [Protestant] identity in a negative history, a history of martyrdom and resistance to Catholic ecclesiastical structure, Parker searched for it precisely in the resistance of English ecclesiasts to foreign-imposed Catholic doctrine' (Robinson, 1998: 1082).
33 Indeed, it seems likely that Parker was consecrated under the Sarum Pontifical since Cranmer's ordinal of 1549/50 had been removed from the statutes under Mary and the older pontifical form restored as the only permissible form. The 1549 ordinals were not restored until later in Elizabeth's reign, and even then not as the 'only' form – the pontifical was not forbidden and could still be used legally for the consecration of an Archbishop of Canterbury, as well as the coronation of a monarch. The 1896 *Apostolicae Curae* of Leo XIII only referred to the validity of Anglican orders as affected by the practice of 1563–1662 – it does not refer to Parker.
34 Such a link was made explicit in the anonymously authored *The Book of Martyrs, or the History of Paganism and Popery*, published in 1764.
35 In *Of the Church* (1606); cited in Barnett, 1999:18.
36 From the 1570s, recusants were those who refused to recognise the Anglican Church and maintained their adherence to Rome. However, many of the penalties prescribed under the recusancy laws were so severe that many judges refused to implement them, and in certain areas of the country such as Lancashire, a strong Catholic following remained.
37 The 1778 Catholic Emancipation Act rewarded the loyalty of British Roman Catholics to the British cause in the ongoing war with America. However, Catholics were still denied the vote and full freedom of worship.
38 After the riots, Gordon was acquitted on a charge of high treason in 1781. He converted to Judaism and in 1793 died insane in Newgate prison.
39 The Act of Settlement of 1701 had prevented Catholics and anyone married to a Catholic from succeeding to the throne; thus, when Queen Anne died in 1714, Roman Catholics with a strong claim to the throne were passed over in favour of the staunchly Protestant Elector of Hanover, who succeeded as George I. Roman Catholics to this day are not permitted to succeed to the throne or act as regent, and are barred from certain high offices such as that of Lord Chancellor and Keeper of the Privy Seal. It will, of course, be interesting to see whether such barriers are finally removed if and when Prince Charles succeeds to the throne, given that Camilla is a Roman Catholic.

40 William Lambarde, an Elizabethan lawyer, characterised the Pope as the 'witch of the world', for example (Read, 1962: 101 cited in Thomas, 1991: 79). Of course, the reverse was also true, with Catholics inferring that Protestants were not only heretics but witches (Waite, 2003: 106–7), and the Jesuits in particular claiming that Calvinists specifically were agents of the Devil (ibid.: 105).

41 And indeed, still are on evangelical websites: 'If our Protestantism would slide back into Catholicism and witchcraft and paganism, it would be because we have forsaken the authority of the Word of God' (http://www.gospelchapel. com/Sermons/John/12.htm). See also http://www.cuttingedge.org/ce1059.html and http://www.remnantofgod.org/page6.htm#occult. I am not here including those who recognise elements of Catholicism and various forms of witchcraft or indigenous practices as syncretic, and therefore successfully combine them in traditions such as Santeria and Voodoo, Christo-paganism, or otherwise retain indigenous witchcraft practices within Catholicism.

42 Protestant informers hunted Catholic priests and were rewarded with £100 on conviction. It was not until the Catholic Relief Act of 1778 that Catholic priests were no longer liable to life imprisonment.

43 Though this was by no means the beginning of such a trend, it certainly became more pronounced. In 1611, for example, the sub-dean of Wells, Thomas James, had felt it necessary to issue *A Treatise on the corruption of Scripture, Counsels and Fathers … Together with a sufficient answere unto … the unknowne Author of the Grounds of the old religion and the new.* In 1628, Joseph Hall, then Bishop of Exeter, published *The old religion: a treatise wherein is laid downe the true state of the difference betwixt the Reformed and the Romane Church; and the blame of this schisme is cast upon the true Authors.* From the English College at Douai in 1672 had come *A brief Survey of the olde religion, which may serve as a guide to all passengers, yet members of the militant church, desirous to know … the old-good-way to Heaven.*

44 So called after the series of publications by its leaders, *Tracts for the Times* (1833–41).

45 A loose affiliation of high church Anglicans, predominantly from Oxford University.

46 Though the movement began partly as a response to concerns that the 1829 Catholic Emancipation Act would lead many Anglicans to Rome.

47 The term first emerged in 1838.

48 Including calls from some radical Whig politicians for the reorganisation of the church as, effectively, a government department. See Yates, 1983: 9.

49 The Cambridge Evangelical C. G. Gorham, in 1847, was appointed to the living of Brampford Speke in the diocese of Exeter, then under the Tractarian bishop Henry Phillpotts. Phillpotts subjected Gorham to lengthy theological examination, after which he decided that the latter held doctrines not in keeping with those taught by the Church of England, and refused to institute him. Having unsuccessfully taken action in the Court of Arches in 1848, Gorham appealed to the Judicial Committee of the Privy Council, who decided in his favour. That a purely doctrinal matter had been pronounced upon by a lay tribunal, thus undermining the independence and authority of the church, was the last straw for high-profile Tractarians such as Manning. Gorham was eventually instituted by the Evangelical Archbishop of Canterbury, John Bird Sumner.

50 See Chapter 4 for further discussion.

51 Charles I was beheaded in 1649 and was regarded by some as a martyr; it was said that he had been offered his life if he would renounce the historic episcopacy of the Church of England, which he refused to do, maintaining that the church was truly Catholic and thus should retain the Catholic episcopate. Believing in a sacramental Church of England, Charles, along with his Archbishop of

Canterbury, William Laud, insisted on the liturgy celebrated with all the ceremony and vestments included in the Book of Common Prayer, thus earning them the hostility of the Presbyterians and all who saw in his policies too close a relationship with the Roman Catholic Church. Charles remains the only person to be canonised by the post-Reformation Church of England. The feast of St Charles, King and Martyr (30 January) was removed from the calendar of the church in 1859 without the consent of Convocation, and was not restored until the publication of the Alternative Service Book in 1980. See http://www. anglicanhistory.org/charles/index.html for more information on the appreciation of King Charles.

52 http://www.skcm.org/SKCM/SKCM_Today/skcm_today.html. The Anglican Catholic Society of King Charles the Martyr was founded by Mrs Ermengarda Greville-Nugent in 1894, its initial objective being 'intercessory prayer for the defence of the Church of England against the attacks of her enemies' (http://www.skcm.org/SKCM/skcm_main.html) and 'to work for the preservation and furtherance of the Catholic inheritance within the Church of England' (http://www.skcm.org/SKCM/History/history_skcm.html). See http://www.anglicanhistory.org/charles/litany.html for a litany by the founder of the Society that clearly relates Charles' sacrifice to that of Christ.

53 See Chapter 2, where the Non-Jurors are discussed in terms of the *episcopi vagantes*.

54 Through which Scottish Presbyterians avowed to maintain their religion.

55 This was in resistance to the attempt to enforce the use of the Prayer Book in Scotland, and with the aim of abolishing the episcopacy.

56 Between 1841 and 1863, 88 works of post-Reformation high church divines were reprinted and edited. The library included, for example, the works of William Laud (1573–1645), William Beveridge (1637–1708) and John Cosin (1594–1672), as well as those of sixteenth-century clerics and nineteenth-century Anglo-Catholics. The library was never completed. For a list of contents, see http://www.anglicanhistory.org/lact/index.html.

57 The *Apostolicae Curae* of Pope Leo XIII, issued in September 1896, declared the Anglican apostolic succession invalid on the grounds that the 1549 ordinal of Edward VI made no reference to the sacrificial function of the priest. The official response of the Archbishops of Canterbury and York, *Saepius Officio* (1897), continues to claim unbroken apostolic succession.

58 14 October 1850 (quoted in Norman, 1968: 64).

59 This clearly ignores the fact that Dissenters and Non-conformists such as Baptists, Methodists, Quakers, Unitarians, the Scottish Kirk and Unitarians admitted no state interference in their practices and refused to accept Royal Supremacy. However, having no foreign papal figure at their head to interfere, they were not regarded as a dangerous and disloyal element of British society.

60 *The Reformation Journal*, vol. I (1851–2), Preface, p.v (in Norman, 1968: 66).

61 Russell, *Hansard*, cxvi, p. 246, 7 February 1851 (in Norman 1968: 76).

62 Ritualism was a later development of the Oxford Movement, undertaken by the second generation of Anglo-Catholics. See Chapter 4 for further discussion.

63 *Hansard*, cxci, p. 924, Debate on Gladstone's motion for a Committee on the Irish Church, 3 April 1868 (cited in Norman, 1968: 22).

64 Pugin, 1851, *An Earnest Address on the Establishment of the Hierarchy*, London, p. 1. He then went on to refer to Protestantism as a 'sort of disease or fungus' (cited in Norman, 1968: 64). At the close of his *Present State of Ecclesiastical Architecture* (1843: 158, reproduced on www.victorianweb.org/art/architecture/pugin/polemic.html, accessed May, 2006), Pugin had basically declared Protestantism to be the child of Satan, and called for men to 'stand forth the

avowed champions of Catholic truth or Protestant error', applying themselves to 'the holy work of England's conversion'.

65 *Present State of Ecclesiastical Architecture* (1843: 158).

66 Claims as to the genuine nature, or otherwise, of the manuscript and information reputedly provided to Leland by Maddelena are irrelevant to the concerns of this chapter. The reader is instead referred to Hutton, 1999, Magliocco, 2002, Pazzaglini, 1998, and Clifton, 1998.

67 Jarcke, 'Ein Hexenprozess', in *Annalen der Deutchen und Auslandischen Criminal-Rechts-Pflege* 1, p. 450; Mone, 'Uber das Hexenwesen', in *Anzeiger fur Kunde der Teutschen Vorzeit* 8, pp. 271–5, pp. 444–5, cited in Hutton, 1996: 11.

68 Murray was referring to the Roman god Dianus, rather than to the goddess Diana whom Leland had cast as the witches' goddess in *Aradia*, and who gave her name to that branch of feminist witchcraft known as 'Dianic'.

69 Karl Pearson (1857–1936), Professor of Applied Mathematics at University College London and founder of statistics. Oates and Wood (1998: 20ff) state that he was heavily influenced by 'Erich Neumann's concept of "mother-right" (matriarchy)', evinced in his essay 'Woman as Witch'. Since Neumann's work was not available until 1955, one assumes that they actually meant to refer to J. J. Bachofen's *Myth, Religion and Mother Right*, which was published in 1870 and therefore would have been available to him. Pearson was a founder member of the Men and Women Club (1885) which was dedicated to exploring the role of men and women in society, and he had a huge range of interests outside his academic field. His essay 'anticipated several themes which appear in Murray's theories' and he was an important influence on her ideas (see Oates and Wood, 1998: 20ff).

70 See ibid.: 11; Oates and Wood attribute this emphasis to two succeeding editors of *Folklore*, A. R. Wright (1923–32, and President of the Society 1927–8) and E. O. James (1932–58). Murray joined the Society in 1927 and acted as President 1953–5; Gardner joined in 1939 and became a member of its Council in March 1946, though he seems to have been rather ineffective (see Heselton, 2003: 172). Leland was also a member, and *Aradia* was published by the Society's publisher (see Oates and Wood, 1998: 14).

71 See Burr, 1922 and Ewen, 1938.

72 It is, of course, wrong to assume that Gardner definitely read either of these simply because they appear to have been in his library. The contents of his library are problematic, with several books listed which were not published until after his death, and the lack of any of Murray's works in the list. The latter could simply have been given away or borrowed by friends who neglected to return them – there is no doubt that he read and absorbed her work.

2 *EPISCOPI VAGANTES* AND HETERODOX CHRISTIANITY

1 As far as I have been able to ascertain, this link was first noted by Morgan Davis (2002). Both Davis and Heselton link the Ancient British Church to the Old Catholic Movement, which is understandable given the confusion surrounding the heterodox churches. This and the following chapter seek to clarify the situation and show that the Ancient British Church into which Gardner was ordained, and indeed the vast majority of heterodox churches are not part of the Old Catholic Movement.

2 Heselton, 2003: 140.

3 Though I can find no resolutions from that conference pertaining to the irregular bishops.

4 Anson was in fact an oblate-brother of the Caldey Island Benedictine community from 1910–24, and was one of the twenty monks who, with Abbot Aelred Carlyle, converted to Roman Catholicism on 5 March 1913.

5 In preparing the final draft of this book, it came to my attention that further material is located at the St Ephrem Institute in Solna, Sweden. Access to these documents at such a late stage was, unfortunately, impossible.

6 I.e. they claimed right of succession.

7 Of course, given the existence of women bishops within the Anglican Communion, even if not yet within the Church of England or the Roman Catholic or Orthodox Churches, such language is now outdated.

8 Ironically, petitions to Rome on this issue led directly to the issuing of the Bull *Apostolicae Curae* by Pope Leo XIII in 1896. Before this time, the Roman Catholic Church had made no official pronouncement on the validity of Anglican orders.

9 Thus, when Charles Edward Stuart died in 1788, ending James' line of succession, they saw no reason to withhold the oath to George III.

10 William Sancroft, Canterbury; Thomas Ken, Bath and Wells; Francis Turner, Ely; Thomas White, Peterborough; William Lloyd, Norwich; Robert Frampton, Gloucester; John Lake, Chichester; William Thomas, Worcester; and Thomas Cartwright, Chester.

11 Literally, 'permission to elect', the *congé d'élire* was a licence from the Crown to the dean and chapter of a cathedral to elect a specific, named person to a vacant see, the appointment of bishops being vested in the Crown under the 1534 Annates Statute. See Cross and Livingstone, 1983: 332.

12 Langford, (1965) 2001 on http://anglicanhistory.org/nonjurors/langford1.html.

13 It was not until 1724 that Archbishop Wake, now fully apprised of the correspondence, wrote to the representatives of the Orthodox Church informing them,

> that certain schismatic priests of our own church have written to you under the pretended titles of archbishops and bishops of the Church of England, and have sought your communion with them … a few of the clergy, fewer still of the bishops, have seceded from us; have persuaded many of the people to their side; and have established congregations separating from the Church. Finally they have reached such a degree of madness that, upon the death of the first authors of this schism, they have consecrated for themselves new bishops to succeed to their places; and it is these who have presumed to write to you. These have tried to seduce you from the communion of our Church.
>
> (Cited in Langford, ibid.)

14 In this case, Jerusalem, since the Non-Jurors had postulated the primacy of this (see Langford, [1965] 2001, proposal 1), presumably because they believed it to be the source of English Christianity (see Chapter 1). Langford explains,

> … if the Non-Jurors, or rather the Catholic and Orthodox remnant of the British Churches, want to submit to the patriarch of Jerusalem, well and good: they could be received into his patriarchate; *but then*, he, and only he, would be canonically empowered to consecrate British bishops (which means presumably he would also have to re-consecrate the Non-Juror bishops).
>
> (Langford, ibid.)

This the Non-Jurors could not accept.

15 Langford, (1965) 2001, proposal 5.

16 Those of Nicaea I (325 CE), Constantinople I (381 CE), Ephesus (431 CE) and Chalcedon (451 CE). That the authority of these councils was upheld probably has more to do with the fact that their decisions were acceptable to Hooker and Andrewes, rather than vice versa.

17 And their secession significantly weakened the influence of the Caroline Divines, who had triumphed at the Restoration of 1660. According to Cross and Livingstone (1983: 57), Anglicanism then entered a period of decline which continued until the rise of the Oxford Movement.

18 Literally 'beyond the mountains', i.e. beyond the Alps. This position stemmed from a desire to regain control over the Gallicanism of the French Church, which sought to keep itself largely independent from Rome. The Ultramontanist position was eventually entrenched in Roman Catholicism at the First Vatican Council, not least through the declaration of Papal Infallibility.

19 The Jansenists were followers of the Utrecht theologian Cornelius Otto Jansen (1585–1638), who spent much of his life in France, studying in Paris before becoming Bishop of Ypres in 1636. His work on St Augustine, *Augustinus* (published posthumously in 1640), was declared heretical by the Sorbonne in 1649 and by Pope Innocent X in 1653. The controversy centred on Jansen's claim that it is impossible to do good works without God's grace, which is irresistible. Persecuted by the Jesuits, many Jansenists fled to the more tolerant atmosphere of the Netherlands, and by the beginning of the nineteenth century, Jansenism remained in France only as an underground movement among French Catholic intellectuals.

20 There is not a single headquarters for all the Old Catholic churches. Each church developed its own national headquarters, and maintains them to the present day. They thus exist independently of each other, rather than seeking a replacement for the Vatican elsewhere than Rome. Their churches are in full communion with each other, and with the Anglican Church since 1932, though cordial relations with Anglicanism go back to 1874. Indeed, the 75th anniversary of the agreement of full communion between the Anglican and the Old Catholic churches of the Union of Utrecht was celebrated at the Old Catholic Congress in Freiburg (Germany), 7–11 August 2006, and was attended by the present Archbishop of Canterbury, Rowan Williams. See http://www.utrechter-union. org/english/bodies_1.htm.

21 According to http://philtar.ucsm.ac.uk/encyclopedia/christ/west/oldcat.html, the Old Catholic Church has never been particularly large, numbering some 400,000 members throughout the world. The largest churches are to be found in USA (62,611), Poland (52,400), Germany (28,000), Austria (22,000), Switzerland (16,000), the Netherlands (10,000), and the Czech Republic (3,000).

22 These differences are not important to the present study, but for information they related to the acceptance of decrees of the Synod of Jerusalem (1672), the Sacrament of Penance, invocation of Saints, alterations in the liturgy, and the attitude towards the Pope. See Brandreth, 1947: 14.

23 Mathew, *The Catholic Church of England* (n.p. or d.: 20ff) and *An Episcopal Odyssey* (1915: 21ff); cited in Brandreth, 1947: 14.

24 As the former Honourable General Secretary of the Church of England's Council on Foreign Relations, Douglas had had a great deal of communication with the Old Catholics and counted many among them personal friends.

25 Principal of Amersfort when Gul, Kennick's predecessor, consecrated Mathew.

26 Mathew intended Williams to succeed him as head of the 'Old Roman Catholic (pro-Uniate) Rite in Great Britain'. According to Brandreth (1947: 19), he is therefore the only legitimate successor of Mathew's movement. Brandreth (ibid.) describes him as 'theologically orthodox' with a small movement which

has been 'entirely free from scandal since he succeeded to the headship of it'. He had not yet appointed a successor in 1947.

27 Although from Wedgwood onwards, all bishops in this line are Theosophists rather than members of the Old Catholic Church, and have no connection with Mathew or his other lines of succession. Until 1930, consecrations were carried out only by Wedgwood and Leadbeater.

28 Anson, 1964: 342–3. Some Church of England clergy were openly expounding theosophical ideas, for example Rev. L. W. Fearn in Westminster, Rev. C. W. Scott-Moncrieff, and Rev. W. F. Geikie-Cobb at St Ethelburga's, Bishopsgate, though he later left the church to promote Co-Masonry. However, two resolutions regarding theosophy were passed at the same 1920 conference which had considered Mathew. Resolution 64 stated:

> The Conference, while recognising that the three publicly stated objectives of the Theosophical Society do not in themselves appear to be inconsistent with loyal membership of the Church, desires to express its conviction that there are cardinal elements in the positive teaching current in theosophical circles and literature which are irreconcilable with the Christian faith as to the person and mission of Christ and with the missionary claim and duty of the Christian religion as the message of God to all mankind. The Conference warns Christian people, who may be induced to make a study of theosophy by the seemingly Christian elements contained in it, to be on their guard against the ultimate bearing of theosophical teaching, and urges them to examine strictly the character and credentials of the teachers upon whose authority they are encouraged or compelled to rely.
> (http://www.anglicancommunion.org/acns/archive/1920/1920-64.htm
> (accessed March 2006))

29 Freemasonry which admitted women. Some Masonic Lodges in France had admitted women to the Craft during the eighteenth century, but these lodges had their own supreme councils. However, in 1882 a Lodge under the jurisdiction of the Supreme Council 33rd of France initiated a woman and was struck off. Consequently, they formed a new group, which came to England in 1902 and became known as Co-Masonry. Annie Besant was initiated in 1902.

30 For the charges brought against Leadbeater, see Owen, 2004: 105–7.

31 Extract from a letter from Leadbeater to Besant, in Jinarajasada, 1952, cited in Anson, 1964: 348.

32 Though many members of the LCC were also members of the Theosophical Society, this was by no means a requirement, and the Church was never an official part of the Society.

33 Both women and men can be ordained to any of the orders, including bishop.

34 This branch is called Forward in Faith. The other, liberal branch is represented by Affirming Catholicism, a Catholic-Anglican society that stresses a progressive approach in relation to issues of gender and sexuality, as well as social justice and the environment. See www.forwardinfaith.com and www.affirmingcatholicism.org.uk.

35 Not much is known about his early life, not even his date of birth or the correct spelling of his name – I have adopted Anson's spelling; Brandreth gives Julius Ferrete as his name, and Mar Georgius (Newman) gives Julius Ferrette. He was apparently born to Protestant parents and received into the Catholic Church during his youth.

36 The name by which a number of Monophysite churches, including the Syrian Church, are known. It derives from Jacob Baradeus, Bishop of Edessa (541–78), who saved the Monophysite heretics from total extinction due to persecution.

Not to be confused with Jacobite supporters of the deposed James II and the claims of the House of Stuart to the English throne, such as the Non-Jurors. See also n. 42 below.

37 Later, as Ignatius Peter III, Patriarch of Antioch.

38 Mar Bedros had allegedly obtained permission from Patriarch Mar Ignatius Jacobus II to begin some sort of reunion movement, for which he required a director in Europe. Ferrette was supposedly 'dispatched as Patriarchal Legate for Western Europe, with authority to erect indigenous Orthodox Churches, under an autonomous patriarchate of their own, and not in any way subject to Antioch' (Mar Georgius [Hugh George de Willmott Newman], 1958: 3). Anson reports that this embellishment of the Ferrette story did not emerge until some eighty years later and no documentary evidence has to date been produced (Anson, 1964: 35). The formation of such 'autonomous patriarchates' does not lie within the authority of a patriarch, which rather makes a nonsense of such claims.

39 In the 'Pastoral Letter' affixed to the book; cited in Brandreth, 1947: 45.

40 He lived on the hospitality of Fr George Nuggee for some months, and impressed Dr Frederick George Lee, a founder of the revived Order of Corporate Reunion who himself underwent an irregular consecration (see Chapter 4). Pusey was never taken in by Ferrette, and refused to write the introduction for Lee's *Essays on the Reunion of Christendom* if Ferrette's contribution were included.

41 The exact date is not known.

42 Not to be confused with the Jacobite church – here it refers to supporters of the deposed James II and the claims of the House of Stuart. See section on the Non-Jurors earlier in this chapter. Neo-Jacobitism was very much in evidence among the Decadents of the 1890s, as well as among Anglo-Catholics as part of their inheritance from the Caroline Divines and Non-Jurors. It was also popular among occultists; perhaps most famously, Samuel Lidell Mathers added 'MacGregor' to his name as part of his attempt to create for himself a Stuart lineage, and entertained an 'endless parade of exiled royalty' (Greer, 1995: 158) at his home in Paris. Following him, Edward Alexander Crowley adopted the Scottish variant of his name, Aleister, and Gerald Gardner likewise claimed Scottish ancestry, dressed in Scottish regalia, and appears to have been a chevalier of the Illustrious and Knightly Order of the Crown of Stuart, according to a certificate dated 1957 lodged in his library (see www.newwiccanchurch.net/gglibrary/index.htm).

43 Morgan's royalist sympathies are well evinced in his 1849 work, *Notes on Various Distinctive Verities of the Christian Church*, in which he inveighs against 'the Puritanism that in former days had deluged England with the blood of her noblest and most loyal citizens; [and] immolated on the altar of its ferocious hypocrisy, gentry, aristocracy, and king' (1849: 42). Unsurprisingly, Oliver Cromwell comes in for a ferocious attack, for 'no language is too expressive to indicate abhorrence of this fanatic mixture of blood and hypocrisy' which led Cromwell to '[hew] his way through the lives of his fellow-subjects, over desperate battle-fields, burning towns and slaughtered garrisons, to the throne of his murdered sovereign' (ibid.: 81). The title page to his *St Paul in Britain* is inscribed '*Ecclesia Britannica ab incunabulis Regia et Apostolica*' ('The British Church was from its Cradle Apostolical and Royal'), a claim he follows up in Conclusion 16, with reference to 'her present majesty, Queen Victoria ...' (1861: 216).

44 During his lifetime, the Welsh language was being suppressed by the British Government. Morgan was a vigorous defender of his native language, and was one of the organisers of the 1858 Llangollen eisteddfod which celebrated Welsh culture. In a letter dated 24 September 1857, he appealed to the Prime

Minister, Henry John Temple, Viscount Palmerston, against the appointments of 'unqualified' bishops in St Asaph (Thomas Vowler Short) and Bangor (Christopher Bethell) who are 'utterly ignorant of, and hostile to, the language of the Principality' (the correspondence is reproduced in Thomann, 2001: 25–42). He had already asked the Archbishop of Canterbury, John Moore, to remove Vowler Short in 1855, without success. See also Morgan's 1859 'Ballads of the Cymry: The English Bishop in Wales', written under his bardic name Môr Meirion (reproduced in Thomann, ibid.: 46–7). According to Cross and Livingstone, between 1715 and 1870, no Welsh bishop could preach in Welsh at the time of his appointment (1983: 1457), though some later learned the language.

45 'A Chapter of Secret History', *Church Times*, 28 April 1922, p. 4.
46 Transcribed and available on http://www.llangyfelyn.org/dogfennau/british_kymry.html, accessed 28 March 2006.
47 A copy of the 1948 edition, published by Covenant, is listed among the books of Gardner's library http://www.newwiccanchurch.net/gglibrary/index.htm, accessed 29 March 2006.
48 Pryce counted ten: Bran, Saints Paul, Peter, Simon Zelotes, Philip, James the Great, and John, Aristobulus, Joseph of Arimathea, and missionaries sent by Eleutherius at the request of King Lucius. See Pryce, 1878: vi.
49 Mar Georgius, 1958: 8, cited in Anson, 1964: 44.
50 Though Morgan continued to live and work in England, the country he hated, until his retirement in 1888, and death the following year in Sussex.
51 This, at any rate, is the line of succession according to the story told by Mar Georgius, who was consecrated into this line in 1944, but no convincing evidence to prove the links has yet come to light.
52 Later 'elected' as His Holiness Mohoran Mar Basilius Abdullah III, Sovereign Prince Patriarch of Antioch, though no one taking part in the election had ever been in communion with the See of Antioch and neither Crow nor anyone else of the Ferrette succession is recognised by the Syrian Church.
53 Their correspondence lasted from May 1944 to September 1947, some three months prior to Crowley's death.
54 See notes to the Manifesto of the Gnostic Catholic Church, http://www.hermetic.com/sabazius/mfstnotes.htm , accessed 14 March 2006.
55 See Heselton, 2003: 204–5.
56 Though by 1947 they were out of communion with each other. See Brandreth, 1947: 51, n. 1.
57 See Chapter 3.
58 Presumably they had only just become aware of these.
59 All quotations from this document are taken from the 'Notice from the Syrian Patriarchate of Antioch and All the East', reprinted as Appendix A in Brandreth, 1947: 70.
60 Resolutions 27 and 28: 'Reunion of Christendom' read:

> We regret that on a review of all the facts we are unable to regard the so-called Old Catholic Church in Great Britain (under the late Bishop Mathew and his successors), and its extensions overseas, as a properly constituted Church, or to recognise the orders of its ministers, and we recommend that, in the event of any of its ministers desiring to join our Communion, who are in other respects duly qualified, they should be ordained sub conditione in accordance with the provisions suggested in the Report of our Committee. The Conference recommends that the same course be followed, as occasion may require, in the case of persons claiming to have received consecration

or ordination from any 'episcopi vagantes,' whose claims we are unable to recognise.

(www.anglicancommunion.org/acns/archive/1920/1920-27.htm,
accessed April 2006)

The resolve of the Anglican bishops was reiterated in Resolution 54 of the Lambeth Conference of 1958 (www.anglicancommunion.org/archives/1958/1958-54.htm, accessed February 2006).

61 Despite its name, this church is not to be confused with the churches of the Old Catholic Movement.

62 Grafton claimed that Vilatte simply got those under his charge to sign a piece of paper; some of them were children, and only one was a clergyman, who stated that his signature was forged (Anson, 1964: 107).

63 The *patronado* agreement of the sixteenth century had allowed the King of Portugal to nominate bishops in Portuguese colonies. On 2 January 1887 Leo XIII established a new hierarchy for India and Ceylon, which undermined the close links felt between Indian Catholics and Portugal. Resenting the transfer of power to French or Italian bishops, they formed the Patronado Association, which petitioned King Luis I of Portugal to get the royal patronage restored.

64 Fr Ignatius was a celibate Anglo-Catholic mission preacher who worked for a time with famous Anglo-Catholic slum worker, Fr Charles Fuge Lowder at St Georges-in-the-East, London. His aim, however, was to revive the Benedictine Order in the Church of England, and in 1869 he acquired a site for his monastery at Capel-y-ffin, four miles from Llanthony, in South Wales. He had been in America raising money for his establishment in 1890–1, where he was publicised as 'The Druid of the Welsh Church' and claimed to belong to an Ancient British Church, older than any except Antioch and Jerusalem. This may well have been Morgan's Church, given its Welsh nationalist overtones and links with revived Druidry. Upon his death, the buildings of Capel-y-ffin passed to the Anglican Benedictines of Caldey Island who used it as a holiday home. As mentioned in n. 4, most of them converted to Rome in 1913 and the community moved to Prinknash Grange in Gloucestershire in 1928, where they remain.

65 Of which more in Chapter 3.

66 Arthur Calder-Marshall, *The Enthusiast*, 1962: 258 cited in Anson, 1964: 114.

67 Henry St John, 'Introduction', in Anson, 1964: 17.

68 Ward's Abbey of Christ the King, for example, which will be discussed in the next chapter. I can only assume that St Badoc's Chapel, Holborn, listed as the place of Gardner's ordination, was a private chapel; I have been unable to find any trace of it.

69 Gardner's claims to hold a doctorate may be in keeping with this tendency among the wandering bishops, though they themselves may simply have regarded themselves as continuing the practice of doctorates in divinity being handed out from Lambeth Palace. Gardner's doctorate from the 'Meta Collegiate Extension of the National Electronic Institute' is listed among the contents of Gardner's library (www.newwiccanchurch.net/gglibrary/index.htm).

70 Under Henry VIII, loyalty to the Pope was treason; the reformers, on the other hand, were heretics.

71 The episcopacy was regarded as a legitimate form of church governance, but was not considered to be divinely ordained or a part of the Church's very essence – i.e. it was an *adiaphora*, important but not essential. Apostolic succession instead became a matter of right doctrine rather than right consecrations, see for example, John Jewel (1522–71), Bishop of Salisbury, to his opponent Thomas Harding (1565: 130): 'It is not sufficient to claime succession of place:

It behooveth us rather to have regarde to the Succession of Doctrine' (1567: Part 2, Ch. 5, Div. 1, p. 130).

3 CHURCHES GNOSTIC AND AGNOSTIC

1 Tackett and Langlois, 1980: 355.
2 See http://users.skynet.be/la.mission/petite_eglise.htm, accessed 26 June 2006.
3 Marian devotion in France mushroomed in the nineteenth century, as did religious orders, particularly for females. Major apparitions were recorded at Paris (1830), La Salette (1846), Lourdes (1858), and Pontmain (1870). Nearly 400 female orders were established by 1880, with 135,000 female religious in 1878 (Blackbourn, 1991: 781–2).
4 The reign of the Paraclete was the third status prophesied by Joachim of Fiore, coming after the reign of the Father (power and fear) and that of the Son (expiation and revelation). It would be characterised by love and atonement. His followers believed that there would no longer be any need for the institutions of the Roman Church. The persecution of the church, the Revolution, and the transformations that followed encouraged apocalyptic speculation, and by the nineteenth century the new age of the Paraclete was firmly embedded in the minds of many occultists, spiritualists and heterodox Christians, especially in France. See Reeves ([1976] 1999) and Gould and Reeves (2001).
5 The image of the suffering woman/mother, identified with the virgin Mary, was seen as an instrument of social progress and co-redemptrix with Christ, assimilated to his life and suffering. In Éliphas Lévi's work, *Le rosier de mai ou la guirlande de Marie* (1839), she is crucified with her son. Lévi was influenced by the Joachimite *Spiridion* (1839) of George Sands, and unsurprisingly sees the secrets of the mother's love as a revelation which will come with the reign of the Paraclete (*L'assomption de la femme*, 1841). See Laurant, 2005: 689–90.
6 Joachim saw Elijah as typifying the Holy Spirit, a view that Vintras seems to have shared. See Gould and Reeves, 2001: 215.
7 Connections made between John the Baptist and Elijah occur in the gospels (e.g. Matt., 11:15; Luke, 1:17; John, 1:19–21) and have been associated ever since. Given Vintras' claim to be the second Elijah, it is perhaps not surprising that Boullan should claim to supersede him as the New Testament John the Baptist.
8 Huysman's novel also told of the coming reign of the Paraclete, the reign of the (gnostic) Gospel of John and of the Holy Spirit (Huysman, 1891: 8). See also McIntosh, [1972] 1975: 188.
9 Though sex magic was by no means limited to heterosexual intercourse.
10 Toth (2005: 402), for instance, argues that Jean Bricaud 'had a great admiration for Vintras, and valued the form of sexual magic sanctioned by the latter', thus explaining the ties between Bricaud and Theodor Reuss of the OTO.
11 Robert Baldick, *The Life of J.-K. Huysmans*, cited in McIntosh, [1972] 1975: 181 (no page reference provided). King also includes a version of this citation [1971] 2002: 181, but provides no reference. Elsewhere, it is cited as being written by Jean Bricaud in a biography of Boullan: 'Since the Fall from grace resulted from an illicit act of love, the Redemption of Humanity can only be achieved through acts of love accomplished in a religious manner'. It was believed that 'guilty love must be combated through pure love, through a sexual approach, but in a heavenly manner, to the spirits in order to raise oneself: this is the union of wisdom' (http://www.gnostique.net/ecclesia/EG_II.htm, accessed 9 May 2006).
12 Baldick, in McIntosh ibid.
13 Boullan and his followers were said to copulate with the spirits of the dead, including Alexander the Great and Cleopatra.

14 The influence of sex magic on Gardner and on Wiccan practice today is enormous, though it is often played down and underestimated; this will be explored in Chapter 5.

15 Maria de Mariategui, Lady Caithness, was a disciple of Anna Kingsford of the Hermetic Society and a prominent spiritualist.

16 First century Samaritan magician, regarded by early Christian anti-heretical writers as the founding father of Gnosticism, the arch-heretic 'from whom all heresies derived' (Ireneus, *Adversus haereses*, I, 32, 2). See van den Broek, 2005a: 1069–73.

17 The Valentinians were an important heretical current in the second and third centuries CE, forming their own community outside the nascent Catholic Church of the majority. They taught a trinity of Father, Mother and Child, and had both exoteric and esoteric teachings.

18 The name given to the Cathar lords.

19 For further information, see Toth, 2005: 401.

20 Papus had, in effect, founded this Martinist Order in 1887.

21 Giraud had been consecrated exactly six years earlier by Vilatte, on 21 June 1907.

22 Who would of course be excommunicated if their membership in such a secret society were known.

23 The magic of apostolic succession was generally believed by wandering bishops with occult leanings, bishops having greater magical powers than priests, which goes some way to explaining the speedy rise to the episcopy of the majority of these men; very few seem to have settled for mere priestly orders.

24 Bricaud had allied himself with dissident organisations of the Roman Church and instituted the 'Gnostic Legates' in 1912, a title which was given to many personalities of the occult world (Toth, 2005: 402).

25 The British section was called Mysteria Mystica Maxima (MMM).

26 According to Tau Apiryon, its first recorded public celebration was not until 19 March 1933, in California ('Introduction to the Gnostic Mass', www. hermetic.com/sabazius/intromass.htm, accessed 14 March 2006).

27 The EGU was eventually 'put to sleep' by its last head, Robert Amberlain (Tau Jean III) in 1960, in favour of his own *Église Gnostique Apostolique*, which he had founded in 1958.

28 The various lines of succession were set out in the newsletter *Gnostic Gnews*, of which only four issues were produced (between December 1988 and September 1989).

29 See www.hermetic.com/sabazius/history_egc.htm, accessed 14 March 2006.

30 See Part 2 of the correspondence between P.-R. Koenig and David Scriven ('Sabazius'), 1 September to 29 November 1996, on http://cyberlink.ch/~koenig/dplanet/html/s2.htm, accessed 17 May 2006.

31 See www.hermetic.com/sabazius/history_egc.htm, accessed 14 March 2006.

32 See Davis, 2002: 6–8; Heselton, 2003: 136. The initial foundation in 1929 was called the Confraternity of the Kingdom of the Wise.

33 Furse preached the sermons at the first two Anglo-Catholic Congresses held at the Albert Hall, London 29 June–1 July 1920, and 10–12 July 1923. He consecrated Ward's Abbey 'on the understanding that it should be used only by members of the Community'. Letter from Furse to Brandreth, 14 August 1939, cited in Anson, 1964: 285.

34 Gardner noted ([1959] 2004: 46) that the Abbey church contained a picture of Christ and of the feminine Holy Ghost on the right and left hand sides of the altar respectively. The latter was

shown as a woman in white, the White Goddess. The priests of this church told me some years ago that Christ was born of the Father, conceived by the Holy Ghost, and that only a woman could conceive. ... This Mother and Son worship is not so different from the cult of the witches, although it may be heresy to say so.

(Gardner, ibid.)

This seems to be an echo of Valentinian gnosticism (see n. 17, above), but whether Gardner means this is a Wiccan heresy or a Christian heresy is unclear.

35 Anson, 1964: 285 and Heselton, 2003: 137. Ward is presumably referring to the refusal of the Church of England to ordain Fr Ignatius (Lyne) to the priesthood and the opposition to his attempts to revive the Benedictine monastic life at Capel-y-ffin. See Morse-Boycott (1933), who calls the monastery, 'a memorial in stone that must ever remain a permanent reproach to the Church he served so nobly', though 'detested and persecuted by fellow-Churchmen'. Ward had been able to ride the wave of the Anglo-Catholic establishment of religious communities. Ignatius, however, had been an early pioneer, unsupported and at times persecuted, the traditions of the religious life still being associated (negatively) with Roman Catholicism. According to Morse-Boycott (1933), it was his ordination 'at the hands of a wandering old Catholic bishop, who was an adventurer' (i.e. Vilatte) that finally discredited him 'in the eyes of the Church that denied him the priesthood'. See also Chapter 2, n. 64.

36 See Thomann (2001: 10), who notes that '[t]he strange tradition of Anglican Clergy receiving episcopal consecration outside the Anglican communion but continuing to serve in it had its beginnings with Morgan and the OCR [Order of Corporate Reunion]'.

37 Established as an open-air museum, the Abbey Folk Park contained as an exhibit a 'reconstruction' of a sixteenth-century witch's cottage. This was later bought and transplanted to a plot of land adjacent to the naturist club near St Albans. Gardner's coven held regular meetings there until his death in 1964.

38 According to Davis, Gardner 'received a consecration from Ward into the Orthodox Catholic Church in England' (Davis' research into Gardner is ongoing and as such is difficult to date; this quotation was found on page 8 of the version available on www.geraldgardner.com in September 2005). This is inaccurate, however. Although Davis is aware that a certificate confirming this is contained within the collection of Gardnerian material housed in Toronto and mentioned by Kelly (1991: 32), he states Gardner was consecrated as a bishop, rather than ordained priest, and incorrectly names both the presiding bishop and the church. The 'diploma' is indeed listed among Gardner's papers in Toronto, but clearly states that it is an ordination, not a consecration. It is signed by Dorian, Bishop of Caerleon, of the Ancient British Church and witnessed by W. Ohly and M. S. Sanders, not by Ward. See http://www.newwiccanchurch.net/gglibrary/index.htm, accessed 28 March 2006. I am most grateful to Philip Heselton for furnishing me with a copy of the certificate.

39 Though Gardner did own a copy of 'The Liturgy of the Orthodox Catholic Church in England' from 'The Chancellor's Office, The Abbey of Christ the King', produced in 1938.

40 This may be the church now known as 'Christ the Saviour', Winton, Bournemouth, which is part of the British Orthodox Church now overseen by de Willmott-Newman's nephew, Mar Seraphim.

41 See http://orthodoxcatholicnew.tripod.com/id7.html, accessed January 2006. Some of Ward's Abbey Folk Park collection is also in Australia, at the Abbey Museum of St Michael's Church (also derived from Ward) – see www.abbey museum.asn.au/history.htm.

42 It was still being used at the time of publication of Anson's book in 1964, though the living quarters had become an artists' colony, as had Fr Ignatius' monastery at Capel-y-ffin. Anson, 1964: 292, n. 1.

43 Ward had entrusted the clergy of the Orthodox Catholic Church to the care of Mar Georgius before leaving for Cyprus, and presumably gave him the right to use the Cathedral of Christ the King.

44 Anson provides no reference for this quotation.

45 Again, Anson provides no reference for this quotation.

46 This goes some way to clearing up Heselton's question as to how Gardner was ordained into a Church which had ceased to exist, since it had become part of the Catholicate of Mar Georgius (de Willmott-Newman). His speculation is that 'Dorian, Bishop of Caerleon, had an affection for the Ancient British Church and continued using the name' (Heselton, 2003: 142). In fact, it was the Ancient British Church of Mar Pelagius (Morgan), of the Ferrette succession, that had, in a sense, ceased to exist. It was merged on 2 November 1897 with the Nazarene Episcopal Ecclesia (founded by James Martin), the United Armenian Church of the British Isles and the Free Protestant Church of England (both founded by Leon Chechemain), into a new church called the Free Protestant Episcopal Church of England. According to Thomann (2001: 11), Morgan's church 'apparently retained some pro-forma independence', but its merger 'with these Protestant groups would not have been according to Morgan's wishes for his British Church'. It survived as part of the Metropolis of Glastonbury when the Free Protestant Episcopal Church of England was united with Mar Georgius' Catholicate of the West, but had more or less ceased to operate as an independent organisation. It was this Ancient British Church that Dorian Herbert revived, at least on paper, after his consecration by Mar Georgius and before ordaining Gardner.

47 So he informed the *Bournemouth Daily Echo*, 11 August 1953, cited in Anson, 1964: 296.

48 In 1899, Breton language activists decided to launch a gorsedd after being initiated by the Welsh gorsedd in Cardiff in August of that year. The first Breton Gorsedd was held on 1 September 1900.

49 The Polish Mariavite Church (*Mariae vitam (imitans)* – '(imitating) the life of Mary') emerged in 1893 with the vision of a Tertiary sister Maria Franciszka Feliksa Kozlowska. After years of persecution by the Polish bishops and Jesuits, in December 1906 they were excommunicated by the Roman Catholic Church, but legalised as a 'tolerated sect' by the Russian authorities. The desire for continued apostolic succession led them to turn to the Old Catholics. A Warsaw priest, Jan Maria Michal Kowalski was consecrated as an Old Catholic bishop by the Archbishop of Utrecht in October 1909, but after the death of Kozlowska in 1921, Kowalski took steps to modernise the church by advocating the marriage of clergy to nuns and the priesthood of women. Such measures were unpopular among the Mariavites themselves, but they also led the Old Catholics to sever connections with them in 1924.

50 His suspicions were correct – such orders would not have been accepted as valid.

51 He was not the first Frenchman to think this way. In the previous century, Ernest Renan (1823–92) believed that the Celtic races – which to him meant the Bretons – would shape the religion of the future. See Gould and Reeves, 2001: 159, 167.

52 More commonly spelled Tudwal, the saint was a sixth century (d. 564) Welsh monk, said to be the son of Hoel I Mawr, a legendary king of Brittany who served as one of King Arthur's loyal allies, also associated with the story of Tristan and Iseult. Tudwal studied in Ireland before adopting an eremitic life on

Saint Tudwal's Island East, off the Llyn Peninsula in North West Wales. He later emigrated to Brittany, where he settled with seventy-two followers in Lan Pabu and established a monastery, then became Bishop of Tréguier where he founded another monastery. This was one of the sees suppressed under the decree of 14 November 1789, on 12 July 1790.

53 Anson, 1964: 317.

54 According to Anson (1964: 318, n. 4), these included baptisms in the sea at midnight, conducted naked, which apparently scandalised the Bretons. It is not known whether such rites were ever part of Druidry, but they were certainly part of early Christian practice, when nudity was used to underline the death and rebirth symbolism of the baptismal rite of initiation. Tugdual may simply have been acting according to the notion that early Christians and Druids overlapped significantly in terms of belief and practice. See Hippolytus:

> *Blessing of font*
> 1 And at the hour when the cock crows they shall first [*of all*] pray over the water.
> 2 [*When they come to the water, let the water be pure and flowing.*]
>
> *The neophytes*
> 3 And they shall put off their clothes.
> 4 And they shall baptise the little children first ....
> 5 And next they shall baptise the grown men; and last the women, who shall [all] have loosed their hair and laid aside the gold ornaments [which they were wearing]. Let no one go down to the water having any alien object with [them].
>
> (Hippolytus, *Trad. Ap.*, 21: 1–5 in Dix, 1968: 33)

See also Easton (1934: 45) and Kevin P. Edgecomb *The Apostolic Tradition of Hippolytus of Rome*, Berkeley, California, http://www.bombaxo.com/hippolytus. html, accessed 5 January 2007.

55 The title 'His Whiteness' probably stems from one of the two states of sentient existence expounded in nineteenth-century Welsh Druidry, the 'Gwynfydolion' ('the beings of the happy, literally "white" state' – Morgan, 1861: 67). Humans were characterised as fallen Gwynfydolion attempting to re-enter 'gwynfyd' (see Morgan, 1861: 67–9). Using 'His Whiteness' as a title suggests that Tugdual felt himself to have re-entered that state of happiness. Presumably, the tradition of Druids wearing white robes – begun at Morgan's eisteddfod of 1858 – reflected aspiration to this state.

56 Titles listed next to his photograph in Anson, 1964: 314 facing.

57 Including the Druid Michel Raoult, Bishop of Iltud.

58 He was consecrated on 16 August 1980 by Mar Seraphim (Newman-Norton) assisted by Yves Marie Joseph Laigle, Albert Ronald Coady and Guy Robert Marie le Mentec. Mar Seraphim himself had been consecrated on 9 July 1977 by his uncle, Mar Georgius (de Willmott-Newman), assisted by Peter Martin Smethurst and Michel Raoult. The lineage of the monastery today thus stems from Ferrette, whereas Tugdual's came via Vilatte. For further information see www.orthodoxie-celtique.net.

59 See www.abbess.org.uk/orthodox/about.html, accessed January 2006.

60 See www.abbess.demon.co.uk/orthodox/saintepresence/hermitage-en.html, accessed January 2006.

61 Nephew and successor of Mar Georgius (de Willmott-Newman). Also W. B. Crow's successor in the Order of Holy Wisdom.

62 The British Eparchy of the *L'Église Orthodoxe Celtique* is now overseen by Mgr Stephen (Stephen Robson), consecrated by Mäel Bliss in 1999. See www.celticorthodox.org.

63 However, the Coptic Church of Egypt is not in communion with the Orthodox Church because of doctrinal differences and because they are no longer regarded as maintaining apostolic succession. Despite a great deal of respect for the Coptic Church, the website of the Orthodox Church states:

> we cannot be in communion with them, because of their rejection of the Ecumenical Councils of and after Chalcedon, and at least the ambiguity of whether they still persist in the Monophysite heresy. Certainly, their piety in some quarters and grace under persecution in Egypt is to be admired.
>
> (www.orthodox.net/links/orgs.html, accessed 25 February 2006)

The Coptic Church in Egypt claims, however, to have never believed in monophysitism, and that the Council of Chalcedon misunderstood the Coptic beliefs in the fifth century. Either that, or

> they wanted to exile the Church, to isolate it and to abolish the Egyptian, independent Pope, who maintained that Church and State should be separate. … Whether it was a conspiracy from the Western Churches to exile the Coptic Church as a punishment for its refusal to be politically influenced, or whether Pope Dioscurus didn't quite go the extra mile to make the point that Copts are not monophysite, the Coptic Church has always felt a mandate to reconcile 'semantic' differences between all Christian Churches.
>
> (http://www.coptic.net/EncyclopediaCoptica/, accessed 30 March 2006)

64 See Chapter 2.

65 Named after one of the first leaders, Jean Cottereau, traditionally nicknamed Jean Chouan, marquis de la Rouerie (John the owl, marquess of Mischief). The rising began in February 1791, and the whole of Western France rose in March 1793 after the proclamation of the Republic in January of that year. Thereafter, the Chouans continued to provoke fear in the minds of the authorities, so much so that in 1870 the Breton army was abandoned without arms in the camp of Conlie because it was feared they were an army of Chouans.

66 Presumably, this is the same Michel Raoult who assisted in the consecration of Newman-Norton, consecrator in turn of Mäel Bliss (de Brescia) of the Monastère de Sainte-Présence.

67 Brittany was after all 'the sleepy backwater which Romantics visited to pursue their vision of a lost world, notable for its ancient Celtic language and its fervent Catholicism', according to Heywood (1995: 794), though of course the latter was what Tugdual was trying to replace.

68 Druidry in particular was not meant to be a religion *per se*, and attempts to make it a religious rather than philosophical system were responsible for splits and schisms.

69 These links had been revised by the publication of *The Druid Renaissance* (Carr-Gomm, 1996), by which time Carr-Gomm and other contributors to the volume had come to understand that the Druids were persecuted by the Christians just as other opposing groups of people were. The idea of a harmonious conversion and mutual influences is still valued, though as a myth which assists in ongoing dialogues between Christian and non-Christian Druids, and between Druids and Christians.

70 See earlier in this chapter. Nichols ([1975] 1992: 118) describes him as the man 'who fostered and spread Martinism from being a very small, very worthy group as left by Louis-Claude de St Martin, into the large movement it is today'.

71 Nichols records these visits ([1975] 1992: 117), also noting that the Welsh Gorsedd refused to have any further links with Brittany so long as the *Gorsedd Breizh* was on friendly terms with the English Druids, an outlook which obviously annoyed him.

72 *Gerald Gardner: Witch* is an account of Gardner's life as told by Gardner to his friend, the Sufi mystic Idries Shah who published the 'biography' under the name of Jack Bracelin in 1960.

73 There are indications that she believed quite literally in Hell (Bracelin, [1960] 1999: 19). Gardner comments in his own work on 'the grim Christian doctrines of the Last Judgement, and of Heaven being reserved for a chosen few, while the greater part of mankind were menaced with Hell and Purgatory' ([1959] 2004: 148).

74 Gardner, [1959] 2004: 18.

75 As will be seen in the next chapter, Catholic ritual is a different matter entirely.

76 Gardner is aware of this, and notes that

> [a] Church of England which derived its authority from Henry VIII was in a weak position; but a Church deriving its authority from Joseph of Arimathea was a very different matter; almost equally dangerous was the tradition of an ancient civilisation independent of Rome altogether.
>
> (Gardner, [1959] 2004: 46)

77 Like Gardner, historians such as Hugh Trevor-Roper and Norman Cohn reeled from the excesses of Stalin and Hitler. See, for example, Cohn, 1975: 89.

78 See Chapter 2, n. 47.

79 Gardner, [1959] 2004: 237–8.

80 *Contra* Clifton, 2004: 269 who claims that once Gardner had worked out what 'Wica' ought to be, 'he would never look back to Druids, esoteric Christianity, or OTO-style magic'. There is plenty of evidence that Gardner in fact maintained his activities in the Ancient Druid Order. He took Doreen Valiente along to the Midsummer ritual at Stonehenge the day after her initiation in 1953, bringing with him the sword the Order used (see Valiente, 1989: 39–40). This was a year before Ross Nichols joined the Order, and given that Gardner and Nichols were good friends who shared common interests until Gardner's death, it seems strange to suggest that the latter would suddenly drop all interest in Druidry. The style of Christianity in which he was ordained was heterodox rather than esoteric. And there is a great deal of 'OTO-style magic' in Wicca.

81 Heselton, 2003: 145.

82 Heselton stresses that Gardner, though enjoying appearing in a dog collar from time to time, was 'not active' in the Church. As may now be clear, this is beside the point – these churches were made up predominantly of bishops, with a few priests and deacons and hardly any laity.

83 Clifton, 2004: 269.

4 REDISCOVERING RITUAL

1 From the Greek 'leitourgia', meaning 'work'. It was used in Hellenistic Greek to denote an act of public service, and was then employed to refer to an act of service or ministry, later confined to the idea of service to God, specifically in the celebration of the Eucharist. See Davies, 1986: 314.

2 Crowley, 1998: 171.

3 Though this of course ignores the attraction of Wicca to those of a Catholic religious background, including Crowley herself, who retain a love of ritual.

4 Instituted by Pope Urban IV in 1264 and inspired by the Eucharistic visions of Juliana of Liège.

5 Johannes Kepler (1571–1630) provided the first accurate description of image formation on the retina in his 'Dioptrics' of 1611.

6 The Greeks held two opposing theories of vision. Extromission, introduced by Empodocles *c*.450 BCE and later advanced by Plato, taught that the eye emits invisible fire that, on touching the object, revealed its colours and shape. Intromission, introduced by Aristotle, taught that the objects emit images of themselves through space to the eye. Both had been challenged by Arab scholars by the tenth century, intromission by al-Kindi (*c*.806–*c*.66) and extromission by al-Hasan (*c*.965–1040), but like much Arab learning it was either not known or ignored in medieval and early modern England.

7 Muir mistakenly identifies this as the extromission theory, but the identification remains valid.

8 Indeed, no consensus has emerged since.

9 In *The End of Modern Ritualism* (1874), an Anglican layman claimed that reunion with Rome would mean 'decadence, moral and material, the utter abnegation of all moral virility, the encouragement of vice, filth, and idleness, the declension of patriotism, and the death of all vital personal religion'. Quoted in Reed, 1998: 236.

10 The Greek 'mysterium' had in any case become institutionalised in the legal Roman mindset, Latinised as 'sacraments'.

11 In the century following the Protestant Reformation, the 'hokey cokey' rhyme and dance had already taken shape as a means of showing how laughable Catholic ritual was, mimicking the manner in which the laity were perceived to follow the mumbled words and covert actions of the priests and generally pointing to a lack of depth, since gestures and half-heard words are 'what it's all about'. An early variant is cited in Robert Chamber's *Popular Rhymes* (1826), but its origins are believed to be seventeenth century.

12 Christian obsession with the Eucharist as the body of God led to the idea that anti-Christian rituals required bodies, particularly Christian bodies, that could be used in an inversion of the Eucharistic liturgy, hence the blood libel accusations against Jews and witches which have persisted to this day.

13 That the Protestant Reformation itself can be interpreted as a ritual protest, moving out from the universities to become a mass movement through changing the laity's experience of the Eucharist, employing traditional ceremonies in new ways as well as introducing new ones (see Muir, 1997), now seems something of a paradox. Likewise, Anglo-Catholicism began in the universities, with the Oxford Movement, and became a mass movement because it changed the laity's experience of ritual.

14 Popularly referred to as 'smells and bells' or even 'gin and lace'.

15 Walter Walsh's 1897 publication *The Secret History of the Oxford Movement*, for example, is an undisguised and scathing attack on all aspects of ritualism, '[t]he gravest indictment that has yet been made against the High Church party', according to the *Baptist* (in Walsh, end material). Within a year of publication, it was in its fourth edition and had sold over 20,000 copies, aided no doubt by the rallying cry of the evangelical Church Association which supplied a six-page leaflet appealing for funds for the back of the fourth edition (1898). In this, the Association appealed for support

> [b]ecause it is necessary to oppose Ritualism, as helping to thrust upon the unwary the Popery which was cast out at the Reformation, and which made

England cringe to a foreign potentate, kept back the Bible from our people, deluged our land with superstition and ignorance, and burned our Protestant Reformers.

16 Edward Burne-Jones and William Morris had wanted to establish a brotherhood under the patronage of Sir Galahad whilst undergraduates at Oxford, and all the pre-Raphaelites appealed to a pre-Reformation, if Victorianised, medievalism.

17 Fr Nugee, of St Austin's Priory, another ritualist centre, was a friend of Pater and took in Ferrette in the 1860s.

18 Orthodox liturgy was richer in ceremonial and accoutrements. It also allowed for a different understanding of Christianity, richer than Rome and with claims to a far greater antiquity, especially the Syrian, Antiochan, and Coptic churches. Greek and Russian Orthodoxy were far too recent to be of interest to those seeking a return to 'primitive' Christianity and an apostolic origination for the British Church. In choosing the Eastern over the Western rite for Russia, Grand Duke Vladimir was also apparently impressed with the greater liturgical splendour of the Greek Orthodox Church (see Muir, 1997: 201).

19 Benjamin Jowett wrote to a friend in 1865 that the churches in London seemed to be undergoing 'a sort of aesthetico-Catholic revival'. Quoted in Reed, 1998: 60.

20 Although, as Bradford Verter (2002: 1, 2) has noted, 'there is of course no "natural" connection between alternative sexuality and alternative spirituality; the link between the two had to be forged', despite it being 'a common and indeed an ancient trope within controversial literature to associate alternative spiritual systems with ostensibly abnormal sexual practices'.

21 See Chapter 2.

22 Dr Richard von Krafft-Ebing's *Psychopathia Sexualis: With Especial Reference to Contrary Sexual Instinct: A Medico-Legal Study* had been published in German in 1886 and was available in English by 1892.

23 The first volume of Ellis' *Studies in the Psychology of Sex*, it was co-authored with the married homosexual writer John Addington Symonds. According to Gould and Reeves (2001: 197), Ellis was 'inescapably linked with the concept of a liberation of body and heart'; in Joachimite fashion, 'he believed that the Age of the Spirit could be willed into being if enough people wanted it. It would be an age of individuality, of mystical sexuality, and of love'.

24 Ellis' work was banned in 1898 under the Obscene Publications Act, but the publicity surrounding this prosecution drew attention to homosexuality (Owen, 2004: 108). Of course, the trial of Oscar Wilde in 1895 had already made homosexuality a talking point.

25 Charles Booth saw in the urban, educated men and (especially) women of the upper middle classes a tendency to 'rush into extremes of religious doctrines and practices', providing a natural recruiting ground 'for occultism, new religions, new forms of old ones, or conversion to Rome' (Reed, 1998: 175).

26 A view expressed by muscular Christians such as Charles Kingsley. See Reed, 1998: 219–23; Hilliard, [1982] 2006: 6.

27 The list of what was and was not permissible included the 'six ritual points': altar lights, illegal vestments, the mixed chalice, the eastward position, elevation of the chalice and paten, and use of unleavened bread. For the text of the PWRA, see 'Legislation related to Liturgy in the Church of England' at Project Canterbury, www.anglicanhistory.org/pwra/index.html. cf. Bale's denunciation of Augustine of Canterbury as the anti-Christ who introduced candles, vestments, altar cloths, hymns and relics, mentioned in Chapter 1.

28 The consecration was carried out in utmost secrecy, and it is not known exactly who the consecrating bishops were – in *Dr Lee of Lambeth*, Brandreth says they

were popularly believed to have been a Greek, a Copt, and either a Roman or Old Catholic, but all evidence was destroyed in Lee's lifetime (in Anson, 1964: 76). See also 'A Chapter of Secret History', *Church Times*, 28 April 1922, p. 5. Whoever raised him to the episcopate, Lee certainly knew plenty of the *episcopi vagantes*, including Mar Pelagius (Morgan), Ferrette and Vilatte (see Chapter 2 for Pusey's refusal to write for a book edited by Lee which was to include an essay by Ferrette).

29 See 'A Statement of the Society of the Holy Cross Concerning the Order of Corporate Reunion ...', reproduced at Project Canterbury, www.anglicanhistory. org/ssc/ocr.html, accessed 23 June 2006.

30 This was particularly so after the declaration of papal infallibility in 1870; henceforth, an even greater emphasis was put on *Anglo*-Catholicism.

31 For example, the Guild of St Mary the Virgin in Oxford, founded in 1844, later becoming the Brotherhood of the Holy Trinity. In 1851 the Guild of St Alban the Martyr was initiated in Birmingham, and between 1845 and 1860, sixteen sisterhoods and communities for women were founded, fourteen of which have survived to the present. See Reed, 1998: 50.

32 In fact, few if any members were known until 1877, when the society's membership roll was published in the *Rock*. Just prior to this, on 14 June in the House of Lords, Lord Redesdale had exposed the privately printed manual for confessors *The Priest in Absolution* by Rev. J. C. Chambers (1817–74), the remaining stock and copyright of which had been purchased by the SSC on Chambers' death. The two events combined led to almost half the members leaving the SSC as their identity was discovered. See Walsh, 1898: 78–9.

33 Walsh (1898: 89) erroneously cites this as p. 205 and ascribes authorship to a male, since it was authored anonymously.

34 The concept of the 'naughty' priest, well established in French literature, began to appear in English tales such as 'The Priest and the Acolyte', which appeared in the single issue of *The Chameleon*, edited by John Francis Bloxam. It was used by the prosecution in the trial of Oscar Wilde in 1895 though actually written by Bloxam himself (Hilliard, 2006: 14).

35 The evangelical Dean of Carlisle, in 1867, declared that Anglo-Catholic priests, 'assumed the form and garb of superior holiness, which is but a cover and concealment of the paganism and popery of the heart which lies within'. Quoted in Anson, 1955: 233.

36 Both he and his sister, Christina Rossetti, were Anglo-Catholics.

37 Cf. Gardner and the worship of beauty by the witch cult, mentioned in Chapter 6.

38 All quotations from Pater, (1889) 1924: 248. In *Marius the Epicurean* (1885), Pater elaborated his ideal of the aesthetic life, opposing his cult of beauty to bare asceticism, and advocating the stimulating effect of the pursuit of beauty as an ideal of its own. The 'Divine Service' described in Chapter 23 of *Marius* is reputed to be based on the Mass as celebrated by Fr Nugee.

39 A notable figure in this revival was Augustus Welby Pugin, favoured architect for Anglo-Catholic churches and communities. See Chapter 1.

40 This included both the preservation of ruins *as* ruins, such as Tintern Abbey, as well as their rebuilding, as at Llandaff Cathedral.

41 Swinburne even called the *Idylls* 'Morte d'Albert, or Idylls of the Prince Consort' (Drabble, 2000: 1002).

42 He also arranged the Medieval court at the Great Exhibition of 1951.

43 Neale identified the Medieval period as a time of perfection in church architecture and symbolism, a 'Divine illustration of Catholic teaching. ... The unrivalled symbolic beauty of the Medieval Church was providentially intended as a timeless principle illustrating how sacramental signs and instruments convey

the grace of God' (de Hart, 1997). Neale also despaired that the Tractarians had 'missed one great principle, namely that of Aesthetics, and it is unworthy of them to blind themselves to it' (cited in Lough, 1975: 55).

44 See de Laura (1969). Cf. William James:

> The early Greeks are continually held up to us in literary works as models of the healthy-minded joyousness which the religion of nature may engender ... [but] the beautiful joyousness of their polytheism is only a poetic modern fiction.
>
> (James, 1985: 142)

45 Unpublished manuscript, c.1859, used as the epigraph for the journal *Studies in Medievalism*, http://www.medievalism.net/.

46 Both Pater and Arnold advocated a return to Hellenism and a resistance to 'Hebraic' values, although Pater didn't actually use the term Hebraic. See Uglow, 1990: xii.

47 See Uglow, 1990: xii. Pater, 'Coleridge', *Westminster Review*, January 1866.

48 J. W. Burgon, Dean of Chichester, quoted in Reed, 1998: 226.

49 Such a view had no basis on historical fact, since academic study of English history still began with the Reformation, emerging 'from an age of darkness and corruption' (Wilson, 2003: 138) in which nothing worthwhile had existed. In 1841, Thomas Arnold, Regius Professor of History at Oxford, had written, 'I could not bear to plunge myself into the very depths of that noisome cavern, and to toil through centuries of dirt and darkness' (cited in ibid.: 282). By the 1930s, the rediscovery of the Medieval world was very much underway, but, according to Wilson, it has still not penetrated the popular imagination (ibid.:138), which remains either filled with romanticised versions of the Middle Ages or ignores them.

50 Gardner, [1959] 2004: 115, discussed in Chapter 5.

51 That Gardner's eldest brother was at Oxford during Gerald's youth, i.e. in the 1880s, at the height of these Movements, is not necessarily suggestive of any influence, since Gardner reports that he remembers very little about him (Bracelin, [1960] 1999: 14).

52 Rountree, 2006 (abstract).

53 See Chapter 1, notes 40 and 41. In addition see the virulently anti-Catholic http://www.revolting.com/1.2/chick/vatican.html.

54 Hopman and Bond, 1995: 273. Thanks are due to Aidan Harris for pointing out this source.

55 Jewish Pagans and witches are becoming more noticeable, particularly in North America and amongst women who are comfortable with an identity incorporating both Judaism in Paganism and Paganism (usually in the form of Goddess worship) within Judaism. Starhawk is perhaps the most notable example of a Jewish witch (or 'Jewitch') who is 'increasingly happy to retain Jewish traditions within her Paganism, claiming that as she grows older both her Jewish and her Pagan identities have strengthened' (Raphael, 1998: 202).

56 In 1978, Lloyd reported 45 per cent Roman Catholic and 27.5 per cent Protestant; Adler in 1986 found 23.5 per cent Roman Catholic, 39.2 per cent Protestant, and 5.4 per cent Jewish; Ludeke in 1989 reported 49 per cent Roman Catholic, 40 per cent Protestant, and 10 per cent Jewish.

57 This is fair enough, given that it was simply a comment based on Crowley's extensive knowledge of the Wiccan population of Britain and Europe over twenty years rather than an argument based on an examination of data.

58 It is, of course, a rather Christian-centred approach to assume that anyone choosing a different religion of their own volition on reaching maturity *must* be rebelling

against Christianity, but the Christian heritage of the discipline of religious studies often leads scholars to make such assumptions. That such rebellion is not the case is effectively proved by Melissa Harrington's work (2000), which shows that conversion motifs among Wiccans are predominantly mystical and concerned with recognition of oneself as a witch rather than revealing any disaffection with Christianity. Indeed, as I pointed out in an earlier article,

> no research has to my knowledge been published to suggest that Wiccans move straight from Christianity to Wicca, and fieldwork suggests that there is usually a gap of some years between people feeling that Christianity is no longer relevant to their lives and finding Wicca. A straightforward disaffection or disillusionment with Christianity is therefore unlikely to be the main cause of Wiccan membership.
>
> (Pearson, 2003a: 176)

59 The name for Wiccan and Pagan weddings.
60 The Wheel of the Year incorporates eight festivals: Imbolc (1 February), Spring Equinox (*c.*21 March), Beltane (1 May), Midsummer (*c.*21 June), Lammas (1 August), Autumn Equinox (*c.*21 September), Samhain/Hallowe'en (31 October), and Yule (*c.*21 December). For a description of these festivals, the reader is referred to Crowley, Vivianne, 1996: 157–70; Farrar and Farrar, 1989; Harvey, 1997: 1–13; Samuel, 1998: 132–3, 140 n. 35–7.
61 Some Wiccans have indicated a strong sense of déjà vu when encountering Wicca after Catholicism (personal communications).
62 Cf. the Apostolic letter of Pope John Paul II dated 4 December 1988, celebrating the twenty-fifth anniversary of *Sacrosanctum Concilium*:

> Bread and wine, water and oil; and also incense, ashes, fire and flowers, and indeed almost all the elements of creation have their place in the Liturgy as gifts to the Creator and as a contribution to the *dignity* and *beauty* of the celebration.
>
> (cited in Elliot, 1995: 55)

63 The *Proskomide* is the preparation of the bread and wine for the Eucharist, the *Prothesis* more properly the table on which this is done. Both terms are used somewhat interchangeably by liturgical writers.
64 See Introduction, n. 16.
65 A somewhat Eliot-esque phrase. See Eliot, 1944.
66 In contrast to what Richard Roberts (1998) has termed 'narrative time' and 'hierarchised space', Wiccan ritual maintains spatiality and temporality as fluid constructs; indeed, time is deemed to be non-existent in the Wiccan circle – no watches may be worn in the ritual space and it is considered by Wiccans to be *detemporalised*. According to Berger (1979: 42), the 'categories of ordinary existence are transformed, especially the categories of space and time. Recurringly the supernatural is conceived of as being located in a different dimension of space or of time'.
67 '[S]timulating an awareness of the hidden side of reality' (Starhawk, 1989: 27) which, S. Gablik laments, we have lost –

> we no longer have the ability to shift mind-sets and thus to perceive other realities, to move between the worlds. ... One way to access these worlds is through ritual where something more goes on than meets the eye – something sacred.
>
> (Gablik, 1992: 22 in Carpenter, 1996: 65)

68 Written by Doreen Valiente. See Crowley, Vivianne, 1996: 87; Farrar, [1971] 1991: 13.

69 See Chapter 5.

70 Binding, scourging and sex are discussed in greater detail in Chapter 5.

71 And as Roof and Taylor insist, we should remember that, through his course on anatomy, James 'literally "taught the body"' (1995: 200).

72 Defined by Karel Werner as 'concentration; unification; deep meditative absorption in some yoga systems ... regarded as a state of higher cognition ...' (1997: 135).

73 Though it should be noted that in the one study of conversion to Wicca the mystical motif was cited most often, suggesting that people become involved in Wicca as a direct result of what they perceive to be mystical experience (Harrington, 2000).

74 Grimes, discussed in Bell, 1997: 183.

75 As Clifford Geertz (1973) has argued, instead of functioning purely to create social solidarity, rituals provide enacted narratives that allow people to interpret their own experience – they produce a story people tell themselves about themselves.

76 Gerholm cited in Parkin, 1992: 13.

77 This may itself be a legacy of Gardner's involvement in heterodox Christianity since, as noted in Chapter 3, the heterodox churches tended to be made up solely of bishops and priests rather than priests and laity.

5 SEX AND THE SACRED

1 Formed in 1827 by a dissatisfied Church of Ireland minister, John Nelson Darby, and a lapsed Roman Catholic, Edward Cronin, who sought greater purity than they believed possible in the corruption they saw in their own churches.

2 The highest initiatory grade in the Golden Dawn, supposedly reserved for the Third Order of the non-incarnated Secret Chiefs.

3 Godwin, 1994: 256. According to Godwin, 'Randolph had a typical nineteenth-century horror of masturbation, and neither he nor [Peter] Davidson [a founder of the HB of L] had the slightest tolerance for homosexuality' (ibid.: 361). It should be noted that the teachings of the HB of L stressed that sex magic had only two purposes, these being the spiritual elevation of the partners, and the benefit such elevation could confer on any child so conceived (ibid.: 358), i.e. it was not for the purpose of achieving anything through intense concentration at the moment of orgasm, as Crowley later described.

4 The Victorian era saw the cataloguing of sexual deviance, in such works as Krafft-Ebing's *Psychopathia Sexualis* (1886), and prison sentences for homosexuality (most famously Oscar Wilde, 1895). See Foucault ([1976] 1998).

5 Godwin develops the concept from Sangharakshita's claims that it is necessary to signal one's emotional, as well as intellectual rejection of Christianity, which may require one to commit blasphemy. The work of many occultists who break various sexual and religious taboos is, Godwin argues, a form of therapeutic blasphemy that allows them to free themselves from Christian indoctrination (ibid.). See Sangharakshita (D. P. E. Lingwood), 1989.

6 Urban, 2003: 139.

7 It is not my aim in this chapter to trace the history of sex magic, which has already been quite adequately covered (see Godwin, 1994, Chapter 16 and Urban, 2006. Unfortunately, Urban's book was not published until October 2006, after this work had gone to press; I therefore mention it here on the basis of the publisher's outline of its contents).

8 The magical or 'true' Will is represented in Wicca and many magical groups by the phallic wand.

9 Liber DCCCXXXVII, 'The Law of Liberty', section II, first published in *The Equinox* III (I), 1919. Available on www.sacred-texts.com/oto/lib837.htm, accessed 4 January 2007. This section contains a number of passages which were later incorporated into the Charge of the Goddess used in Wicca.

10 He envisioned the abbey as a magical colony from which to launch the new (third) aeon of which Crowley considered himself to be the chosen prophet. This was to be the Age of Horus (the child), superseding that of the Father and that of the Mother (cf. Valentinian gnosticism's trinity of Father, Mother, Child, noted in Chapter 3, n. 17). Shadows of Joachim of Fiore emerge here once again, and it may well be that Crowley was using a gnostic adaptation of the three statuses, given the presence of Joachimite ideas within the French heterodox influences on Reuss and the OTO. Crowley's new aeon seemed not to be destined to begin in Sicily after all, however, as Crowley was expelled by Mussolini in 1923.

11 See Rabelais, 1985: 150–1.

12 Rabelais is included in the list of saints contained in the Gnostic Mass. See http://www.hermetic.com/sabazius/gnostic_mass.htm, accessed 13 March 2006.

13 Blake, 'The Garden of Love', in *Songs of Experience*. Crowley was an admirer of William Blake, who he regarded as a great religious teacher (Crowley, 1978: 395). This is unsurprising given Blake's insistence in *Jerusalem*, Ch. 1, 10:20–1, that 'I must create a System or be enslav'd by another Man's'. Blake's cult of the child may also have influenced Crowley's change to the Joachimite progression, from Father to Son to Spirit, to Father to Mother to Child. Although Crowley did not include Blake in the list of saints of the Gnostic Mass, he was later added, in 1997, by Patriarch Hymenaeus Beta.

14 'Homilies on 1 John, VII, 8', in Burnaby 1955: 316. Sometimes rendered *Ama deum, et fac quod vis* ('Love God, and do what you will').

15 I.e. not as the licence to 'do what you like', as it is often misrepresented, but as a basis for choosing one's own spiritual (and moral) path through life, which requires dedication and self-knowledge.

16 See Gay ([1969] 1996: 196ff) for a discussion of Diderot's similar argument for the love of liberty versus the hypocritical fetters of the Christian sexual code.

17 See Chapter 3.

18 Gardener, (1959) 2004.: 115. See also p. 210: 'When the Church made marriage a Sacrament, they were right; but when they added that it was ordained for the procreation of children and for that alone, they were a thousand thousand times wrong.' Of course, according to the Book of Common Prayer marriage is not simply for the purposes of procreation but because man cannot contain his lust and for the 'mutual benefit' of husband and wife.

19 'Thou hast conquered, O pale Galilean; The world has grown grey from thy breath./We have drunken of things Lethean,/And fed on the fullness of death.' See Gardner, [1959] 2004: 125. Swinburne was a favourite poet of Crowley, and is to be found in the list of Saints of the *Ecclesiæ Gnosticæ Catholicæ*, recited towards the close of the Gnostic Mass. See http://www.hermetic.com/sabazius/gnostic_mass.htm, accessed 14 March 2006.

20 For example, the charges against the Cathars in the twelfth century were almost identical to those levelled against witches. To both are ascribed a doctrine of dualism between God and the Devil, both are accused of secret assemblies, and both are charged with indulging in promiscuous sexual orgies. See Trevor-Roper (1969: 113) and Cohn (1975: x, 260–2). Cohn also notes that the same charges were levelled against early Christians by pagans (ibid.: ix).

21 Hutton 2003d: 200–1 notes a few examples, including Epiphanius' claims that the Barbelo gnostics enacted nude rites, and Hippolytus' denunciations of the

Naasene gnostics for the practice of an all-male nocturnal nude rite. Always in the claims made by ecclesiastics whose aim was to root out aberrant Christian traditions, there is no evidence from either the writings of heretics themselves or from their confessions.

22 Against the various gnostic sects was levelled an accusation based on extreme dualism – since they claimed that the body is not important, it therefore wouldn't matter what was done with it, whether that be never washing, extreme asceticism, or the gratification of every sexual desire.

23 Second-century gnostic sect, founded by Carpocrates in Alexandria who 'taught the practice of every sort of immorality and the cultivation of every kind of sin' (John of Damascus, *On Heresies*, 27). They were accused of magic and sexual immorality. For example, Irenaeus of Lyon, writes, 'They practise also magical arts and incantations; philters, also, and love-potions; and have recourse to familiar spirits, dream-sending demons, and other abominations' (*Adv. Haer./Against Heresies* 1.25.3). Clement of Alexandria, in a letter to Theodore discovered in 1958 writes, 'You did well in silencing the unspeakable teachings of the Carpocratians. For these are the "wandering stars" referred to in the prophecy, who wander from the narrow road of the commandments into a boundless abyss of the carnal and bodily sins'. Eusebius claimed that it was because of the activities of the Carpocratians that all Christians came under 'the infamous and most absurd suspicion that we practised unlawful commerce with mothers and sisters, and enjoyed impious feasts' (*Hist. Eccl./Ecclesiastical History* 4.7.11).

24 Crushed at the beginning of the fourteenth century. Neo-Templar organisations such as the OTO, ignoring the complete lack of evidence for the practices alleged to be part of Templar rituals, play upon the associations with sexual deviance in their higher grade rituals.

25 See Gardner, 2004: 213ff.

26 For an excellent account tracing this development, see Hanegraaff 1995b, particularly the section entitled 'The making of a stereotype'.

27 Goldberg, B.Z. *The Sacred Fire: The Story of Sex in Religion* (1931); Goodland, R. *A Bibliography of Sex Rites and Customs* (1931); Dane, V. *Naked Ascetic* (1933); Potter, LaForest, *Strange Loves: A Study of Sexual Abnormalities* (1937); Bose, D.N. (ed.), *Tantras: Their Philosophy and Occult Secrets* (n.d. listed, but certainly published by 1946, with many subsequent reprints).

28 See Vivianne Crowley, 1996: 188. The blessing of the cakes in Crowley's Gnostic Mass reads: 'Lord most secret, bless this spiritual food unto our bodies, bestowing upon us health and wealth and strength and joy and peace, and that fulfilment of will and of love under will that is perpetual happiness' (http://www.hermetic.com/sabazius/gnostic_mass.htm, accessed 15 March 2006).

29 See Chapter 4.

30 The male holds the chalice, the female symbol, and the female holds the male symbol, the athame.

31 See Vivianne Crowley, 1990a: 47 for an account of her initiation.

32 Apparent because, as Jeremy Carrette notes (2005: 15), '[p]ain, the body and religious practices have a long history, but this is not the modern invention of S&M'.

33 Kelly claims that 'the rites can be boiled down to a set of practices designed to induce sexual excitement by scourging, and that this was Gardner's distinctive personal contribution to, and main emotional investment in [Wicca]' (Hutton, 1999: 235), though it seems that there were more complex issues at work, including Gardner's asthma, which disabled him from other more energetic mechanisms for entering trance states, and genuine belief that bondage and scourging were idiosyncratic ways of attaining an ecstatic trance. As Hutton

discerns (ibid.), Gardner's novels are not works of flagellant fiction and his scrapbooks, though containg some erotic images of 'pretty, nude young women', are not concerned with binding or flagellation. He concludes, '[t]his is not the profile of a straightforward flagellant'.

34 It is also a symbol of discipline – of the self as well as others, and more importantly the former. As Vivianne Crowley states, the scourge is a tool which it is important we make and consecrate ourselves; for it is a symbol of the self-discipline that is necessary to follow an initiatory path. The teaching given with the scourge in the first degree was that the initiate should be willing to suffer to learn (1996: 199).

35 There are eight magical weapons, or working tools, in Wicca – the sword, black-handled knife or athame, white-handled knife or boline, wand, pentacle, censer, cords, and scourge. The two knives are taken from the *Key of Solomon*; the rest derive from the Golden Dawn via Crowley, apart from the scourge, which seems to come directly from Crowley. The chalice, regarded as a magical tool by both the Golden Dawn and Crowley is not regarded as such in Wicca. See Hutton, 1999: 229.

36 WITCH was formed at Hallowe'en 1968 as the 'action wing' of New York Radical Women. Raphael (1998: 136) describes them as 'something of an anarchic sisterhood enjoining a theatrical form of feminist praxis'. They hexed the Chase Manhattan bank, and invaded the Bride Fair at Madison Square Gardens dressed as witches. Describing witches, the collective wrote: 'they bowed to no man, being the living remnant of the oldest culture of all' (WITCH, 'Spooking the patriarchy', cited in Purkiss, 1996: 9).

37 See also her analysis of film noir: 'women are active, not static symbols, are intelligent and powerful, if destructively so, and derive power, not weakness from their sexuality' (ibid.: 121).

38 'crones are the survivors of the perpetual witchcraze of patriarchy … which is the entire period of patriarchal rule' (Daly, 198: 14–15).

39 A peremptory look on internet fetish sites showed a prevalence of PVC 'Goth-Witch-Vamp' outfits for the dominant woman; there seems to be no equivalent for men!

40 It remains a moot point as to whether this is an image which reflects what women really are rather than a fantasy about what woman is or should be. Among early political feminists, not only was any idea of female spirituality shunned, but there were also concerns that the use of the witch stereotype (by WITCH, Daly, *et al*.) would harm their cause.

41 Written by Doreen Valiente. The full text of the Charge can be found in Farrar (1971) 1991: 172–3, and an annotated version appears in Crowley, Vivianne 1996: 189–191; myriad versions are available on the internet. Valiente's original version, written in verse, is in Valiente, 1989:61–2. See also n. 9, above.

42 Out of respect for Wiccan secrecy, I have given here words from the literary source from which the charge derives, rather than the charge itself. Interestingly, Chapter 22 of Cabell's *Jürgen* was based on Aleister Crowley's most sexual rite, the Gnostic Mass. Crowley lambasted 'the smut-smeller society' which had suppressed *Jürgen* as obscene, though it at last made Cabell famous (see Crowley, 1978: 738–9).

43 Cf. Winckelmann's belief in the 'salutary effects of climate, health, naturalism and nudity enjoyed by the ancients and not by clothed, corrupted, and lifeless moderns' (Howard, 1982: 122; see also ibid.: 125). This belief was shared by William Blake, a reputed nudist, who 'found justification for nudism in Christian and esoteric theory and practice. Like Winckelmann and other creative contemporary thinkers, he held that nudism was sacred and salutary' (ibid.: 129).

44 See, for instance, *Love's Enchantment (Der Liebeszauber)*, Flemish School 1670–80, which was used as the cover of Keith Thomas' *Religion and the Decline of Magic*. Luhrmann (1994: Plate 4) notes that modern witches sometimes point to this painting as a piece of historical evidence for working in the nude. A further example which Luhrmann points out is an engraving called *The Four Witches* (1497) by Albrecht Dürer (ibid.: Plate 1). Hutton (2003d: 203) notes that representations of the nude witch were prominent in North European, particularly German, art from the sixteenth century on, which may have simply been a reflection of contemporary attitudes which did not generally allow the drawing of nude females. It should be remembered that there are also numerous representations of the witch in art which, whilst often depicting the witch as female, also paint her fully-clothed – Goya's *Conjuro* and *The Sabbat* (both *c.* 1794–5), for example.

45 See Crowley, Vivianne (1996: 98) for provenances from the Celts and the Mysteries of Isis and Osiris; Valiente (1993: 73 and 1989: 102) cites ancient Greek and Roman practices of working nude or 'in loose flowing garments', the Villa of the Mysteries in Pompeii is thought to provide evidence of nudity during a ritual of initiation (1989: 59), and tantric worship 'gives further meaning to the custom of ritual nudity, which is found in the east as well as the west' (1989: 141). She reports Pliny's observation that women and girls in ancient Britain performed religious and magical rites in the nude (1989: 99), but provides no reference for this.

46 Merchant here relies on Christopher Hill, 1972: 251–7.

47 Cf. Chapter 3, n. 54 in the present volume. Also Salomonsen, 2002: 225: 'Ritual nudity ... symbolizes the innocence of beginnings, of conversions, of being born again'.

48 Hutton's assertion that Wicca may be 'taking a Christian stereotype of bad behaviour and giving it positive connotations' (Hutton, 2003d: 207) stands despite this, for Vintras' heterodoxy, and Ranters and Quakers of the first half of the seventeenth century were certainly regarded as deviant by more orthodox Christianity.

49 A somewhat gnostic echo, the implication being that the spiritual focus is 'higher' than recognising the naked body.

50 'What is peculiar to modern societies is not that they consigned sex to a shadow existence, but that they dedicated themselves to speaking of it *ad infinitum*, while exploiting it as *the* secret' (Foucault, [1976] 1998: 35).

51 Cf. Foucault's 'tolerant familiarity with the illicit' (ibid.: 3).

52 See Valiente:

> The traditional ritual nudity has for its purpose the free flow of power from the naked bodies of the participants ... when a circle of naked or loosely robed dancers gyrates in a witchcraft ceremony, the power flowing from their bodies rises upwards towards the centre of the circle, forming a cone-shape which is called the Cone of Power.
>
> (Valiente, 1993: 73)

Similar reasons are also cited by Russell (1991: 169) from his fieldwork, where witches reported that nudity 'increases their contact with the powers of nature ... erases class distinctions ... [allows them] to appear before the gods as they were born, with nothing to hide ... [and] gives them a salutary sense of freedom'.

53 A fact also noted by Luhrmann (1994: 249), although she does not elaborate on it, except to point out that nudity is contained within the circle.

54 Luhrmann does not make it clear on what evidence she bases this observation.

55 Cf. Crowley, Vivianne, 1996: 107.

56 Turner takes as his example St Francis, to whom 'poverty and nakedness were both expressive symbols of communitas and instruments for attaining it' (1969: 146).
57 Wildman, Laura (lwildman@medusa.sbs.umass.edu), 28 May 1999, *Witches' Bodies*. E-mail to Nature Religion Scholars List (natrel-l@uscolo.edu).
58 One need only observe the covers of some of the books aimed at the teen witches, mentioned in the introduction – Ravenwolf's has four teenage girls, none of whom are remotely overweight, whilst the girl on Horne's cover could easily be described as 'Barbie doll'. See the related and growing industry of Goddess commodities (e.g. Adams *et al.*, 2004; Simpson, 2001; Wishart, 2003).
59 Yates, 1991: 25. Hutton notes the Chaldean Oracles which also suggest a devotee casting off not only clothes but the world and the flesh in order to ascend in spirit (2003d: 199). Cf. the myth of the descent of Inanna.
60 For the conservative nature of tantra, see Urban, 2000.
61 Wicca has also been accused of homophobia, largely due to Gardner's proclivities, despite the open bisexuality of Alex Sanders and other high profile figures of the past 40 years. Phallocentric heterosexuality has been very much the 'normal' sexual expression at the centre of Wicca. Whilst gays, lesbians and bis have been welcome in Wicca, their involvement has often been besieged with problems because of the notion that gender polarity is necessary for effective magic. Many have left and sought a more queer friendly magical life in, for example, shamanism and the heathen *seidr* practices. Gay Wiccans are now challenging the accepted norms of Wiccan practice and belief, not only by conducting same-sex initiations but by remaining within what we might call 'mainstream Wicca', arguing eruditely, and inviting others to their rituals. As a result, many of the beliefs propagated by Gardner are now being questioned and there appears to be a greater willingness to experiment with the sexual energies expressed between people of varying persuasions and inclinations, including transexuals and androgynes as well as gays, lesbians and bisexuals.
62 Thus, whilst Wicca might subvert Christian notions of religion by collapsing the boundaries between religion and magic, it merely plays with the disruption of imagined Christian attitudes towards sexuality.
63 Even in the Great Rite the missionary position remains the norm.
64 The overlaps between Wiccan S/M symbolism and rhetoric and the physical spirituality of some S/M practitioners remains unexplored, and issues of power, abuse, and gender are only just beginning to be recognised. A brief comparison between Wiccan initiation and the S/M dungeon, for example, suggests a common conceptual ground, yet the physical actuality expressed and embraced in S/M is rarely found in Wicca except in cases where a genuine combination of S/M and Wicca exists for the individual.

6 THE MAGIC OF THE MARGINS

1 Tylor is the 'father of anthropology'. In 1871 he produced *Primitive Culture*, and in 1884 Oxford University created a readership in anthropology for him; in 1886, he became the first professor of the new discipline.
2 See also Owen's descriptions of some of those who populated such 'bourgeois' organisations as the Hermetic Order of the Golden Dawn, Owen 2004: 1 and 3, and Butler, 2004: 212, who insists that initiates were drawn 'from all walks of life'.
3 Evans-Pritchard, 1937: 30, 201.
4 Thomas, [1971] 1991: 794.
5 Although ambiguities are evident in the works of Christian mages such as Marsilio Ficino, who attempted to reconcile the practice of magic to Christian

doctrine, particularly as expounded by Augustine in his *City of God*, this is largely because the Hermetic passages relating to the animation of statues with the powers of the cosmos seemed to breach the Second Commandment (see Hanegraaff, 1999: 1ff).

6 Tylor's work was, of course, just a little too early to take note of the Golden Dawn. By the time Malinowski was writing the comments quoted above, the Order had collapsed. It was also, of course, supposed to be a secret society, and therefore inaccessible to academic study by outsiders.

7 See Butler (2004: 212): 'Four more temples and twelve years [after its foundation], the Order, in its original form, self-destructed in the midst of a scandalous court case and general insurrection'. See also Francis King, [1970] 1989: 66–78.

8 Butler (2004: 213) notes six fundamental changes to Western magic made by the Golden Dawn, that made magical practice relevant for the late nineteenth century and beyond. These are (1) group rather than solitary practice; (2) institutionalised format instead of the transmission of magical knowledge from individual or textual authority; (3) loss of an intermediary spirit and a focus on direct communication through invocation or evocation; (4) change in magical goals from material gain to personal transmutation; (5) dominance of the imagination; (6) equality of women. Of these, the fourth is debatable. Butler herself states that this emphasis was 'a restatement of the Renaissance goal' (ibid.: 221), and see later in this chapter.

9 See Martin, 1989: 98–124.

10 See Gilbert, 2005: 1164–5.

11 See Hutton, 1999: 184–5.

12 See Ashcroft-Nowicki, 1986, for example, mentioned later in the chapter in relation to 'spiritual alchemy'.

13 Hanegraaff, 1998: 80.

14 A grimoire is a book containing spells and rituals, 'The Key of Solomon' being perhaps the most famous. Many grimoires circulated in the Middle Ages as handbooks of magic, drawing on ancient Egyptian, Greek, Latin and Hebrew texts.

15 One might also argue the same for some heathen traditions which contain the 'intuitive and largely feminine based magic' of *seidr*; the 'highly ceremonial form of magic known as *galdr*'; and the 'talismatic [*sic*] magic' of the runes, known as *taufr* (Pete Jennings, 1998: 18–19). Jennings adds his personal view that '[t]here is nothing more magical for me than seeing a delicate plant forcing its way up through a crack in the concrete to flower. It knows its will and is doing it'.

16 Cited in Harvey, 1997: 88. Harvey provides no source for the quotation and I have as yet been unable to trace the exact phrase in Fortune's works.

17 Again, cf. Böehme: '[Magic] is a creatrix according to the understanding and lends itself to good or evil. ... By Magic is everything accomplished, both good and bad. ... In that which is good it is good, and in that which is evil it is evil' ([1620] 1989: 5: 11 and 19).

18 Ashcroft-Nowicki, 1986: 21–2.

19 Wax dolls made to represent people, used principally for healing.

20 The reflection of the macrocosm in the microcosm is a key Hermetic principle embedded within the magic and philosophy of the Western Esoteric Tradition and thence transferred to Wicca.

21 The other three are 'correspondences', 'living nature', and 'imagination and mediation'. In addition, there are two 'relative' elements that frequently occur alongside the four fundamental elements. These are the 'praxis of the concordance', the attempt 'to establish common denominators between two different traditions or even more, among all traditions, in the hope of

obtaining an illumination, a gnosis, of superior quality' (Faivre, 1994: 14), and 'transmission', i.e. teaching via initiation.

22 As opposed to mere 'transformation', which implies a change more or less limited to outward appearance.

23 Such as the Wheel of the Year.

24 See Chapter 4 for an outline of the Wiccan ritual framework.

25 This was not just the 'magic' of the Mass, but also Medieval ritual magic, largely the domain of clerics who had almost exclusive access to both books and literacy. See Kieckhefer, [1989] 1992.

26 See Allen, 2005.

27 See Lelli, 2005.

28 See Ciliberto, 2005.

29 Many manuscripts collectively known as the *Corpus Hermeticum*, the authorship of which was attributed to the mythical Egyptian figure Hermes Trismegistos, Thrice-Great Hermes, were extant in the fifteenth century. The manuscripts were thought to date from vast antiquity, long before Plato and even longer before Christ – indeed, Hermes Trismegistos was believed by some to be a contemporary of Moses, and by others to have lived at the same time as Noah. The *Corpus* was, however, misdated and it is now known that the writings were by various authors and of varying dates, being 'the records of individual souls seeking revelation, intuition into the divine, personal salvation, gnosis, without the aid of a personal God or Saviour, but through a religious approach to the universe' (Yates, [1964] 1991: 22). Isaac Casaubon (1559–1614), in his *De rebus sacris et ecclesiaticis exercitationes XVI* of 1614, finally disproved the pre-Christian provenance of the Hermetic manuscripts. For further information, see van den Broek, 2005b: 487–99.

30 See Yates, 1991: 86.

31 Yates (1991: 15) notes that Hermes is always either positioned first or second only to Zoroaster in this genealogy, demonstrating 'the extreme importance which Ficino assigned to Hermes as the *fons et origo* of the wisdom tradition which led in an unbroken chain to Plato'.

32 Hermes Trismegistos, the Egyptian sage to whom the *Corpus Hermeticum* is attributed, was called the first great theologian (see preface to Ficino's translation of the *Corpus* – 'Thus, he was called the first author of theology, and Orpheus followed him, taking second place in the ancient theology …'). Ficino later moved Zoroaster ahead of Hermes Trismegistos. Cf. Copenhaver, 1995: xlviii. Magic, or at least the so-called 'learned magic' evinced in Neoplatonism and the Hermetica, is distinctly gnostic in its concern with bridging the gap between the human and the divine, the microcosm and the macrocosm.

33 Bruno's *De umbris idearum* of 1582 might be a possible source for the Wiccan 'Book of Shadows', following from the *Liber de umbris* attributed to Solomon by the fourteenth century magician Cecco d'Ascoli. The concept of the Book of Shadows is certainly a continuation of an Hermetic theme popularised and developed in Renaissance esotericism whereby 'the light of divinity [is sought] through having an intention of will towards shadows or reflections of it' (Yates, 1991: 195). Yates further suggests that

> Bruno's 'shadows of ideas' *are* the magical images, the archetypal images in the heavens which are closer to the divine mind than things here below. And it is even possible that Ficino, in his frequent uses of the word 'shadows', may sometimes mean this too.
>
> (Yates, 1991: 197)

34 Long a Catholic enclave, Oxford University had by this time become Protestant, largely through the forced eviction of many of its college masters and the drain of Catholic students, or those with Catholic tendencies, to Jesuit seminaries at Douai and elsewhere in continental Europe.

35 Bruno was burned at the stake, as a heretic and magician, in Rome on 17 February 1600.

36 See Muir, 1997, Chapters 3 and 4, and, of course, Bakhtin, 1940.

37 Cited in Styers, 2004: 37, no reference given.

38 Thomas, [1971] 1991: 69.

39 Pausinius (*c*.160 CE) thought Plato had developed this from Chaldean or even Indian sources. See During, 2002: 5.

40 Due to the preference for the more Attic term *goês* instead of *magos* (Bremmer, 2002: 11).

41 Cf. Flood (1999: 231): 'Orientalist discourse ... contrasts the East as feminine, irrational, exotic, sensual, female, despotic, and backward, with the West as masculine, rational, sober, moral, male, democratic, and progressive ... the Orient becomes a projection of what the West does not wish to acknowledge about itself...'. Wax and Wax argued that it had become

> clear that the basis of the distinctions between magic and religion (or magic and science) is not the attitudes and conduct of the primitive peoples in whose lives magic plays such a major role. Rather, these distinctions stem from the rationalistic orientation of Western civilisation (and its highly rational scholars).
>
> (cited in Hanegraaff, 1998: 80)

42 See also Luhrmann, 1994: 8–10.

43 Breckenridge and van de Veer, 1993: 12.

AFTERWORD: THE CHRISTIAN HERITAGE

1 A situation that I intend to rectify in a future book.

2 As William Warburton (1698–1779), Bishop of Gloucester (from 1759), is reputed to have said in answer to a question from Lord Sandwich, 'orthodoxy is my doxy; heterodoxy is another man's doxy', reported in Joseph Priestley's *Memoirs*, vol. 1, 1807: 372. Gardner paraphrases the aphorism [1959] 2004: 108.

BIBLIOGRAPHY

Adams, Jessica, Jelena Glisic and Anthea Paul (2004) *21st Century Goddess: The Modern Girl's Guide to the Universe*, London: Corgi Adult.

Adler, Margot (1986) *Drawing Down the Moon: Witches, Druids, Goddess-Worshippers, and other Pagans in America Today*, Boston, MA: Beacon Press.

Alexander, Jeffrey C. (1995) *Fin de Siècle Social Theory: Relativism, Reduction and the Problem of Reason*, New York: Verso.

Allen, Micheal J. B. (2005) 'Ficino, Marsilio', in Hanegraaff, W. J. (ed.), *Dictionary of Gnosis and Western Esotericism, Vol. I*, Leiden/Boston, MA: Brill, pp. 360–7.

Anonymous (1895) 'The Latter Day Pagans', in *The Quarterly Review*, 182, London: John Murray, pp. 31–58.

Anson, Peter F. (1964) *Bishops at Large: Some Autocephalous Churches of the Past Hundred Years and their Founders*, London: Faber & Faber.

—— (1955) *The Call of the Cloister*, London: SPCK.

Ashcroft-Nowicki, Dolores (1986) *The Ritual Magic Workbook: A Practical Course of Self-Initiation*, London: Aquarian Press.

Aston, M. (1964) 'Lollardy and the Reformation: Survival or Revival', in *History*, xlix (166), pp. 149–70.

Bachofen, J. J. ([1870] 1967) *Myth, Religion and Mother-Right: Selected Writings*, edited by Joseph Campbell, Princeton, NJ: Princeton University Press.

Baker, James W. (1996) 'White Witches: Historic Fact and Romantic Fantasy', in Lewis, James R. (ed.), *Magical Religion and Modern Witchcraft*, Albany, NY: SUNY, pp. 171–92.

Bakhtin, Mikhail ([1940] 1984) *Rabelais and His World*, trans. Helen Iswolsky, Bloomington, IN: Indiana University Press.

Barnett, S. J. (1999) 'Where Was Your Church Before Luther? Claims for the Antiquity of Protestantism Examined', in *Church History*, 68 (1), pp. 14–41.

Barrow, Logie (1986) *Independent Spirits: Spiritualism and English Plebeians 1850–1910*, London: Routledge and Kegan Paul.

Baudelaire, Charles (1992) *Selected Writings on Art and Literature*, trans. P. E. Charvet, Harmondsworth: Penguin.

—— ([1930] 1990) *Intimate Journals*, trans. Christopher Isherwood, London: Picador.

—— (1989), *The Poems in Prose*, ed. and trans. Francis Scarfe, London: Anvil Press.

Bauman, Zygmunt (1999) 'Postmodern religion?', in Heelas, Paul (ed.) *Religion, Modernity, and Postmodernity*, Oxford: Blackwell, pp. 55–78.

—— (1988) *Freedom: Concepts in the Social Sciences*, Milton Keynes: Open University Press.

Baumann, Gerd (1992) 'Ritual Implicates "Others": Rereading Durkheim in a Plural Society', in Coppet, Daniel de (ed.), *Understanding Rituals*, London: Routledge, pp. 97–116.

Bell, Catherine (1997) *Ritual: Perspectives and Dimension*, New York: Oxford University Press.

—— (1992) *Ritual Theory, Ritual Practice*, New York: Oxford University Press.

Bentley, James (1978) *Ritualism and Politics in Victorian Britain: An Attempt to Legislate for Belief*, Oxford: Oxford University Press.

Berens, Jessica and Kerry Sharp (eds) (2002) *Inappropriate Behaviour: Prada Sucks! and other Demented Descants*, London: Serpent's Tail.

Berger, Helen A. (1999) *A Community of Witches: Contemporary Neo-Paganism and Witchcraft in the United States*, Columbia, SC: University of South Carolina Press.

Berger, Peter L. (1979) *The Heretical Imperative: Contemporary Possibilities of Religious Affirmation*, New York: Anchor Press (Doubleday).

Berman, David (1990) *A History of Atheism in Britain: From Hobbes to Russell*, London: Routledge.

Besant, Annie (1910) *Popular Lectures on Theosophy*, Madras: The Theosophist Office.

—— (1910) *The Path of Discipleship*, Benares: Theosophical Publishing Society.

—— (1909) *The Changing World*, London: Theosophical Publishing Society.

Blackbourn, David (1991) 'The Catholic Church in Europe since the French Revolution: A Review Article', in *Comparative Studies in Society and History*, 33 (4), pp. 778–90.

Blake, William (1927) 'The Garden of Love', in Songs of Experience, *Poems and Prophecies*, ed. Max Plowman, London: J. M. Dent & Sons Ltd.

—— (1804–20) 'Jerusalem', Chapter 1, in Plowman, Max (ed.) *William Blake: Poems and Prophecies*, London: J. M. Dent & Sons Ltd, pp. 164–92.

Blavatsky, H. P. (1975) *Studies in Occultism*, London: White Lion Publishing.

—— (1960) *Isis Unveiled*, Pasadena, CA: Theosophical University Press.

Bocking, Brian (2001) 'Religious Studies: the New Queen of the Sciences', paper presented at the British Association for the Study of Religion annual conference, October 2000 at the University of London, SOAS.

Böehme, Jacob ([1620] 1989) *Sex Puncta Mystica or A Short Explanation of Six Mystical Points*, trans. John Rolleston Earle, www.facsicle.com/issue02/imagining-language/bohme3.html.

Bonewits, Isaac ([1971] 1989) *Real Magic*, York Beach, ME: Samuel Weiser.

Bossy, John (1985) *Christianity in the West: 1400–1700*, Oxford: Oxford University Press.

Bowman, Marion (2002) 'Contemporary Celtic Spirituality', in Pearson, Joanne (ed.), *Belief Beyond Boundaries: Wicca, Celtic Spirituality and the New Age*, Aldershot: Ashgate, pp. 55–101.

—— (1996) 'Cardiac Celts: Images of the Celts in Paganism', in Harvey, Graham and Charlotte Hardman (eds), *Paganism Today: Wiccans, Druids, the Goddess and Ancient Earth Traditions for the Twenty-First Century*, London: Thorsons, pp. 242–51.

Bracelin, Jack ([1960] 1999) *Gerald Gardner: Witch*, Thame: I-H-O Books.

Brandreth, Fr Henry R. T. (1947) *Episcopi Vagantes and the Anglican Church*, London: SPCK.

—— (1947) *The Œcumenical Ideals of the Oxford Movement*, London: SPCK.

Breckenridge, Carole A. and Peter van de Veer (1993) *Orientalism and the Postcolonial Predicament*, Philadelphia, PA: University of Pennsylvania Press.

Bremmer, Jan (2002) 'The Birth of the Term "Magic"', in Bremmer, Jan N.and Jan R. Veenstra (eds), *The Metamorphosis of Magic from Late Antiquity to the Early Modern Period*, Leuven/Paris/Dudley, MA: Peeters, pp. 1–11.

Briggs, Robin (1996) *Witches and Neighbours: The Social and Cultural Context of European Witchcraft*, London: HarperCollins.

Brilioth, Rev. Yngve (1925) *The Anglican Revival: Studies in the Oxford Movement*, London: Longmans, Green & Co.

Bristow, Joseph (1997) *Sexuality*, London: Routledge.

Brown, Callum G. (2001) *The Death of Christian Britain*, London: Routledge.

Bruce, Steve (2002) *God is Dead: Explaining Secularization*, Oxford: Blackwell.

Bruno, Giordano ([1584] 1992) *The Expulsion of the Triumphant Beast*, trans. and ed. Arthur D. Imerti, Lincoln, NE: University of Nebraska Press.

Buber, Martin (1961) *Between Man and Man*, trans. Ronald Gregor Smith, London: Collins.

Burgess, Right Revd Thomas (Bishop of St David's) (1815) *Tracts on the Origin and Independence of the Ancient British Church; of the Supremacy of the Pope, and the Inconsistency of All Foreign Jurisdiction with the British Constitution; and on the Differences Between the Churches of England and of Rome*, London: F. C. & J. Rivington.

—— (1813) *The First Seven Epochs of the Ancient British Church: A Sermon Preached at St. Peter's Church, Carmarthen on the Second of July 1812, at the Anniversary Meeting of the Society for Promoting Christian Knowledge, and Church Union, in the Diocese of St. David's*, London: F. C. & J. Rivington.

Burnaby, John (ed.) (1955) *Augustine: Later Works*, London: SCM Press.

Burr, G. L. (1922) 'A Review of M. A. Murray's *Witch Cult in Western Europe*', in *American Historical Review*, 27 (4), pp. 780–3.

Butler, Alison (2004) 'Making Magic Modern: Nineteenth-Century Adaptations', in *The Pomegranate*, 6 (2), pp. 212–30.

Cabell, James Branch ([1921] 1984) *Jürgen*, London: Unwin Books.

Cabot, Laurie with Tom Cowan (1990) *Power of the Witch*, London: Michael Joseph.

Carmichael, Alexander ([1900; 1928 ff.] 1997) *Carmina Gadelica: Hymns and Incantations*, Trowbridge: Redwood Books.

Carpenter, Dennis D. (1996a) 'Emergent Nature Spirituality: An Examination of the Major Spiritual Contours of the Contemporary Pagan Worldview', in Lewis, James R. (ed.), *Magical Religion and Modern Witchcraft*, New York: SUNY, pp. 35–72.

—— (1996b) 'Practitioners of Paganism and Wiccan Spirituality in Contemporary Society: A Review of the Literature', in Lewis, James R. (ed.) *Magical Religion and Modern Witchcraft*, Albany, NY: SUNY, pp. 373–406.

—— (1995) *Spiritual Experiences, Life Changes, and Ecological Viewpoints of Contemporary Pagans*, Saybrook Institute, San Francisco, California, unpublished PhD thesis.

Carrette, Jeremy (2005) 'Intense Exchange: Sadomasochism, Theology and the Politics of Late Capitalism', in *Theology and Sexuality Special Issue: Dangerous Sex*, 11 (2), pp. 11–30.

Carrette, Jeremy and Richard King (2005) $*elling Spirituality: The Silent Takeover of Religion*, London: Routledge.

Carr-Gomm, Philip (1996) (ed.) *The Druid Renaissance: The Voice of Druidry Today*, London: Thorsons.

Chadwick, Owen (1992) *The Spirit of the Oxford Movement: Tractarian Essays*, Cambridge: Cambridge University Press.

Chambers, Robert (1826) *Popular Rhymes of Scotland*, Edinburgh: C. Smith & Co.; London: James Duncan.

Chesterton, G. K. (1926) *The Catholic Church and Conversion*, New York: Macmillan.

Ciliberto, Michele (2005) 'Bruno, Giordano (Filippo)', in Hanegraaff, W. J. (ed.), *Dictionary of Gnosis and Western Esotericism, Vol. I*, Leiden/Boston, MA: Brill, pp. 206–13.

Clark, J. C. D. (2000) 'Protestantism, Nationalism, and National Identity, 1660–1832', in *The Historical Journal*, 43 (1), pp. 249–76.

Clifton, Chas (2004) Review of Philip Heselton, *Gerald Gardner and the Cauldron of Inspiration*, in *The Pomegranate*, 6 (2), pp. 267–70.

—— (1998) 'The Significance of Aradia', in Leland, Charles Godfrey, *Aradia or the Gospel of the Witches*, trans. Mario and Dina Pazzaglini, Blaine, WA: Phoenix Publishing Inc., pp. 59–80.

Cohn, Norman (1975) *Europe's Inner Demons*, New York: Basic Books.

Copenhaver, Brian (1995) *Hermetica: The Greek Corpus Hermeticum and the Latin Asclepius in a new English Translation with notes and introduction*, Cambridge: Cambridge University Press.

Couliano, Ioan (1987) *Eros and Magic in the Renaissance*, trans. Margaret Cook, Chicago, IL: Chicago University Press.

Coward, Barry ([1980] 1994) *The Stuart Age: England 1603–1714*, Essex: Longman Group Ltd.

Crawford, Deborah (1993) 'St Joseph in Britain: Reconsidering the Legends, Part I', in *Folklore*, 104 (1/2), pp. 86–98.

—— K.E. (1994) 'St Joseph in Britain: Reconsidering the Legends, Part II', in *Folklore*, 105, pp. 51–9.

Cross, F. L and E. A. Livingstone (1983) *The Oxford Dictionary of the Christian Church*, Oxford: Oxford University Press.

Crowley, Aleister (1996) *The Law is For All: The Authorized Popular Commentary on liber al vel legis*, Tempe, AZ: New Falcon Publications.

—— (1993) *Thelema*, London: Suhal.

—— ([1930] 1990) *The Forbidden Lecture: Gilles de Rais*, Oxford: Mandrake Press.

—— ([1910] 1985) *The World's Tragedy*, Las Vegas, NV: Falcon Press.

—— (1978) *The Confessions of Aleister Crowley: An Autohagiography*, Harmondsworth: Arkana.

—— (1973) *Magick*, ed. John Symonds and Kenneth Grant, Harmondsworth: Arkana.

—— (1972) *The Magical Record of the Beast 666: The Diaries of Aleister Crowley 1914–1920*, London: Gerald Duckworth & Co. Ltd.

—— *Liber XV: Ecclesiae Gnosticae Catholicae Canon Misae*, on www.otohq.org/oto/
115.html (accessed April 2000).

—— ([1913]1970) *The Book of Lies Which is also Falsely Called Breaks: The
Wanderings or Falsifications of the One Thought of Frater Perdurabo (Aleister
Crowley), Which Thought is Itself Untrue*, York Beach, ME: Red Wheel/Weiser.

—— (1904) *Liber AL vel Legis, sub figura CCXX, The Book of the Law, as delivered
by XCII = 418 to DCLXVI*, available at www.sacred-texts.com/oto/engccxx.htm
(accessed 4 January 2007).

Crowley, Vivianne (1998) 'Wicca as Nature Religion', in Pearson, Joanne E., Richard
H. Roberts and Geoffrey Samuel (eds), *Nature Religion Today: Paganism in the
Modern World*, Edinburgh: Edinburgh University Press, pp. 170–179.

—— ([1989] 1996) *Wicca: The Old Religion in the New Millennium*, London:
Thorsons.

—— (1995) 'Wicca as Modern-Day Mystery Religion', in Harvey, Graham and
Charlotte Hardman (eds), *Paganism Today: Wiccans, Druids, the Goddess and
Ancient Earth Traditions for the Twenty-First Century*, London: Thorsons,
pp. 81–93.

—— (1994) *Phoenix From the Flame: Pagan Spirituality in the Western World*,
London: Thorsons.

—— (1990a) 'Priestess and Witch', in Matthews, Caitlin (ed.), *Voices of the Goddess:
A Chorus of Sibyls*, Northants: Aquarian Press, pp. 45–66.

—— (1990b) 'The Initiation', in Jones, Prudence and Caitlin Matthews (eds), *Voices
from the Circle: The Heritage of Western Paganism*, London: Aquarian Press,
pp. 65–82.

Culpepper, Emily (1978) 'The Spiritual Movement of Radical Feminist Consciousness',
in Needleman, Jacob and George Baker (eds.), *Understanding the New Religions*,
New York: Seabury Press.

Daly, Mary ([1978] 1981) *Gyn/Ecology: the Metaethics of Radical Feminism*, London:
The Women's Press.

Davies, J. G. (ed.) (1986) *A New Dictionary of Liturgy and Worship*, London:
SPCK.

Davies, J. H. T.(1999) 'Paganism and Magical Ethics', in *Pagan Dawn*, Beltane 1999,
pp. 28–9.

Davies, Owen (1999) *Witchcraft, Magic and Culture 1736–1951*, Manchester:
Manchester University Press.

Davis, Morgan (2002) *From Man to Witch: Gerald Gardner 1946–1949*, available at
www.geraldgardner.com (accessed November 2005).

Davis, R. W. and R. J. Helmstadter (1992) *Religion and Irreligion in Victorian Britain:
Essays in Honor of R. K. Webb*, London: Routledge and Kegan Paul.

De Hart, Scott D. (1997) 'The Influence of John Mason Neale and the Theology
of Symbolism', available at http://anglicanhistory.org/essays/dehart1.pdf (accessed
February 2006).

De Laura, David J. (1969) *Hebrew and Hellene in Victorian England: Newman,
Arnold, and Pater*, Austin, TX: University of Texas Press.

De Santillana, Giorgio (1965) Review of Frances A. Yates, *Giordano Bruno and the
Hermetic Tradition* in *American Historical Review*, 70, p. 455.

Dix, Gregory (ed.) (1968) *The Apostolic Tradition of St Hippolytus of Rome*, London:
SPCK.

Drabble, Margaret (ed.) (2000) *The Oxford Companion to English Literature*, Oxford: Oxford University Press.

Duffy, Eamon (1992) *The Stripping of the Altars: Traditional Religion in England 1400–1580*, New Haven, CT and London: Yale University Press.

Dunstan, Petà (2006) 'Some Thoughts on Identity in Anglican Religious Life', in *Religious Life Review*, 41 (2002), and Nicholas Stebbing CR (ed.) (2003) *Anglican Religious Life*, Dublin: Dominican Publications, reproduced on Project Canterbury, 2006, www.anglicanhistory.org/academic/dunstan_identity2002.pdf (accessed June 2006).

—— (2004) 'Bishops and Religious 1897–1914', in *Anglican Religious Life Journal*, 1, reproduced on Project Canterbury, www.anglicanhistory.org/academic/dunstan_bishops2004.pdf (accessed June 2006).

During, Simon (2002) *Modern Enchantments: The Cultural Power of Secular Magic*, Cambridge, MA: Harvard University Press.

Durkheim, Émile ([1912] 1965) *The Elementary Forms of the Religious Life*, New York: Free Press.

Dworkin, Andrea (1974) *Woman Hating*, New York: Dutton, Chapter 7: 'Gynocide: The Witches', pp. 118–50.

Eagleton, Terry (1995) 'The Flight from the Real', in Ledger, Sally and Scott McCracken (eds), *Cultural Politics at the Fin de Siecle*, Cambridge: Cambridge University Press, pp. 11–21.

Easton, Burton Scott (1934) *The Apostolic Tradition of Hippolytus*, Cambridge: Cambridge University Press.

Eliade, Mircea (1976) *Occultism, Witchcraft and Cultural Fashions: Essays in Comparative Religions*, Chicago, IL: University of Chicago Press.

Eliot, T. S. (1944) *Four Quartets*, London: Faber and Faber.

Elliot, Peter J. (1995) *Ceremonies of the Modern Roman Rite*, San Francisco, CA: Ignatius Press.

Ellis, Havelock and John Addington Symonds (1897) *Sexual Inversion*, London: Wilson & Macmillan.

Evans-Pritchard, E. E. ([1937] 1976) *Witchcraft, Oracles and Magic Among the Azande*, Oxford: Clarendon.

Ewen, C. L. (1938) *Some Witchcraft Criticisms: A Plea for the Blue Pencil*, n.p.

Ezzy, Doug (2006) 'White Witchcraft and Black Magic: Ethics and Consumerism in Contemporary Witchcraft', in *Journal of Contemporary Religion*, 21 (1), pp. 15–31.

—— (2003) 'New Age Witchcraft? Popular Spell Books and the Re-enchantment of Everyday Life', in *Culture and Religion*, 4 (1), pp. 47–65.

—— (2001) 'The Commodification of Witchcraft', in *Australian Religion Studies Review*, 14, (1), pp. 31–44.

Fairfield, Leslie P. (1976) *John Bale: Mythmaker for the English Reformation*, Lafayette, IN: Purdue University Press.

Faivre, Antoine (1994) *Access to Western Esotericism*, New York: State University of New York Press.

—— (1988) 'The Children of Hermes and the Science of Man', in Merkel, Ingrid and Allen G. Debus (eds), *Hermeticism and the Renaissance: Intellectual History and the Occult in Early Modern Europe*, London/New Jersey/Ontario: Associated University Presses, pp.424–35.

Faivre, Antoine and Karen-Claire Voss (1995) 'Western Esotericism and the Science of Religions', in *Numen*, 42, pp.48–77.

Faivre, Antoine and Jacob Needleman (eds) ([1992] 1993) *Modern Esoteric Spirituality*, London: SCM Press.

Farrar, Stewart ([1971] 1991) *What Witches Do: A Modern Coven Revealed*, London: Robert Hale Ltd.

Farrar, Janet and Stewart Farrar ([1981] 1989) *Eight Sabbats for Witches*, London: Robert Hale Ltd.

Flood, Gavin (1999) *Beyond Phenomenology: Rethinking the Study of Religion*, London: Cassell.

Ford, Michael (2005) *Luciferian Witchcraft*, Lulu.com.

Fortune, Dion ([1935] 1987) *The Mystical Qabalah*, London: Aquarian Press.

—— (1938) *Sane Occultism*, London: Inner Light Publishing Society. (First published in 1929 by Rider & Co. London.)

Foucault, Michel ([1976] 1998) *The Will to Knowledge: History of Sexuality, Volume 1*, Harmondsworth: Penguin.

—— ([1966] 1987) 'Maurice Blanchot: the Thought from the Outside', in *Foucault/Blanchot*, trans. Jeffrey Mehlman and Brian Massumi, New York: Zone Books, pp. 7–60.

Fowden, Garth (1986) *The Egyptian Hermes: A Historical Approach to the Late Pagan Mind*, Princeton, NJ: Princeton University Press.

Frazer, Sir James G. (1990) *The Golden Bough*, London: Macmillan.

Gage, Matilda Jocelyn ([1893] 1972) *Women, Church and State*, New York: Arno Press.

Gallagher, Ann-Marie (2000) 'Woven Apart and Weaving Together: Conflict and Mutuality in Feminist and Pagan Communities in Britain', in Griffin, Wendy (ed.), *Daughters of the Goddess: Studies of Healing, Identity and Empowerment*, Walnut Creek, CA: AltaMira Press, pp. 42–58.

Gardner, Gerald B. ([1959] 2004) *The Meaning of Witchcraft*, York Beach, ME: Red Wheel/Weiser.

—— (1954) *Witchcraft Today*, London: Rider.

—— ([1949] 1993) *High Magic's Aid*, London: Pentacle Enterprises.

Gay, Peter ([1969] 1996) *The Enlightenment, An Interpretation: The Science of Freedom*, London and New York: W. W. Norton and Co.

Geertz, Clifford (1973) *The Interpretation of Culture: Selected Essays*, New York: Basic Books.

Gellner, Ernest (1992) *Postmodernism, Reason and Religion*, London: Routledge.

Gennep, Arnold van ([1911] 1960) *The Rites of Passage*, trans. Monika B. Vizedom and Gabrielle L. Caffee, London: Routledge and Kegan Paul.

Georgius, Mar (Hugh George de Willmott Newman) (1958) *The Man from Antioch, being an Account of Mar Julius, Bishop of Iona, and of his Successors, the British Patriarchs, from 1866 to 1944*, Glastonbury: n.p.

Geraghty, Tony (2000) 'The Bull (and a Few Sacred Cows) Sacrificed: Mithras, Hutton and Others Invite You to the Wake', review of *The Triumph of the Moon*, in *Pagan Dawn*, 135, pp. 37–8.

Giddens, Anthony (1991) *Modernity and Self-Identity: Self and Society in the Late Modern Age*, Stanford, CA: Stanford University Press.

Gilbert, Robert A. (2005) 'Waite, Arthur Edward', in Hanegraaff, W. J. (ed.), *Dictionary of Gnosis and Western Esotericism, Vol. II*, Leiden/Boston, MA: Brill, pp. 1164–5.

—— (ed.) (1987) *The Hermetic Papers of A. E. Waite: The Unknown Writings of a Modern Mystic*, Northants: Aquarian Press.

—— (1983) *The Golden Dawn: Twilight of the Magicians*, Northants: Aquarian Press.

Ginzburg, Carlo (1992) *Ecstasies: Deciphering the Witches' Sabbath*, New York: Penguin.

Godwin, Jocelyn (1994) *The Theosophical Enlightenment*, New York: SUNY.

Gould, Warwick and Marjorie Reeves (2001) *Joachim of Fiore and the Myth of the Eternal Evangel in the Nineteenth and Twentieth Centuries*, Oxford: Clarendon Press.

Gransden, Antonia (1980) Review of J. P. Carley (ed.) *John of Glastonbury, Cronica sive Antiquitates Glastoniensis Ecclesie* in *English Historical Review*, 95 (375), pp. 358–63.

Graves, Robert ([1948] 1984) *The White Goddess: A Historical Grammar of Poetic Myth*, London: Faber & Faber.

Greenwood, Susan (2000) *Magic, Witchcraft and the Otherworld: An Anthropology*, Oxford: Berg.

—— (1996) 'The Magical Will, Gender and Power in Magical Practices' in Harvey, Graham and Charlotte Hardman (eds), *Paganism Today: Wiccans, Druids, the Goddess and Ancient Earth Traditions for the Twenty-First Century*, London: Thorsons.

Greer, Mary K. (1995) *Women of the Golden Dawn: Rebels and Priestesses*, Rochester, Vermont: Park Street Press.

Grimes, Ronald (1990) *Ritual Criticism: Case Studies in its Practice, Essays on its Theory*, Columbia: University of South Carolina Press.

Grosz, Elizabeth and Elspeth Probyn (eds) (1995) *Sexy Bodies: The Strange Carnalities of Feminism*, London: Routledge.

Hanegraaff, Wouter J. (ed.), with Antoine Faivre, Roelof van den Broek and Jean-Pierre Brach (2005) *Dictionary of Gnosis and Esotericism*, Leiden: Brill.

—— (1999) 'Sympathy or the Devil: Renaissance Magic and the Ambivalence of Idols', in *Esoterica* I (II), p. 1–44. Available http://www.esoteric.msu.edu/VolumeII/Sympdevil.html.

—— (1998) *New Age Religion and Western Culture: Esotericism in the Mirror of Secular Thought*, New York: SUNY.

—— (1995a) 'Empirical Method and the Study of Esotericism', in *Method and Theory in the Study of Religion*, 7 (2), pp. 99–129.

—— (1995b) 'From the Devil's Gateway to the Goddess Within: The Image of the Witch in Neopaganism', in Kloppenberg, Ria and Wouter J. Hanegraaff (eds), *Female Stereotypes in Religious Traditions*, Leiden/New York: E.J. Brill, pp. 213–42.

Hardie, Titania (1998a) *Hocus Pocus: Titania's Book of Spells*, London: Quadrille Publishing Ltd.

—— (1998b) *Bewitched: Titania's Book of Love Spells*, London: Quadrille Publishing Ltd.

Hardie, Titania and Sara Morris (1998) *Titania's Oraqle: A Unique Way to Predict Your Future*, London: Quadrille Publishing Ltd.

Harding, Thomas (1565) *A Confutation of a Booke Intituled An Apologie of the Church of England*, Antwerp.

Hardy, Rob (1997) 'Interview', in *Pagan Dawn*, 122, p. 21.

Harrington, Melissa (2000) 'Conversion to Wicca?', in Bowman, Marion and Graham Harvey (eds), *Pagan Identities*, special issue of DISKUS, http://web.uni-marburg. de/religionswissenschaft/journal/diskus/ harrington.html (accessed July 2006)

Harris, Elizabeth Furlong Shipton (1847) *From Oxford to Rome: and How it Fared with Some Who Lately Took the Journey*, London: Longman, Brown, Green & Longman.

Harris, Tim (2006) *Restoration: Charles II and his Kingdoms*, Harmondsworth: Penguin.

Harrison, Jane Ellen ([1903] 1962) *Epilogomena to the Study of Greek Religion*, New York: University Books.

Harvey, David (1989) *The Condition of Postmodernity: An Enquiry into the Origins of Cultural Change*, Oxford: Blackwell.

Harvey, Graham (1997) *Listening People, Speaking Earth*, London: Hurst & Co.

Heselton, Philip (2003) *Gerald Gardner and the Cauldron of Inspiration: An Investigation into the Sources of Gardnerian Witchcraft*, Berkshire: Capall Bann.

—— (2000) *Wiccan Roots: Gerald Gardner and the Modern Witchcraft Revival*, Berkshire: Capall Bann.

Heywood, Colin (1995) 'Review of Michel Legrée (1992) *Religion et Cultures en Bretagne, 1850–1950*, Paris: Fayard', in *English Historical Review*, June, pp. 794–5.

Hill, Christopher ([1958] 1990) *Puritanism and Revolution: Studies in Interpretation of the English Revolution of the 17th Century*, Harmondsworth: Penguin.

—— (1972) *The World Turned Upside Down: Radical ideas During the English Revolution*, New York: Viking Press.

Hilliard, David ([1982] 2006) 'UnEnglish and Unmanly: Anglo-Catholicism and Homosexuality', in *Victorian Studies*, 25, pp. 181–210, reproduced at Project Canterbury, http://anglicanhistory.org/hilliard_unenglish.pdf (accessed April 2006).

Hobsbawm, Eric and Terence Ranger (eds) (1992) *The Invention of Tradition*, Cambridge: Canto (Cambridge University Press).

Holzhausen, Jens (2005) 'Valentinus and Valentinians', in Hanegraaff, W. J. (ed.), *Dictionary of Gnosis and Western Esotericism, Vol. II*, Leiden/Boston, MA: Brill, pp. 1144–57.

Hopman, Ellen E. and Lawrence Bond (1995) *People of the Earth: The New Pagans Speak Out*, Rochester, VT: Inner Traditions.

Horne, Fiona (2002) *Witchin': A Handbook for Teen Witches*, London: HarperCollins.

Howard, Seymour (1982) 'William Blake: The Antique, Nudity, and Nakedness: A Study in Idealism and Regression', in *Artibus et Historiae*, 3 (6), pp. 117–49.

Howe, Ellic ([1922] 1972) *The Magicians of the Golden Dawn*, London: Routledge and Kegan Paul.

Hudson, Nicholas (1994) *Writing and European Thought 1600–1830*, Cambridge: Cambridge University Press.

Hume, Lynne (1997) *Witchcraft and Paganism in Australia*, Melbourne: Melbourne University Press.

Huson, Paul (1970) *Mastering Witchcraft: A Practical Guide for Witches, Warlocks and Covens*, London: Corgi.

Hutton, Ronald (2007) 'Crowley and Wicca', in Bogdan, Henrik (ed.), *Aleister Crowley: An Anthology*, New York: SUNY.

—— (2003a) 'Glastonbury: Alternative Histories', in Hutton, R. (ed.), *Witches, Druids and King Arthur*, London and New York: Hambledon and London, pp. 59–85.

—— (2003b) 'Living with Witchcraft', in Hutton, R. (ed.), *Witches, Druids and King Arthur*, London and New York: Hambledon and London, pp. 259–94.

—— (2003c) 'The Great Debate', in *The Cauldron*, 108 (May), pp. 9–16.

—— (2003d) 'A Modest Look at Ritual Nudity', in Hutton, R. (ed.), *Witches Druids and King Arthur*, London and New York: Hambledon and London, pp. 192–214.

—— (1999) *The Triumph of the Moon: A History of Modern Pagan Witchcraft*, Oxford: Oxford University Press.

—— (1998) 'The Discovery of the Modern Goddess', in Pearson, Joanne E., Richard H. Roberts and Geoffrey Samuel (eds), *Nature Religion Today: Paganism in the Modern World*, Edinburgh: Edinburgh University Press, pp. 89–100.

—— (1996) 'The Roots of Modern Paganism', in Harvey, Graham and Charlotte Hardman (eds), *Paganism Today: Wiccans, Druids, the Goddess and Ancient Earth Traditions for the Twenty-First Century*, London: Thorsons, pp. 3–15.

—— ([1991] 1993) *The Pagan Religions of the Ancient British Isles: Their Nature and Legacy*, Oxford: Blackwell.

Huysman, J.-K. ([1891] 2001) *The Damned = Là Bas*, trans. and introduction Terry Hale, Harmondsworth: Penguin.

—— ([1884] 1959) *Against Nature*, trans. Robert Baldick, Harmondsworth: Penguin.

Hyland, William P. (1999) 'Bishop Richard Challoner and the Idea of the Primitive Church', in *Touchstone: A Journal of Mere Christianity*, www.touchstonemag.com/archives/article.php?id=12–02–016–f (accessed 16 March 2006).

James, William ([1902] 1985) *The Varieties of Religious Experience*, Harmondsworth: Penguin.

Jenkins, Keith (ed.) (1997) *The Postmodern History Reader*, London: Routledge.

Jennings, Hargrave ([1870] 1887) *The Rosicrucians: Their Rites and Mysteries*, London: J. C. Hotten.

Jennings, Pete (1998) 'Some advice on Norse Tradition Magic', in *Pagan Dawn*, Samhain, pp. 18–19.

Jerry, C. (1998) 'Magic-free Paganism', letter in *Pagan Dawn*, Samhain, pp. 38–9.

Jewel, Right Rev'd John (Bishop of Salisbury) (1567) *A Defence of the Apologie of the Churche of Englande, Conteininge an Answeare to a certaine Booke lately set foorthe by M. Hardinge, and Entituled, A Confutation of etc.*, London: Henry Wykes.

Jinarajasada, C. (1952) *Extracts from Letters of C. W. Leadbeater to Annie Besant, 1916–1923*, Adyar: Theosophical Publishing House.

Jones, Edwin (2003) *The English Nation: The Great Myth*, Stroud: Sutton Publishing.

Jones, Norman L. (1981) 'Matthew Parker, John Bale, and the Magdeburg Centuriators', in *Sixteenth Century Journal*, 12 (3), pp. 35–49.

Kellner, Hans (1998) '"Never Again" is Now', in Fay, Brian, Philip Pomper and Richard T. Vann (eds), *History and Theory: Contemporary Readings*, Oxford: Blackwell, pp. 225–44.

Kelly, Aidan (1991) *Crafting the Art of Magic, Book 1*, St Paul, MN: Llewellyn.

Kieckhefer, Richard ([1989] 1992) *Magic in the Middle Ages*, Cambridge: Cambridge University Press.

King, Francis ([1971] 2002) *Sexuality, Magic and Perversion*, Los Angeles, CA: Feral House.

—— ([1970] 1989) *Modern Ritual Magic: the Rise of Western Occultism*, Bridport: Prism Press.

—— ([1970] 1972) *Ritual Magic in England, 1887 to the Present Day*, London: New English Library.

King, Richard (1999) *Orientalism and Religion: Postcolonial Theory, India, and the Mystic East*, London: Routledge.

Lagorio, Valerie M. (1971) 'The Evolving Legend of St Joseph of Glastonbury', in *Speculum: A Journal of Mediaeval Studies*, XLVI (2), pp. 209–31.

Lamond, Frederic (1997) 'The Long View' in *Pagan Dawn* 122, Imbolc 1997, p. 20.

Langford, Rev. H. W. ([1965] 2001) 'The Non-Jurors and the Eastern Orthodox', available on http://anglicanhistory.org/nonjurors/langford1.html (accessed March 2006).

Latham, Cassandra (2002) 'A Walk on the Wild Side', video for Open University course AD317 *Religion Today: Tradition, Modernity and Change* (Academic consultant: Dr Jo Pearson).

Laurant, Jean-Pierre (2005) 'Lévi, Éliphas', in Hanegraaff, W. J. (ed.), *Dictionary of Gnosis and Western Esotericism, Vol. II*, Leiden/Boston, MA: Brill, pp. 689–92.

La Vey, Anton (2003) *The Satanic Witch*, Los Angeles, CA: Feral House.

Leach, Edmund (1976) *Culture and Communication: The Logic By Which Symbols are Connected*, Cambridge: Cambridge University Press.

Leland, Charles G. ([1890] 1990) *Aradia: Gospel of the Witches*, Blaine, WA: Phoenix Publishing Inc.

Lelli, Fabrizio (2005) 'Pico della Mirandola, Giovanni', in Hanegraaff, W. J. (ed.), *Dictionary of Gnosis and Western Esotericism, Vol. II*, Leiden/Boston, MA: Brill, pp. 949–54.

Lévi-Strauss, Claude (1966) *The Savage Mind*, London: Weidenfeld and Nicholson.

Lloyd, S. M. (1978) *The Occult Revival: Witchcraft in the Contemporary United States*, PhD thesis, Dissertation Abstracts International, 39: 6205A University Microfilms No. AAC7906899.

Lough, A. G. (1975) *John Mason Neale: Priest Extraordinary*, Devon: A. G. Lough.

Ludeke, J. C. (1989) *Wicca as a Revitalization Movement Among Post-Industrial, Urban, American Women*, PhD thesis, Iliff School of Theology, Dissertation Abstracts International, 50: 2951A University Microfilms No. AAC9004182.

Luhrmann, T. M. ([1989] 1994) *Persuasions of the Witch's Craft: Ritual Magic in Contemporary England*, Basingstoke: Macmillan.

MacCulloch, Diarmaid (1991) 'The Myth of the English Reformation', in *The Journal of British Studies*, 30 (1), pp. 1–19.

Macdonald, A. J. (1945) *Episcopi Vagantes and Church History*, London: SPCK.

MacGregor, Geddes (1990) *The Everyman Dictionary of Religion and Philosophy*, London: J. M. Dent & Sons.

—— (1999) *Religion and the Return of Magic: Wicca as Esoteric Spirituality*, PhD thesis: Lancaster University.

—— (1998) 'Assumed Affinities: Wicca and the New Age', in Pearson, Joanne E., Richard H. Roberts and Geoffrey Samuel (eds), *Nature Religion Today: Paganism in the Modern World*, Edinburgh: Edinburgh University Press, pp. 45–56.

Pengelly, James, Robert Hall and Jem Dowse (1997) *We Emerge: The History of the Pagan Federation*, London: The Pagan Federation.

Pike, Sarah M. (1996) 'Rationalizing the Margins: A Review of Legitimation and Ethnographic Practice in Scholarly Research on Neo-Paganism' in Lewis, James R. (ed.) *Magical Religion and Modern Witchcraft*, New York: SUNY, p. 353–72.

Priestley, Joseph (1807) *Memoirs*, Vol. 1, London: J. Johnson.

Pryce, Revd John (1878) *The Ancient British Church: A Historical Essay*, London: Longmans, Green & Co.

Purkiss, Diane (1996) *The Witch in History: Early Modern and Twentieth Century Representations*, London: Routledge.

Pye, Michael (1998) 'A General Theory of Religious Innovation', paper presented at BASR Conference, 'Religion and Innovation', University of Lampeter, September.

Rabelais, François ([1534/1532] 1985) *Gargantua* and *Pantagruel*, Harmondsworth: Penguin.

Radcliffe-Brown, A. R. (1948) *The Andaman Islanders*, Glencoe: Free Press.

Randolph, Paschal Beverly (1874) *The History of Love*, Toledo, OH: Randolph Publishing Co.

Raoult, Michel (1996) 'The Druid Revival in Brittany, France and Europe', in Carr-Gomm, Philip (ed.), *The Druid Renaissance: The Voice of Druidry Today*, London: Thorsons, pp. 100–22.

Raphael, Melissa (1998) *Introducing Thealogy*, Sheffield: Sheffield Academic Press.

Rappaport, Roy (1979) *Ecology, Meaning and Religion*, Richmond, CA: North Atlantic Books.

Ravenwolf, Silver (2003) *Solitary Witch: The Ultimate Book of Shadows for the New Generation*, St Paul, MN: Llewellyn Publications.

—— (1998) *Teen Witch: Wicca for a New Generation*, St Paul, MN: Llewellyn Publications.

Read, C. (ed.) (1962) *William Lambarde and Local Government*, Ithaca, NY: Cornell University Press, on behalf of the Folger Shakespeare Library.

Reed, John Shelton (1998) *Glorious Battle: The Cultural Politics of Victorian Anglo-Catholicism*, Nashville, TN: Vanderbilt University Press.

Rees, Kenneth (1996) 'The Tangled Skein: The Role of Myth in Paganism', in Harvey, Graham and Charlotte Hardman (eds), *Paganism Today: Wiccans, Druids, the Goddess and Ancient Earth Traditions for the Twenty-First Century*, London: Thorsons, pp. 16–31.

Reeves, Marjorie ([1976] 1999) *Joachim of Fiore and the Prophetic Future: A Medieval Study in Historical Thinking*, London: SPCK.

Regardie, Israel ([1941] 1989) *The Golden Dawn: The Original Account of the Teachings, Rites and Ceremonies of the Hermetic Order of the Golden Dawn*, St. Paul, MN: Llewellyn Publications.

—— ([1971] 1986) *The Golden Dawn: A Complete Course in Ceremonial Magic – Four Volumes in One: The Original Account of the Teachings, Rites and Ceremonies of the Heremetic Order Of the Golden Dawn (Stella Matutina) as revealed by Israel*

Regardie, with further revision, expansion and additional notes by Israel Regardie, Chris Monnastre and others, under the editorship of Carl Llewellyn Weschcke, St Paul, MN: Llewellyn Publications.

—— (1983) *What You Should Know About the Golden Dawn*, Phoenix, AZ: Falcon Press.

—— (1939) *The Golden Dawn*, Vol. III, Chicago, IL: The Aries Press.

—— (1938) *The Golden Dawn*, Vol. II, Chicago, IL: The Aries Press.

—— (1937) *The Golden Dawn*, Vol. I, Chicago, IL: The Aries Press.

Richardson, Alan ([1987] 1991) *The Magical Life of Dion Fortune: Priestess of the 20th Century*, London: Aquarian Press.

Robbins, R. H. (1959) *Encyclopedia of Witchcraft and Demonology*, London: Peter Nevill.

Roberts, Richard H. (1998) 'Space, Time and the Sacred in Modernity/Postmodernity', unpublished paper presented at the ISA World Congress, Montreal, July.

Robinson, Benedict S. (1998) '"Darke Speech": Matthew Parker and the Reforming of History', in *Sixteenth Century Journal*, 29 (4), pp. 1061–83.

Roof, Wade Clark and Sarah McFarland Taylor (1995) 'The Force of Emotion: James's Reorientation of Religion and the Contemporary Rediscovery of the Body, Spirituality, and the "Feeling Self"', in Capps, Donald and Janet L. Jacobs (eds), *The Struggle for Life: A Companion to William James's The Varieties of Religious Experience*, Princeton, NJ: Society for the Social Scientific Study of Religion and Princeton Theological Seminary, pp. 197–208.

Roper, Lyndal (1994) *Oedipus and the Devil: Witchcraft, sexuality and religion in early modern Europe*, London and New York: Routledge.

Rose, E. E. (1962) *A Razor for a Goat: Witchcraft and Diabolism*, Toronto: University of Toronto Press.

Rountree, Kathryn (2006) 'Reconstructing Paganism in Malta: When Polytheism Meets Catholicism', paper presented at the Association of Polytheist Traditions conference, University of Central Lancashire, Preston, May.

—— (2004) *Embracing the Witch and the Goddess: Feminist Ritual-Makers in New Zealand*, London: Routledge.

Rowland, Christopher (1988) *Radical Christianity: A Reading of Recovery*, Oxford: Polity Press.

Russell, Jeffrey B. ([1980] 1991) *A History of Witchcraft: Sorcerers, Heretics and Pagans*, London: Thames & Hudson.

Said, Edward (1978) *Orientalism*, London: Routledge and Kegan Paul.

Salomonsen, Jone (2002) *Enchanted Feminism: The Reclaiming Witches of San Francisco*, London: Routledge.

—— (1998) 'Feminist Witchcraft and Holy Hermeneutics', in Pearson, Joanne E., Richard H. Roberts and Geoffrey Samuel (eds), *Nature Religion Today: Paganism in the Modern World*, Edinburgh: Edinburgh University Press, pp. 143–56.

—— (1996) *'I Am a Witch – A Healer and a Bender': An Expression of Women's Religiosity in the Contemporary USA*, PhD Thesis: University of Oslo.

Samuel, Geoffrey (1998) 'Paganism and Tibetan Buddhism: Contemporary Western Religions and the Question of Nature', in Pearson, Joanne E., Richard H. Roberts and Geoffrey Samuel (eds), *Nature Religion Today: Paganism in the Modern World*, Edinburgh: Edinburgh University Press, pp. 123–40.

Sangharakshita (D. P. E. Lingwood) ([1978] 1989) *Buddhism and Blasphemy. Buddhist Reflections on the 1977 Blasphemy Trial*, Glasgow: Windhorse Publications.

Sean (1999) 'Star Letter: Magic-Free Paganism?', in *Pagan Dawn*, Imbolc, p. 43.

Sharpe, Kevin (1992) *The Personal Rule of Charles I*, New Haven, CT and London: Yale University Press.

Simpson, Liz (2001) *Awaken Your Goddess: A Practical Guide to Discovering a Woman's Power, a Woman's Glory*, London: Gaia Books Ltd.

Simpson, W. J. Sparrow (1932) *The History of the Anglo-Catholic Revival from 1845*, London: Allen & Unwin.

Sjöö, Monica and Barbara Mor (1987) *The Great Cosmic Mother: Rediscovering the Religion of the Earth*, San Francisco, CA: Harper and Row.

Spong, John Shelby (2002) *A New Christianity for a New World*, New York: HarperSanFrancisco.

Starhawk (1979; 1989; 1999) *The Spiral Dance: A Rebirth of the Ancient Religion of the Great Goddess*, San Francisco, CA: HarperCollins.

—— (1982) *Dreaming the Dark: Magic, Sex and Politics*, Boston, MA: Beacon Press.

Strong, Roy (1999) *The Spirit of Britain: A Narrative History of the Arts*, London: Hutchinson/Julia Macrae.

Styers, Randall (2004) *Making Magic: Religion, Magic and Science in the Modern World*, Oxford: Oxford University Press.

Sutcliffe, Richard (1996) 'Left-Hand Path Ritual Magick: An Historical and Philosophical Overview', in Harvey, Graham and Charlotte Hardman (eds), *Paganism Today: Wiccans, Druids, the Goddess and Ancient Earth Traditions for the Twenty-First Century*, London: Thorsons, pp. 109–37.

Tackett, Timothy and Claude Langlois (1980) 'Ecclesiastical Structures and Clerical Geography on the Eve of the French Revolution', in *French Historical Studies*, 11 (3), pp. 352–70.

Tambiah, Stanley J. ([1990] 1999) *Magic, Science, Religion and the Scope of Rationality*, Cambridge: Cambridge University Press.

Taylor, Eugene (1996) *William James on Consciousness Beyond the Margin*, Princeton, NJ: Princeton University Press.

Telesco, Patricia (1994) *A Kitchen Witch's Cookbook*, St Paul, MN: Llewellyn Publications.

Thomann, Rev. G. H. (2001) *A Short Biography of the Reverend Richard Williams Morgan (1815–1889) the Welsh Poet and Re-Founder of the Ancient British Church: Enquiry into the Origins of Neo-Celtic Christianity, together with a Reprint of Several Works by Richard Williams Morgan and Jules Ferrette, etc.*, Solna, Sweden: St Ephrem's Institute.

Thomas, Keith ([1971] 1991) *Religion and the Decline of Magic*, Harmondsworth: Penguin.

Thompson, Mark (ed.) (1991) *Leatherfolk: Radical Sex, People, Politics and Practice*, Boston, MA: Alyson Publications.

Tiryakian, E. (1974) 'Toward the Sociology of Esoteric Culture', in Tiryakian, E. (ed.), *On the Margin of the Visible: Sociology, the Esoteric and the Occult*, New York: Wiley-Interscience, pp. 257–80.

Toth, Ladislaus (2005) 'Gnostic Church', in Hanegraaff, W. J. (ed.), *Dictionary of Gnosis and Western Esotericism, Vol. 1*, Leiden: Brill, pp. 400–3.

Trevor-Roper, H. R. (1969) *The European Witch-Craze of the 16th and 17th Centuries*, Harmondsworth: Penguin.

Truzzi, Marcello (1974) 'Definition and Dimensions of the Occult: Towards a Sociological Perspective', in Tiryakian, E. (ed.), *On the Margin of the*

Visible: Sociology, the Esoteric and the Occult, New York: Wiley-Interscience, p. 243–55.

Turner, Victor (1969) *The Ritual Process*, Chicago, IL: Aldine Press.

Tylor, Edward B. (1929) *Primitive Culture, Vol. 1*, London: John Murray.

——(1889) *Primitive Culture: Researches into the Development of Mythology, Philosophy, Religion, Language, Art and Custom*, Vol. I, New York: Henry Holt.

Uglow, Jennifer ([1973] 1990) 'Introduction', in Pater, Walter, *Essays on Art and Literature*, ed. Jennifer Uglow, London: Dent.

Urban, Hugh B. (2006) *Magia Sexualis: Sex, Magic and Liberation in Modern Western Esotericism*, Berkeley, CA: University of California Press.

—— (2004) 'The Beast with Two Backs: Aleister Crowley, Sex Magic and the Exhaustion of Modernity', in *Nova Religio*, 7 (3), pp. 7–25.

—— (2003) 'Unleashing the Beast: Aleister Crowley, Tantra and Sex Magic in Late Victorian England', in *Esoterica*, V, pp. 138–92.

—— (2000) 'The Cult of Ecstasy: Tantrism, the New Age, and the Spiritual Logic of Late Capitalism', in *History of Religions*, 39 (3), pp. 268–304.

Ussher, Jane M. (1997) *Fantasies of Femininity: Reframing the Boundaries of Sex*, London: Penguin.

Valiente, Doreen ([1978] 1993) *Witchcraft for Tomorrow*, London: Robert Hale.

—— (1984) 'The Search for Old Dorothy', in Farrar, Janet and Stewart Farrar (eds) *The Witches' Way*, London: Hale, pp. 282–93.

—— (1989) *The Rebirth of Witchcraft*, Blaine, WA: Phoenix Publishing.

Van Baal, Jan (1963) 'Magic as a Religious Phenomenon', in *Higher Education and Research in the Netherlands*, 7 (3/4), pp. 10–12.

Van den Broek, Roelof (2005a) 'Simon Magus', in Hanegraaff, W. J. (ed.), *Dictionary of Gnosis and Western Esotericism, Vol. II*, Leiden/Boston, MA: Brill, pp. 1069–73.

—— (2005b) 'Hermetic Literature I: Antiquity', in Hanegraaff, W. J. (ed.), *Dictionary of Gnosis and Western Esotericism, Vol. I*, Leiden/Boston, MA: Brill, pp. 487–99.

Versluis, Arthur (1986) *The Philosophy of Magic*, London: Arkana.

Versnel, H. S. (1991) 'Some Reflections on the Relationship of Magic-Religion', in *Numen*, 38 (2), pp. 177–97.

Verter, Bradford (2002) 'Occult Eroticism: Black Magicians, Yellow Journalists, and Sex Cults in the 1920s', paper presented at the AAR Annual Meeting, Toronto, November.

Vesta, Dianna (1991) 'Fantasy, Fetish and the Goddess', in Thompson, Mark (ed.), *Leatherfolk: Radical Sex, People, Politics and Practice*, Boston, MA: Alyson Publications, pp. 267–75.

Waite, Gary K. (2003) *Heresy, Magic and Witchcraft in Early Modern Europe*, Basingstoke: Palgrave Macmillan.

Walsh, Walter ([1897] 1898) *The Secret History of the Oxford Movement*, London: Swan Sonnenschein and Co.

Ward, J. S. M. (1944) *The Orthodox Church in England*, n.p.

—— *The Confraternity of Christ the King*, n.p. or d.

Wax, Murray and Rosalie Wax (1963) 'The Notion of Magic', in *Current Anthropology*, 4 (5), pp. 495–518.

—— (1962) 'The Magical World View', in *Journal for the Scientific Study of Religion*, 1, pp. 179–88.

Webb, James (1976) *The Occult Establishment*, La Salle, IL: Open Court.

—— (1971) *The Flight From Reason: Volume 1 of the Age of the Irrational*, London: MacDonald & Co. Ltd.

Weber, Eugen (1988) 'Religion and Superstition in Nineteenth-Century France', in *The Historical Journal*, 31 (2), pp. 399–423.

Werner, Karel ([1994] 1997) *A Popular Dictionary of Hinduism*, London: Curzon.

West, Kate (2002) *The Real Witches' Kitchen: Spells, Recipes, Oils, Lotions and Potions from the Witches' Hearth*, London: HarperCollins.

Whitebrook, J. C. (1945) *The Consecration of the Most Reverend Matthew Parker*, London and Oxford: A.R. Mowbray & Co. Ltd.

Wiener, Carol Z. (1971) 'The Beleaguered Isle. A Study of Elizabethan and Early Jacobean Anti-Catholicism', in *Past and Present*, 51, pp. 27–62.

Wilson, A. N. (1999) *God's Funeral*, London: John Murray.

Wilson, Derek (2000) *The King and the Gentleman: Charles Stuart and Oliver Cromwell, 1599–1649*, London: Pimlico.

Wilson, Edwin ([1998] 2003) *The English Nation: The Great Myth*, Stroud: Sutton Publishing.

Wishart, Catherine (2003) *Teen Goddess: How to Look, Love and Live Like a Goddess*, St Paul, MN: Llewellyn.

Woodhead, Linda (1996) 'Untangling the Historical Roots of Alternative Spirituality', paper presented to the conference *Nature Religion Today*, Lancaster University, Ambleside, April.

—— (1993) 'Post-Christian Spiritualities', *Religion*, 23, pp. 167–81.

Woodman, Justin (2000) *Lovecrafting the Art of Magick: Secularism, Modernity, and Emergent Stellar Spiritualities within Contemporary Occult Discourses*, paper delivered to the British Sociological Association, Sociology of Religion Study Group Conference, *Prophets and Predictions: Religion in the 21st Century*, University of Exeter, April.

Wyschogrod, Edith (1998) *An Ethics of Remembering: History, Heterology and the Nameless Others*, Chicago, IL and London: Chicago University Press.

Yates, Frances A. ([1964] 1991) *Giordano Bruno and the Hermetic Tradition*, Chicago, IL: Chicago University Press.

Yates, Nigel (1983) *The Oxford Movement and Anglican Ritualism*, London: Historical Association.

—— (2000) *Anglican Ritualism in Victorian Britain, 1830–1910*, Oxford: Clarendon Press.

INDEX

Abbey Folk Park 49, 50
aesthetic movement 63, 66, 67, 68
Agrippa, Cornelius 97
altar lights 21, 138 n.27
American Catholic Church 40
Ancient British Church: and the Church
    of England 9, 16, 17, 18; and Dorian
    Herbert 51, 57; and Gardner 27,
    50, 57; as literary invention 26; and
    Morgan 35–6, 37, 38, 41
Anderson, Ebenezer Johnson 48
Andrewes, Lancelot 20, 29, 59
Anglican religious orders 20
Anglicanism: and Catholicism 21, 69;
    development of 9, 21; search for
    authenticity 12–18 see also apostolic
    succession/origins
Anglo-Catholicism 11, 12, 28, 30,
    73, 112; and LCC 33; religious
    communities 27, 65; and ritual 59,
    62–6, 74, 76, 95
Anson, Peter 27–8, 32, 38, 52
anti-Catholicism 61, 64; as 'Englishness'
    18
anti-clericalism 43, 44
Antioch: and W. B. Crow 38; Jacobite
    patriarch of 39; and Old Catholics
    31; Order of 37, 48; Syrian
    Patriarchate 37–8
apostolic succession: and ancient British
    Christianity 11, 14–15, 17, 35, 36,
    53; Church of England claims to 11,
    21, 26, 29, 42, 63; heterodox claims
    to 38, 47, 52; Old Catholic claims
    to 30
Apostolicae Curae 42, 120 n.33, 122
    n.57, 124 n.8
Appolonius of Tyana 46
Argenteum Astrum (AA) 77

Arnold, Matthew 67
Arthurian romance 66
Ashcroft-Nowicki, Dolores 102
Association for the Promotion of the
    Unity of Christendom (APUC) 64–5
athame 70, 83, 84
Augustine of Canterbury 11, 15
Augustine of Hippo 80

Bale, John 16, 26
baptism 60, 87, 134 n.54
Basilius Abdullah III, Mar see Crow,
    William Bernard
beauty, cult of 65–6
Bedros, Mar, Bishop of Emesa 34, 38,
    39
Bell, Catherine 75
Bell, Thomas 13
Berger, Peter 73, 89, 141 n.66
Bernard, Mar see Crow, William
    Bernard
Besant, Annie 32, 33, 114 n.7, 126 n.29
binding 74, 80, 83, 84–5, 92
Blake, William 80, 93, 98, 143 n.13,
    145 n.43
Blavatsky, Helena 33
body: of Christ 12, 60, 104, 137 n.12;
    Christian attitudes towards 81, 107;
    and mystical states 71–2, 74, 84, 86,
    87–8, 104; naked body 73, 88; as
    sacred 76, 82, 90, 92–3; as symbol
    90, 91
Böehme, Jacob 102, 111
Book of Martyrs 16–17
Book of the Law 79
Boullan, Joseph-Antoine 45
Brandreth, Fr Henry R.T. 27, 28 31, 34
de Brescia, Paul-Edouard de Fournier
    52, 55, 135 n.66

Breton Association 54
Breton National Party 54
Breuriez Barzed Breiz 53
Bricaud, Jean 46–7
British Orthodox Church 53
Brittany 52, 53
Bruno, Giordano 105, 106, 149 n.33
Buckland, Raymond 3
Burne-Jones, Edward 66, 138 n.16

Caithness, Lady (Maria de Mariategui)
    46, 99
cakes & wine 70, 83
Calvinists/ism 12, 21, 121 n.40
Caroline divines 20–1, 29, 41, 59
Carpocratians 81
Carr-Gomm, Philip 55, 135 n.69
Cathars/ism 44, 45, 46, 81
Catholic Emancipation Act 18
Catholicate of the West 38, 49
Celtic Church 52, 55
Challoner, Richard 19
Chamberlain, Colin Mackenzie 37, 50
Charge of the Goddess 86, 89, 115
    n.16, 143 n.9
Chechemain, Leon 36
Chesterton, G. K. 22–3
Christ the King: Abbey of 37, 49;
    cathedral of 49, 50; Confraternity of
    48, 50
Christendom, reunion of 36, 38,
    65, 127 n.40, 128 n.60 *see also*
    Association for the Promotion of
    the Unity of Christendom, Order of
    Corporate Reunion
Christianity 11, 60, 67, 70; ancient
    British 10, 13–16, 19, 20, 35–6, 41,
    53; anti-Christian attitudes 61, 65,
    78, 80, 98; and Druids 35, 53–4, 55;
    Gardner and 55–8; gnostic 48, 77;
    heterodox 1, 9, 44, 47, 59; and the
    occult 98–9, 106, 108; and sexuality
    81, 85, 91; and Wicca 1, 9, 10,
    11–12, 58, 112–13
Church of England; as Catholic 10,
    12, 15, 21, 65 *see also* Anglo-
    Catholicism; Anglicanism; apostolic
    succession; *Apostolicae Curae*
circle, Wiccan 84, 85, 89, 90, 91, 92;
    casting of 69–71
Collège Bardique des Gaules 54
Collège Druidique des Gaules 54, 55
Collier, Jeremy 18, 29
colonialism 94, 108–9

Co-Masonry 33
confession 20, 65
conversion 20, 21, 22; of Britain 14–15,
    35
Coptic Church 53
Corpus Hermeticum 105
correspondences 66; systems of 103,
    148 n.21
Council of London 37–8
Council of Trent 20
Cranmer, Thomas 12
creed 38, 51, 57, 74, 95
Cromwell, Oliver 127 n.43
Cromwell, Thomas 12–15, 25, 26, 41
Crow, William Bernard 27, 36–7, 38,
    41
Crowley, Aleister 47, 77; and
    Christianity x, 70, 80, 99; definition
    of magic 102; and Gardner 37;
    possible ordination 47; and sexuality
    46, 77–80, 88; and Wicca 5, 70,
    101, 104, 115 n.16
Crowley, Vivianne 2, 7, 84; attraction
    of Wicca to those of Protestant
    background ix, 69; experience of
    invocation 71–2; and magic 111

Dafo 2
Daly, Mary 86
Danyel, Jean-Pierre (Clodoald) 51–2,
    52–3, 54, 55
Davies, Owen 13
Disraeli, Benjamin 22, 63
divine feminine 46, 86
Doinel, Jules-Benoît Stanislas 46, 47
Doreos, Mar *see* Herbert, Frederic
    'Dorian'
Druidry 9, 26, 37, 52, 54, 57, 99;
    Breton 53–4, 55; and Christianity
    35, 41, 53, 54–55, 56, 58
Durkheim, Emile 96

Eastern Churches Association 64
Eastern Orthodox Church 21
Ecclesiæ Gnosticæ Catholicæ (EGC) 37,
    47, 58, 80,
ecumenical councils 21, 29
Edward VI 12, 16, 18, 122 n.57
effeminacy 63
Église Gnostique 46, 47
Église Johannite des Chrétiens Primitifs
    44, 46
Egyptian 37, 46, 53, 98, 105, 106
eisteddfod 35, 53

INDEX

elements: eucharistic 60–1; four 69, 70
Elizabeth I 12, 16, 18, 21
Ellis, Havelock 63
Encausse, Gérard *see* Papus
esbats 69, 83
Eucharist 20, 60–1, 70, 107

Fabré-Palaprat, Dr Bernard-Raymond 44, 46, 47
Faivre, Antoine 90–1, 103, 105–6,
Farrar, Janet and Stewart 7
feminist consciousness movement 3, 8, 85
Ferrette, Jules 34–5, 38, 39, 52; succession 36, 37, 48, 49, 53
Ficino, Marsilio 105
First Nations Peoples 3
Folklore Society 23, 24
Fortune, Dion 5, 98, 99, 106; and magic 101–2, 104
Foucault, Michel 1, 88
Foxe, John 16–17, 19
France 44, 45; and Brittany 53–4
Fraudulent Mediums Act 9
Frazer, Sir James G. 24, 95, 109
Frederic, Mar *see* Harrington, Charles Aloysius
Freemasonry 33, 44, 84; and magical groups 8, 98, 42; Scottish Rite 46

Gallican Church 40, 46
Gallicanism 44, 53
Gardner, Gerald Brosseau 1–2; formulation of Wicca 2–4, 5, 9, 23–6, 104, 112; and heterodox Christianity 10, 27, 37, 50, 54–8; historical claims of 8; and OTO 37; and naturism 87, 91, 93; and sexuality 81–2; and Ward 37, 49–50
Georgius, Mar *see* de Willmott-Newman, Hugh George
Giraud, Louis-Marie-François 40, 47
Glastonbury 14; and Joseph of Arimathea 14–15, 29; dissolution of abbey 15
Glorious Revolution 28
gnosticism 102; ancient 77, 81, 91; and magic 111; and Western Esoteric tradition, 105, 106 *see also* Carpocratians; Cathars; Magus, Simon; Knights Templar; Valentinus
Gnostic Church 78
Gnostic Mass 47; and Wicca 70, 80, 83, 104

Goddess spirituality 3–4
Goddess, as deity of the witches 23, 24; in Wicca ix, 71–2, 73, 83, 84, 86, 104
Golden Dawn, Hermetic Order of 97–9, 104, 106; and Crowley 77; influence on Wicca 5, 58, 69–70, 104; and magic 88, 101, 102, 148 n.8
Gordon Riots 18
Gothic revival 22, 66, 113
Great Oak 54
Great Oak Forest Celtic College of Broceliande 54
Great Rite 74, 84, 92
Great Work 103–4, 111
Greece, ancient 108
Gregorian Chant 66
Grimes, Ronald 75

Hanegraaff, Wouter 5, 97, 103, 111
Harrington, Charles Aloysius 36, 37–8, 41, 48, 49, 50
Harrison, Jane Ellen 73, 104
Heard, Herbert James Monzani (Archbishop of Selsey) 36, 37, 41
heathen, Heathenism 4, 15, 23, 100, 147 n.61, 148 n.15
Hellenic Paganism 67
Henry VIII 12, 13, 16, 18
Heraclitus 108
Herbert, Frederic 'Dorian' 26, 37, 50, 56, 57
heresy 1, 44, 68, 81, 113
heretics, heretical sects 15, 16, 50, 55, 81, 113
Hermes Trimegistos 106, 108
Hermetic Brotherhood of Luxor (HB of L) 78
hermeticism 98, 100, 106
Heselton, Phillip 10, 27, 50
High Magic's Aid 2
hocus pocus 61
homosexuality 45, 63, 78
Humanism 61
Huss, Jan 18
Hutton, Ronald xi, 4, 8–9, 10, 88, 91
Huysman, J.-K. 45

Idylls of the King 66
Ignatius Peter III, Mar *see* Bedros, Mar, Bishop of Emesa
incense 21, 61, 69, 70, 74, 82, 86

Independent Catholic Church of Ceylon 39

initiation 37; Wiccan 74, 83, 84–5, 92, 103, 112

initiatory religion 77, 84; Wicca as 1, 4–7, 69

interfaith x

invocation 71–3, 74, 86–7, 92, 104

Iolo Morganwg (Edward Williams) 35

Irish, immigrants to Britain 19, 22, 59, 65

Isis 4, 98

James, William 62, 67, 73

Jansenists 30

Jean II, Tau see Bricaud, Jean

Jerusalem 14, 16, 29, 35, 36, 41

Jesus 36, 46, 56, 57, 80

Jews, Judaism 45, 55, 61, 81, 105

Joachim of Fiore 44

Johannes, Tau, Bishop of Lyon see Bricaud, Jean

John, Gospel of 46

John, Mar, Titular Archbishop of Olivet, see Ward, J.S.M.

Joseph of Arimathea 14–15, 35, 36, 41, 53, 56

Julius, Mar, Bishop of Iona see Ferrette, Jules

kabbalah/istic 103, 105, 106

Keble, John 19–20

Kelly, Aidan 68, 72, 84

Key of Solomon 5, 70, 98

King, Edward, Bishop of Lincoln 64

Kingsford, Anna 99

Knights Templar 44, 45, 56, 81

Krafft-Ebing 63

Kredenn Geltiek 54

Kwamin, Mar see Anderson, Ebenezer Johnson

L'Église Gnostique Universelle (EGU) 47

L'Église Orthodoxe Celtique 52

Lambeth Conference 27, 32, 37, 38

Laud, William 21, 59

Law of Liberty 78–9, 80

Leadbeater, Charles Webster 33–4, 63

Lebesque, Phileas 54

Lee, F.G. 65

Leland, Charles Godfrey 23, 24, 87, 89

Lévi, Éliphas 46, 99

Liber XV see Gnostic Mass

Liberal Catholic Church 32–4, 36, 51, 99

Library of Anglo-Catholic Theology 21

liturgy: Catholic 1, 30, 59–61, 70, 76; Church of England 20; LCC 33; Liturgical Movement 20; Orthodox 34, 59, 70

Llanthony, Fr Ignatius of 40, 49

Lloyd, F.E.J. 40, 48

Lollards 15, 61

Lucius, King 14

Luhrmann, Tanya 89, 100

Luther, Martin 60–1

Mackonochie, Fr Alexander Heriot 65

Mäel Bliss see de Brescia, Paul-Edouard de Fournier

magic 10, 93; and Catholicism 11, 12, 33, 61, 104, 105, 107; definitions of 101–2; Mass as magic 33, 107; and modernity 94, 97–9, 110–11; 'othering' of 107–10; and Paganism 100–1, 104; Renaissance 97, 105–7; ritual magic 5, 7, 58, 69, 88, 99; sex magic 45–6, 77–80, 82–5, 92; theories of ix, 13, 94–7, 109–10; Wiccan 74, 87, 101–4, 110–11

Magus, Simon 46

Malinowski, Bronislaw 95, 102

Malta 68

Manning, Henry Edward (Cardinal) 20, 22

Martinist Order 46, 47, 55

Mary Tudor 12, 18

Mass 17, 33, 44, 45, 60, 68, 87, 107

masturbation 45, 77, 78

Mathers, Samuel Liddell 'MacGregor' 77, 97–8, 127 n.42

Mathew, Arnold Harris 30–2, 33; succession 34, 37, 38

matriarchy 4, 7, 8

Mauss, Marcel 96, 109

McCombie, Josephine ('Com') 56

Meaning of Witchcraft, The 2, 24–5, 57

Medievalism 66–8, 113

Michelet, Jules 24, 58

mixed chalice 21, 138 n.27

Monastère de Sainte-Présence 135 n.66

monasteries, dissolution of 12, 15

monastic/ism 12, 14–15, 23, 79, 85

Morgan, Rev Richard Williams 26, 34–6, 41, 51, 53, 55, 57

Murray, Margaret 2, 24–5, 26

mystical 57, 105; and magic, 97, 111; Christian 26, 99; states 73–4

naturist/naturism 51, 58, 87, 88, 93
Neale, John Mason 59, 64
neo-gnosticism 42, 45, 46, 77
Newman, John Henry (Cardinal) 20, 21, 59
Newman-Norton, William Henry Hugo 53, 134 n.58
Nichols, Ross 10, 27, 51, 54–5, 56, 57, 93
Nietzsche, Friedrich 78, 80
Non-Jurors 28–30, 41, 59
nudity: allegations of 81–2; and baptismal rites 134 n.54; ritual 83, 87–93

occult: and Wicca 5–6, 7, 9
Old Catholic Church 10, 30–32, 33, 37, 38, 39
Order of Bards, Ovates and Druids 55
Order of Holy Wisdom 36, 37
Ordo Templi Orientis (OTO) 37, 46, 47, 77, 78
Origen 46
Orpheus 106, 108
Oxford Movement 9, 11, 12, 19–20, 59, 62, 66

Pagan Federation 6, 99
Pagan, Paganism 98; ancient 5, 70, 109; and Catholicism 65, 68; and magic 100–1, 104; studies of 7; types of 4–5; and Wicca 5–6
pagano-papism 34, 62
Papal Infallibility, Declaration of 30
papal interference 13, 22
Papus 46, 47, 55, 78
Paraclete, Age of 44, 45, 46
Parker, Matthew 17, 25, 26, 41
Pater, Walter H. 63, 65–6, 67
patriarchy 4, 85
Patronado Association 39
Pelagius, Mar see Morgan, Rev Richard Williams
Petite Église 43
Pico della Mirandola, Giovanni 105
Pike, Sarah 111
Pilgrimage of Grace 12
Plato 106, 108
Plutarch 108
Plymouth Brethren 70, 77

popery 11, 18, 19, 21, 22, 107
poppets 102
Pre-Raphaelites 66
priest-craft 1, 18, 61, 104, 105
priesthood of all believers 76
Public Worship Regulation Act 59, 63–4
Pugin, Augustus Welby Northmore 22, 66
Pusey, Edward 19, 59

Quakers 87, 122 n.59

Rabelais, François 79–80
Randolph, Paschal Beverley 78, 83
Ranters 87
Real Presence 20, 60
recusancy laws 18
reformations 1, 9, 41, 42, 60, 94, 106; Tudor 11, 20, 35, 44, 66
relics 60, 103
religious experience 62, 73–4
Renaissance 67, 97, 105–8, 111
Reuss, Theodor 27, 47, 77
Ritualist Movement 12, 59, 62–3, 65, 66
Roman Catholic Relief Act 18
Roman Catholicism 12; doctrines 30; and Gardner 55–6; and magic 11, 12, 33, 61, 104, 105, 107; as marginal 1, 13, 25; nineteenth century revival 9, 20, 58, 95; and occultists 99; as 'Old Religion' 11, 13, 19, 22–3, 26; ritual 12, 20, 32, 33, 59, 60–1, 66, 69–70, 76, 106; and secrecy 62, 65; as 'unEnglish' 21, 64; vilification of 17, 18, 61, 62, 64; and Wiccan backgrounds x, xi, 68–9
Romantic Movement 20
Rosicrucians/ism 37, 98
Rossetti, Dante Gabriel 66

sabbats 69, 83
sacerdotalism 61, 63, 76
sacraments 21, 30, 45, 46, 47
sacred space 69, 71, 73, 91
Sainte Église celtique en Bretagne 51
saints, cult of 16, 60
Salomonsen, Jone 7, 89, 102
samadhi 74
Sanders, Alex 2, 7, 104
Saxons 15, 17, 56
Schleiermacher, Friedrich 73

science: and magic 95–6, 97, 102, 109, 110
scourging 74, 83, 84–6, 92
secrecy 81; and Catholicism 19, 62, 65; and Wicca 5, 6, 7, 90
secret societies 55, 84, 112; Anglo-Catholic 63; occult 4, 5, 8, 9, 45; of witches 24
Seraphim, Mar see Newman-Norton, William Henry Hugo
Servants of the Light 102
sexual symbolism 83, 84
sexuality: and the body 76, 92; Christian attitudes towards 81–2; female 86; and magic 10, 58; S/M 83–5, 92; and spirituality 83
Sibley, Churchill 48, 49
Societas Sanctae Crucis (SSC) 65
Society of King Charles the Martyr 20
sociology 94, 110
Solesmes, Abbey of 66
spells 74, 102, 107
spiritual alchemy 102, 103, 104, 111
spiritualism 9, 23, 44, 95
St Albans, Holborn 48, 49
Starhawk 70, 101, 102
Stella Matutina 88, 99
Stevens, Charles Isaac 36
superstition 11, 12, 43, 109
Sutcliffe, Richard 111
Syrian Jacobite Church 39, 52

tabloid sensationalism 82–3, 87
talismans 103
Tambiah, Stanley J. 110
Thelema 37, 47, 77, 79; Abbey of 79, 88; law of 79, 80
Theosophical Society 32–4, 63, 78, 98, 99
therapeutic blasphemy 78
Thirty Nine Articles 20
Thomas, Keith 96–7, 107, 111
Timotheos, Mar see Vilatte, Joseph René
Tractarians 9, 20, 21, 29, 59, 64, 66 see also Oxford Movement
transmutation 6, 103, 107,111
transports 73–4
Tugdual see Danyel, Jean-Pierre (Clodoald)
Turner, Victor 89
Tylor, Edward 95, 109

Ultramontanism 30

un-English 22, 63
Unions of Life 45
Universal Gnostic Church 40
universities, of the epsicopi vagantes 41–2

Valentin II, Tau see Doinel, Jules-Benoît Stanislas
Valentinus 46
Valiente, Doreen 2, 7, 87, 90
Van Baal, Jan 101, 110
Vatican Council, First 30
vestments 20, 40, 138 n.27
Victoria, Queen 63, 64
Vilatte, Joseph René 34, 39–40, 44; succession 36, 38, 47, 48, 49
de la Villemarque, Hersart 53, 54
Vincent, Tau, Bishop of Toulouse see Papus
Vintras, Pierre-Eugène-Michel 44–5, 46, 47, 87
vision, theories of 60

Waite, Arthur Edward 99
Waldenses 17
Ward, J.S.M. 10, 37, 48–50
Weber, Max 96
Wedgwood, James Ingall 32–3
Welsh nationalism 34, 41
Western Esoteric Tradition 90, 97, 105, 111
Westminster, palace of 66
Wheel of the Year 3, 69
Wicca, Wiccans: and Christianity 1, 10, 54, 57–8, 68, 112–3; history of 1–3, 5–6, 7–9, 23–5; and magic 99, 101–4; magical heritage of 98–9; as 'old religion' 11, 23; and Paganism 4–6; as religion and magic 94, 104, 111; religious background 1, 68–9; representations of 82, 83, 86; and ritual 59, 67, 69–76; and sexuality 80, 83–5, 87, 91–2; spread of 3; studies of 7; and Theosophical Society 34; and witchcraft 3–4, 6–7
Wilde, Oscar 66, 138 n.24, 139 n.34
Williams, Bernard Mary 32
de Willmott Newman, Hugh George 36, 37
Willoughby, Frederick Samuel 32, 38
witch, witches: Bruno's portrayal of 106; Gospel of the 23; as identificatory image 4, 8, 85–6; types of 6 see also witchcraft, Wicca

witchcraft 1, 87; as ancient religion 2, 7, 23–5; anthropological study of 3, 4; and Catholicism 1, 10, 19, 61, 68, 93, 104, 107; and Christianity 1, 56, 57, 58, 112–3; commodification of 7; early modern 1, 23–4, 45, 61, 68, 81–2, 85, 104; feminist 3–4, 7, 8; and Gardner 2, 9, 24–5; histories of 9; and Paganism 4–5; persecutions 4, 8, 24; publications on 6; Reclaiming 3; and spiritualism 9; types of 3–7, and Wicca 1, 4–6; 55; as wimmin's religion 85–6
Witchcraft Act 1, 9
Witchcraft Today 2, 24–5
Witches' Rune 71
women priests/ordination of women 33, 42
Woodhead, Linda ix, 113
Wycliffe, John 15, 16, 18

Zwingli, Ulrich 61, 107